Expertise, Communication, and Organiz

Expertise, Communication, and Organizing

Edited by

Jeffrey W. Treem and Paul M. Leonardi

OXFORD
UNIVERSITY PRESS

OXFORD
UNIVERSITY PRESS

Great Clarendon Street, Oxford, OX2 6DP,
United Kingdom

Oxford University Press is a department of the University of Oxford.
It furthers the University's objective of excellence in research, scholarship,
and education by publishing worldwide. Oxford is a registered trade mark of
Oxford University Press in the UK and in certain other countries

© Oxford University Press 2016

The moral rights of the authors have been asserted

First Edition published in 2016

Impression: 1

Published in the United States of America by Oxford University Press
198 Madison Avenue, New York, NY 10016, United States of America

British Library Cataloguing in Publication Data

Data available

Library of Congress Control Number: 2015956092

ISBN 978-0-19-873922-7 (hbk)
       978-0-19-873923-4 (pbk)

Printed in Great Britain by
Clays Ltd, St Ives plc

ACKNOWLEDGMENTS

First and foremost we would like to thank all of the contributors to this book. When we were in the initial stages of this project we generated a list of the foremost scholars studying the intersection of expertise, communication, and organizing—our dream team of authors. Our hope was perhaps half of them would entertain our invitation, but to our immense surprise each of them agreed to participate in this work. The contributors were asked to be bold, provocative, and offer insights that would advance the study of expertise, and each one of them delivered. We could not have asked for better group of scholars to work with and this book is a product of their intellect, generosity, and yes, expertise.

Our goal was to produce a coherent volume that is more than a collection of singular entries. This could not have been accomplished without the participation of the authors in a workshop held in Austin, Texas, in the summer of 2014. The conversations, questioning, and debates that took place during that workshop were invaluable in clarifying the focus of the book and aiding the development of the individual contributions. We would like to thank the Moody College of Communication at The University of Texas at Austin for hosting and funding this workshop. Specifically we want to recognize Roderick Hart for his support of this project from its inception. Following the workshop, a CAREER grant from the National Science Foundation (SES-1057148) provided time and resources to develop material that found its way into this book. Additionally, Northwestern University's School of Communication provided financial assistance that aided in the production of the book.

One area where we certainly lack expertise is in publishing. Throughout this process we were extremely fortunate to have had the guidance and support of our editor David Musson at Oxford University Press, as well as the benefit of his great editorial staff. A special thank you to Clare Kennedy for her patience and counsel throughout this project.

In putting together this book about expertise we were reminded at every step how little we know about so many things, and how much we rely on the kindness and support of others to do our work. In that spirit we want to acknowledge the help of our colleagues and friends who were willing to answer questions or look over materials when asked. Finally, we want to thank our families who despite our glaring lack of expertise in so many areas still love us and encourage us in our efforts.

Jeffrey W. Treem
Paul M. Leonardi

CONTENTS

▨ LIST OF FIGURES

▧ LIST OF TABLES

LIST OF CONTRIBUTORS

Jeffrey W. Treem is an assistant professor of communication studies in the Moody College of Communication at The University of Texas at Austin. His program of research explores the relationship between communication practices and social perceptions of expertise, primarily in organizational contexts. Specifically, his studies examine how communication technologies facilitate recurrent, interactive practices that affect attributions of knowledge individuals make regarding co-workers, and the perceived value of organizational work. Dr. Treem's work appears in publications such as *Journal of Communication, Communication Monographs, Journal of Applied Communication Research*, and *Communication Yearbook*.

Paul M. Leonardi is the Duca Family Professor of Technology Management at the University of California, Santa Barbara. He is also the Investement Group of Santa Barbara Founding Director of the Master of Technology Management Program. Dr. Leonardi's research focuses on how companies can design their organizational networks and implement new technologies to more effectively create and share knowledge. He is particularly interested in how data intensive technologies, such as simulation and social media tools, enable new ways to access, store, and share information; how the new sources of information these technologies provide can change work routines and communication partners; and how shifts in employees' work and communication alter the nature of an organization's expertise.

Mark Aakhus is Professor of Communication in the School of Communication and Information at Rutgers University. His current projects focus on stakeholder engagement in collaborative governance, information systems for open practice, argumentation mining (unstructured data analysis), deliberation/controversy analytics, and design practice for communication. His research investigates the uses of language, argumentation, and social interaction in professional practice, organizational processes, and information systems. This research addresses the competence and creativity of individuals, organizations, and communities in managing complex situations through communication and design.

Bryan Abendschein is a doctoral student in the Department of Communication at the University of Illinois at Urbana-Champaign. His research interests include times of change in families and how interpersonal relationships are managed over time. His work on relational turbulence and social support has been presented at the annual conventions of the National Communication Association and the International Communication Association.

Mark S. Ackerman is the George Herbert Mead Collegiate Professor of Human–Computer Interaction and a Professor in the Department of Electrical Engineering and Computer Science and in the School of Information at the University of Michigan, Ann Arbor. His major research area is Human–Computer Interaction (HCI), primarily Computer-Supported Cooperative Work (CSCW). He has published widely in

HCI and CSCW, investigating collaborative information access in online knowledge communities, medical settings, expertise sharing, and most recently, pervasive environments. Mark is an HCI Fellow and an Association for Computing Machinery (ACM) Fellow. Before becoming an academic, Mark led the development of the first home banking system, had three Billboard Top-10 games, and worked on the X Window System. Dr. Ackerman has degrees from the University of Chicago, Ohio State, and MIT.

Joshua B. Barbour is an assistant professor of communication studies in the Moody College of Communication at The University of Texas at Austin. He studies the confluence of the macromorphic and communicative in organizational life. His research is concerned with how and why individuals, groups, and organizations manage information and meaning and how we can (re)design conversations, change groups, and help individuals to do so with more sophistication. His research has been published in *Communication Research, Communication Monographs, Journal of Applied Communication Research*, and *Management Communication Quarterly*.

William C. Barley is an assistant professor of communication at the University of Illinois at Urbana-Champaign. His research explores how people design and use technology to collaborate across knowledge boundaries in a variety of organizational contexts. Specifically, he is interested in the challenges that emerge as teams seek to communicate with people who have differing expertise, and the strategies those people enact to overcome those challenges. He has studied these processes in a number of settings including automobile engineering, applied weather science, hospitals, service firms, and enthusiast communities.

Patrice M. Buzzanell is a Distinguished Professor in the Brian Lamb School of Communication and the School of Engineering Education (courtesy) at Purdue University. She has edited four books and authored more than 170 articles and chapters, plus proceeding in engineering education, with her research centering on the intersections of career, gender, and communication, particularly in STEM (science, technology, engineering, and math). Dr. Buzzanell is a Fellow and past president of the International Communication Association (ICA), and past president of the Organization for the Study of Communication, Language and Gender (OSCLG) and the Council of Communication Associations (CCA). She has received numerous awards for her research, teaching/mentoring, and engagement, and serves currently on sixteen editorial boards. Dr. Buzzanell has also served in a leadership role for a variety of research projects: Purdue-ADVANCE initiatives for institutional change; the Transforming Lives Building Global Communities (TLBGC) engineering design team in Ghana through the Engineering Projects in Community Service (EPICS); and development and validation of individual engineering ethical development and team ethical climate scales as well as everyday negotiations of ethics in design through National Science Foundation (NSF) funding as Co-PI.

Harry Collins is Distinguished Research Professor and directs the Centre for the Study of Knowledge, Expertise and Science (KES) at Cardiff University. He is an elected Fellow of the British Academy and a winner of the Bernal prize for social studies of science. He has served as President of the Society for Social Studies of Science. His eighteen published books cover sociology of scientific knowledge, artificial intelligence, the nature of expertise, and tacit knowledge. He is continuing his research on the sociology of gravitational wave detection, expertise, fringe science, science and democracy, technology in sport, and a new technique—the "Imitation Game"—for exploring expertise and comparing the extent to which minority groups are integrated into societies. He is currently writing books on science and democracy, on artificial intelligence, on technology in sport, and on the Imitation Game.

Punit Dadlani is a doctoral student in Library and Information Science at the School of Communication and Information at Rutgers University. He has a Bachelor's degree in Philosophy and English and a Bachelor's degree in Information Technology and Informatics from Rutgers University. Prior to pursuing a Ph.D. he worked for eight years in several operational roles in financial IT. His research interests include information behavior in context, social justice, organizational communication, collaboration, and philosophy of information.

Janet Fulk is Professor of Communications at the Annenberg School for Communication, and Professor of Management and Organization at the Marshall School of Business, at the University of Southern California. Her publications include *Policing Hawthorne* (2001, with Gregory Patton and Peter Monge), *Shaping Organizational Form: Communication, Connection and Community* (1999, with Gerardine DeSanctis), and *Organizations and Communication Technology* (1990, with Charles Steinfield), which won the best book award from the National Communication Association in 1990. Her research articles and chapters cover topics including knowledge networks, information technology for strategic alliance networks, social aspects of knowledge and distributed intelligence, social media use, networking strategies of nongovernmental organizations, and online communities. Dr. Fulk's research has been sponsored by a series of grants from the National Science Foundation in the United States, as well as private corporations and governmental organizations. She is a Fellow of both the Academy of Management and International Communication Association.

Ralph A. Gigliotti is assistant director for the Center for Organizational Development and Leadership at Rutgers University, where he is also a doctoral student and part-time lecturer in Communication. His research interests explore the intersection of organizational communication, leadership, and crisis communication, particularly in the context of higher education. He is the former Associate Director for Leadership at Villanova University. Gigliotti's research has been accepted in the *Atlantic Journal of Communication,* the *Journal of Public Affairs Education,* the *Journal of Leadership, Accountability and Ethics,* the *Journal of Student Affairs Research and Practice,* and the *Journal of Leadership Education.*

Rebecca Gill is a Senior Lecturer in the Massey University School of Management, Auckland, New Zealand. Her research questions the contemporary and historical construction of identity in relation to occupational discourse and practice, as informed by social identity, place, and culture. Recent work focuses on how discourses of entrepreneurship and innovation are constructed and shape expectations for work and work identity, regional development, and civic and community life. Dr. Gill's research has been published in *Human Relations, Communication Monographs, Organization, Management Communication Quarterly,* and other outlets.

Christine Goldthwaite is a doctoral student studying organizational and mediated communication in the School of Communication and Information at Rutgers University. Her research interests concern group creative and innovative activity with a focus on collaboration, knowledge sharing, and decision-making in both co-located and virtual teams. She is an active member of the Rutgers research group, Collaboratory for Organizing and Social Media (COSM), and was a 2012–14 Fellow in the Pre-Doctoral Leadership Development Institute at Rutgers University. Before transitioning to academia, she worked in advertising and business-to-business communications serving US and international for-profit and non-profit clients for twelve years.

Naina Gupta is a Senior Lecturer at Nanyang Business School in Singapore. Her research interests include shared cognition and virtuality in teams, social networks, and deviant behavior in both teams and organizations. Her research has appeared in *Management Science, Group Dynamics: Theory, Research, and Practice, Journal of Occupational and Organizational Psychology,* and *Journal of Organizational Behavior.*

Andrea B. Hollingshead is Professor of Communication in the Annenberg School of Communication and Journalism at the University of Southern California. She has joint appointments with the Marshall School of Business and the Department of Psychology. Dr. Hollingshead's research concerns the factors and processes that lead to effective and ineffective knowledge sharing in groups. She has been a co-principal investigator on several large projects funded by the National Science Foundation to develop collaborative technologies for solving practical problems, including one to improve knowledge sharing among first responders. She has co-authored three books, *Research Methods for Studying Groups and Teams, Theories of Small Groups: Interdisciplinary Perspectives,* and *Groups Interacting with Technology,* and has published many articles in top-tier psychology, communication, and management journals.

Pei-Yao Hung is a doctoral student in the School of Information at the University of Michigan, Ann Arbor. He is interested in Human–Computer Interaction, End-User Programming, and Computer-Supported Cooperative Work. He received a BS and MS in Computer Science and Information Engineering from National Taiwan University, Taiwan, and an MS in Information from the University of Michigan.

Allie Kosterich is a doctoral student in the School of Communication and Information at Rutgers University. She is interested in the intersection of organizations and digital technology, particularly within the context of media industry evolution. Her recent research examines the impact of social analytics on the reconfiguration of both media audience and content. In addition, she is looking at the relationship between venture capital funding and the organizational processes of new and legacy media companies. Prior to returning to academia, she worked as a television producer.

Julia Kotlarsky is a Professor of Technology and Global Sourcing at Aston Business School, UK. Her research interests revolve around outsourcing and offshoring of knowledge-intensive business processes and services, knowledge and expertise coordination in ad hoc and complex organizational settings, innovation, digital technologies, and new ways of working. She has published her work in numerous journals including *MIS Quarterly, European Journal of Information Systems, Journal of Strategic Information Systems,* and *Communication Research.* Dr. Kotlarsky has published eight books, among them *The Handbook of Global Outsourcing and Offshoring.* She serves as an Associate Editor for *MIS Quarterly,* Senior Editor for *Journal of*

Information Technology, and is co-founder of the annual Global Sourcing Workshop <www.globalsourcing.org.uk>.

Timothy Kuhn is a Professor in the Department of Communication at the University of Colorado Boulder. His research examines how authority and agency—and, in turn, knowledge, identities, objects, and what we take to be organizations themselves—are constituted in and through communication. His work has appeared in *Academy of Management Review, Communication Monographs, Organization, Organization Studies,* and *Management Communication Quarterly,* among other outlets.

Natalie J. Lambert is a doctoral student in the Department of Communication at the University of Illinois at Urbana-Champaign. She is interested in the development and coordination of organizations in online and real-world contexts. Her research seeks to better characterize the organizational and communication structures that influence intra- and interorganizational coordination, and to illuminate how organizations are formed and change in online contexts using a network perspective and computational methods.

John C. Lammers is a Professor in the Department of Communication and Director of the Health Communication Online Masters of Science Program at the University of Illinois at Urbana-Champaign. His research applies institutional theory to communication among health professionals and organizations. His work has appeared in the *Academy of Management Review, Management Communication Quarterly, Communication Theory, Health Communication,* the *Annals of Internal Medicine,* and the *Annals of Emergency Medicine.*

Wang Liao is a doctoral student studying organizational communication at Cornell University. His research interests include emergent structures and collective behaviors in communication networks. His current research relates to (a) the emergence of hierarchy and related social judgments in interpersonal and group communications and (b) affective mechanisms of identity-based collective behaviors and network evolution. He is also interested in quantitative methods and computational tools for causal inference using observational data.

Ziyu Long is an assistant professor of organizational communication in the Department of Communication Studies at Colorado State University. Her research interests include career design, entrepreneurship, and gendered organizing in the globalized and digitalized workplace. Her research has appeared in such outlets as *Journal of Business and Technical Communication, Communication Yearbook, Management Communication Quarterly, Journal of Business and Entrepreneurship, The Electronic Journal of Communication,* and *Public Relations Review,* as well as a number of edited books and conference proceedings.

Patrick MacDonald is a doctoral student studying organizational communication at Cornell University. His research focuses on the study of organizational networks and intercultural communication. Specifically, he is interested in how the perceptions of negative ties impact organizational effectiveness and efficiency. Additionally, he has a background in communication and instructional design.

David T. Merritt is a doctoral student in Computer Science and Engineering at the University of Michigan, Ann Arbor. He is interested in Human–Computer

Interaction, Computer-Supported Cooperative Work, and Usable Privacy and Security. He received his MS in Computer Engineering from the Air Force Institute of Technology in 2011 and his BS in Computer Engineering from the US Air Force Academy in 2002. He is currently working on effective ways to use mixed expertise in crowdsourcing platforms.

Jens Rennstam is Associate Professor at the Department of Business Administration, Lund University, Sweden. His research interests include organizational control, particularly in knowledge-intensive contexts, knowledge, materiality in organizations, practice theory, gender and sexuality in organizations, branding, and qualitative methods. His work has appeared in journals such as *Gender, Work and Organization, Human Relations, Organization Studies, Research in the Sociology of Organizations,* and *Scandinavian Journal of Management.*

Tobias Reynolds-Tylus is a doctoral student in the Department of Communication at the University of Illinois at Urbana-Champaign. His research interests include health communication and social influence, particularly in the areas of organ and tissue donation and sexual health. His work has been presented at national and international conferences, and in refereed journals including *Journal of Health Communication, Journal of Broadcasting & Electronic Media,* and *Progress in Transplantation.*

Surabhi Sahay is a doctoral student in Library and Information Science at the School of Communication and Information at Rutgers University. She is interested in exploring the implications that participatory designs have for various stakeholder groups during times of organizational change.

Paul A. Sommer is an assistant professor in the School of Communication Studies at Kent State University at Stark. His research revolves around the communicative accomplishment of knowledge work in project-based organizations. Paul is particularly interested in how, why, and to what end information or knowledge is managed, and the role of uncertainty in organizing. His past experience working in residential and commercial construction has provoked his interest in the articulation of expertise, both physically and intellectually.

Bart van den Hooff is Professor of Organizational Communication and Information Systems at the VU University Amsterdam in the Netherlands. His research interests include the interaction between ICTs, organizations, and individuals; enterprise systems; and online interaction and knowledge coordination. His work has been presented at international conferences and published in (among others) *Journal of Management Studies, Organization Studies, Communication Research, Human Communication Research, Journal of the Association for Information Systems, Journal of Information Technology,* and *European Journal of Information Systems.*

Kira A. Varava is a doctoral student in the Department of Communication at the University of Illinois at Urbana-Champaign and a faculty member at Missouri State University. Her research interests focus on health communication and media and primarily include determining what media communicate about health, how they communicate this information, and the potential effects of exposure on viewers.

Kay Yoon is an associate professor in the College of Communication at DePaul University. She studies how people share knowledge and information in collaborative processes and how such knowledge sharing affects the performance of work teams in organizations. Her research investigates cognitive, communicative, and sociocultural barriers to effective knowledge-sharing processes and how those barriers could be mitigated. She teaches a broad range of courses within the realm of Team and Organizational Communication at both undergraduate and graduate levels, including Small Group Communication, Teams and Diversity, Team Information Sharing, Leadership and Diversity Training, and Group Decision-Making.

Y. Connie Yuan is an associate professor in the Department of Communication at Cornell University. Her research interests include group collaboration, social networks, usage of information and communication technology in organizations, and intercultural communication. She has received multiple NSF grants to support her research in these areas. Her works have appeared in all major journals in the field of communication, and Dr. Yuan has been awarded multiple research awards at major conferences in the fields of communication and management.

1 What is Expertise? Who is an Expert? Some Definitive Answers

JEFFREY W. TREEM AND PAUL M. LEONARDI

Why are we qualified to answer the questions, "What is Expertise?" and "Who is an Expert?" And why are we qualified to edit and publish a book about expertise, communication, and organizing? You could say that our expertise on the topic of expertise is demonstrated through our publications on the subject in peer-reviewed academic journals. Or you could argue that our expertise has been developed over years of academic study at established universities and within institutionalized disciplines of knowledge. Perhaps you are confident in our expertise because we were able to produce a physical book, attract contributions from accomplished scholars, and receive support from a respected publisher. However, we suspect you are convinced that we are experts on the subject of expertise merely because we say we are, and you have no obvious reason to doubt this claim. We have communicated to you that we are experts, and that alone is an important influence in you recognizing us as such. In short, we claim expertise. And the more definitively we do it, shows the research, the more likely you are to believe us. Are you convinced?

Our hope is that this book will verify your suspicion that we, and the authors who have contributed chapters, can indeed advance your knowledge regarding the study of expertise and offer an agenda for ongoing research in this domain. But that is just our hope. In fact, if you come to meet either one of us in person, you will quickly find that neither one of us feels qualified as experts on anything, and neither one of us is sure if we have any real expertise to offer. Although such statements surely do not provide a very compelling beginning to a book on expertise, they highlight the broad point, demonstrated over and over again and in various ways by the authors of the various chapters herein: that expertise is a communicative construct. In other words, trying to isolate the attributes of experts, or the qualities that constitute expertise, is likely to be futile because experts do not exist unless there is an audience out there willing to attribute expertise to them and recognize them as experts.

Of course, we do not mean to suggest that objective skill is not an important component of expertise. K. Anders Ericsson's classic studies of expertise making—that it commonly takes no less than 10,000 hours of dedicated practice to develop and hone the skills necessary to become an expert—speak to the importance of actual capabilities. But is a basketball player who has practiced free throws for 10,000 hours and has accumulated a percentage of 92 percent (at the close of the 2014–2015 regular season, Stephen Curry who is a Guard for the Golden State Warriors had the highest free throw percentage of anyone in the NBA at 91.4 percent) an expert if no one knows that she has done so? In a social world, the practical answer is no. To be recognized as an expert, an audience needs to see signs of that person's expertise. This claim entails two assumptions.

The first assumption is that some observer knows what expertise looks like. It only takes a moment to recognize that most people do not know what expertise looks like in most dimensions of practice. For example, by watching a neurosurgeon do his work, could you tell whether or not he is an expert? Compared to you (assuming you are not a neurosurgeon) that person would likely seem like an expert if for no other reason than they had the guts to cut someone's head open. You, knowing full well that you have no expertise in neurosurgery, would never dare to cut someone's head open (hopefully!). But is their intrepidness enough to lead you to consider them an expert? What if they were wearing scrubs and had a nametag with the salutation "Dr" before their name, or the letters "MD" after it? What if the surgery was being performed in a prestigious hospital? What if a crew of nurses and technicians swirled about attending to every need and listening to every command given by the person with the scalpel? What if the surgeon barked commands with confidence and used a set of terms you could not understand? Slowly, an image of an expert begins to come into focus. Interestingly, though, what brings that image into focus is not just the skill of the person in question, but the infrastructure that unfolds around them—each piece of it sending off signals that bolster your view that the person at the activity's center must be an expert, because everyone else seems to think he is.

The surgery is over. Let's say we hand you a document summarizing the success of that surgeon's procedures performed over the last decade. According to the evidence, his surgeries have an 85 percent success rate. Do you still consider him an expert? What if we were to hand you a similar document summarizing the success rate of another surgeon who works at the same hospital? Her success rate for the same surgery is 97 percent. Who is the expert? Who has more expertise?

What we hope to reveal through our onslaught of questions is that it is a very tricky business to recognize expertise. Expertise is rarely something that can be observed directly. Rather, we use the cues available in the environment to infer expertise and, consequently, to name people as experts. The problem is that we can never perceive all elements of the environment at once, and even if we could, the environment is not static. Through the assembly of cues as diverse as name tags, hospital status, and the command-following behavior of nurses, our inferential reasoning may lead us to believe that one surgeon is an expert. But add a second surgeon to the mix, and now we begin to make comparisons. A person who we perceived to be an expert when examining his actions relative to our own may no longer seem like an expert when we compare his actions relative to someone else who holds the same job title or who performs a similar type of work. Thus, the first assumption that observers know what expertise looks like is problematic.

The second assumption is that people who have some kind of objective skill greater than you or greater than others will communicate that skill, such that we have cues available with which to make inferences about their possession of expertise. Communication comes in a great many forms. The most basic form of communication is action. When a person performs an activity in front of others (we see the surgeon wield the scalpel in the operating room, or we see the basketball player make her free throws) they have provided communicative cues that we can use to begin to make inferences about their expertise. If we could see the activities that people perform in the course of their work, we might have some confidence in our ability to cast them as experts. But we live in a peculiar age in which the types of work that we can see are highly rationalized and pre-programmed, while the work that we cannot see is much more holistic and idiosyncratic. Take, for example, the work of people who assemble automobiles on an assembly line. Would you characterize them as experts? If you tour Ford Motor Company's Dearborn assembly plant where they manufacture their highly successful F-150 pickup truck, you can stand on an enclosed platform and watch each assembler do each aspect of his or her job. If you were a worker on the line, not a visitor to the plant, you could also see most of your co-workers and observe every activity they performed. Although there is a tremendous amount of skill involved in ratcheting a bolt to the right level of tension or fastening a grommet on an interior trim panel, most people do not consider automotive assembly line workers to be experts. In fact, the job of an assembler is designed in such a way such that any person should, in theory, be able to step into the role and help to assemble the vehicle. Such separation of rote labor needed to do a job from the expertise required to design the job in the first place harkens back to Fredrick Taylor and the principles of scientific management. Incidentally, individuals whose jobs consist of performing actions that others can easily observe—auto assemblers, fast food clerks, and garbage collectors, to name a few, are not those that we typically characterize as experts.

Contrast these jobs with those of a financial analyst, a computer engineer, a surgeon, or even a public relations professional. What do these people do? What actions do they perform? Most of us have no clue. And if we do have just the slightest clue, it is because we've seen characterizations of their work on television shows and in movies. The work of most people in knowledge-intensive jobs is invisible to would-be observers. So individuals in these roles cannot communicate their expertise simply by working and expecting the rest of us to watch them and attribute expertise to them. We must use other communicative signals to make such inferences. Artifacts provide some clues. For example, the diploma on the wall in the surgeon's office, the computer engineer's membership in the Society for Professional Engineers, and the fact that the financial analyst works on the 80th floor of a skyscraper on Wall Street give us signals through which we can make inferences of expertise. Outputs of work provide another set of clues. We see a complicated Excel spreadsheet filled with equations used for stock valuations, or the results of a finite element analysis of an airplane fuselage, or a healthy patient leaving the operating room and we use these communicative signals to make inferences that the person who produced them must have some expertise. We also, more often than we realize, rely on people's self-reports of their expertise. Put simply, they tell us they are experts, so we believe them. The more confident they are in proclaiming their expertise, the more likely we are to believe them if there are no conflicting cues that would lead us not to trust what they have said. Each of these forms of communication stand in for our own observations of people actually performing activities. So what if someone spent 10,000 hours honing their skills? If we can't see them do it, we have to rely on other cues that they communicate—intentionally or not—to form our impressions and make our attributions about whether or not they have expertise.

The point is that people's evaluations of others' expertise depend on communication. Experts do not always think about communicating their expertise. In fact, the sociologist Erving Goffman (1959) observed that people who are experts spend very little time communicating their expertise to others because they are spending so much time honing their expertise that they have no time left to talk about it. And even if experts wanted to communicate the nature of their expertise, the esoteric nature of their knowledge often makes it difficult to describe. How does a master sculptor describe how she sees the vision for her next work? How does a military sniper sense a subtle change in wind conditions and adjust a shot? If it were so easy to describe, we would be less likely to think of it as expertise. Consequently, audiences play a tremendously important role in the establishment of expertise and the creation of experts. But audiences come in varied types. Target audiences are those people to whom we intend to communicate our messages. Sometimes people in the target audience receive the message, and sometimes they do not. Empirical audiences are those people who hear our message, even though they were not our targets. They are the visitors who happen to be in the recovery room when the surgeon comes to talk to the patient, or the shareholder who reads the report in which the financial analyst is quoted. These members of the empirical audience are exposed to communicative cues that allow them, too, to make inferences about someone's expertise.

Audiences affect the establishment of experts by choosing to ascribe expertise to some individuals and not others. As one example, a few years ago we conducted a field study of computer technicians who provided basic user support to administrators at a federally funded research lab (Leonardi and Treem, 2012). These computer technicians were organized into a department, but they worked alone; none of their co-workers saw them fix a software problem on a user's computer. The only way they could learn what one of their co-workers did was to read the documentation a fellow technician wrote in their knowledge management tool about how they solved a user problem. The target audience was the IT department head, who wanted to see that each technician was doing the work they were supposed to be doing. The empirical audience was comprised of all the other technicians in the department. As technicians began to read each other's documentation, they began to use it (because there were few other available communicative cues to use) to make inferences about who was an expert. Someone who wrote a "crappy" documentation was deemed not to have expertise in the problem they were working on. Someone who wrote an "elegant" documentation was deemed to have expertise, especially when the solution appeared "more elegant" than what someone else had done previously. People who wrote long documentation were also considered to be more expert than people who wrote short documentation—because in the words of one technician, "If you didn't really understand what you did to make it work, you won't have much to say about it and no one cares that you got lucky."

The importance of the empirical audience was made manifest when technicians were empowered by their boss to assign jobs to the person who had the most "expertise" to complete it. To summarize what followed in the most straightforward way possible: all hell broke loose. Some technicians were upset that their co-workers were not assigning them jobs in areas in which they thought they had expertise. Others were upset that their co-workers were assigning them jobs in areas they did not like, even though they felt they had expertise in those areas. Some technicians felt undervalued and quit their jobs. Other technicians began to game the system. They would make up documentation—write things they did not do—in the knowledge management tool to communicate cues that others would use to infer they were experts, even though they themselves did not believe they were. One technician justified such action as follows: "I want to learn how to fix that problem. But if no one thinks I already know how to fix the problem, they won't assign me the job, so I'll never learn. So I have to make up some documentation so they think I know, so that they'll assign me the job and then I can have the chance to really learn it." Although that reasoning is complicated, it is not without warrant. Expertise and communication go hand in hand. It's just not always clear which one is in which hand at which moment.

The goal of this book is to unmask these assumptions about the relationship between communication, expertise, and organizing. In doing so, we hope to build a platform for theorizing about the role of expertise in modern organizations. The scholars who have authored the chapters in this book are all focused on understanding how expertise is constituted through communication, though at very different levels of analysis, in different settings, and through different processes. In what follows, we first provide an overview of why the study of expertise, communication, and organizing is so important for understanding work in the information age. We then highlight the main contributions made by each of the authors in their respective chapters, and we conclude with some overarching themes that we believe will serve as the foundations upon which communicative studies of expertise should be built. Or maybe we should phrase that differently to help you to believe that we are experts. What do you think?

Why Study Expertise, Communication, and Organizing?

For most activities in life expertise, or the engagement of an expert, is not needed to produce a perfectly acceptable outcome. For instance, when you are at the department store picking out clothing you are likely to purchase a fairly flattering pair of blue jeans without consulting a professional stylist to decide which brand, color, or cut to select. However, if you could get the advice of professional stylist before deciding what to buy, would you take it? And what if accessing that type of expertise was a free and easily available part of everyday life? Well, for anyone with an internet connection access to this type of expertise is increasingly a reality. With a few clicks and a bit of typing individuals are exposed to more information than they could process in a lifetime. And this technological platform not only provides people the opportunity to view information in hopes of developing personal knowledge, it also provides greater connectivity that allows people to find, interact, and develop relationships with experts who were previously inaccessible. However, as anyone who has had a friend who is convinced they have cancer after looking up symptoms on WebMD.com knows, simply possessing a plethora of information is not a direct path to expertise. The same technologies that allow individuals to access expertise and experts also allow charlatans, scam artists, or well-meaning novices to claim expertise and market themselves as experts. Turn on a morning talk show, read a newspaper article, or even have a drink with friends and you will likely encounter someone who is eager to share his or her purported expertise. Finding someone claiming to an expert is often not a problem, but whether they will actually provide the expertise you seek—or whether you would even know if they didn't—is a relevant concern.

Workers and organizations face a similar challenge in locating, assessing, and utilizing expertise. However, the stakes are raised a bit when we start to consider the relationship between expertise and organizing. Organizing is a social processes, and therefore carries with it an inherent element of coordination and interdependence. In organizing we count on expertise to provide guidance for how to take action, and we look to experts to take those actions as part of the work of constituting and sustaining organizations. Failures of expertise in organizational contexts have consequences not just for the exposed non-expert, but also for others who hoped to benefit from that expertise. For instance if you watch YouTube videos of Yo-Yo Ma in hopes of becoming an expert cellist, and then try to play Bach's Suite No. 1 in G Major in your room, no one else will likely be meaningfully harmed by the horrible squawks and scratches that would be produced. But if you were to attempt to play cello as a member of a symphony orchestra the whole production would be ruined, the composer might lose his job, and the company would be ridiculed in the musical community. Expertise is critical to organizing because it allows people to *do things*—complete a task, give advice, make a decision, provide a service, delegate responsibility—with a reasonable expectation that the actions taken by experts can be trusted.

Yet at the same time that we look to experts to help us navigate an expansive environment of information, we often know surprisingly little about the individuals and organizations offering expertise. When we access information online we rarely have the chance to ask questions about the source of the material. This invisibility is not an exclusively modern problem—we commonly don't see what a mechanic does to our car or how a chef prepares our food. However, as work is increasingly distributed and mediated by the use of communication technologies, the actions of experts become increasingly distant from those seeking expertise. The result is an organizational environment where expertise is both more accessible and invisible than it has ever been before.

Paradoxically, within such an uncertain and dynamic information environment expertise is extremely valued because it carries with it the confidence individuals and organizations are acting in an appropriate manner. As Mieg (2001, 35) commented in describing the role experts play, "In one sense or another, expert labor, be it expert advice or expert problem solving, is thought to be rational." Whereas knowledge can be understood as the capacity to act, expertise can be understood as the capacity to act with the best, or right, knowledge. Organizational members often have competing claims to knowledge that facilitate a discourse about the best course of action (Kuhn and Jackson, 2008), but invoking expertise produces a sense of discursive closure (Deetz, 1992) that closes off debate. Similarly we seek expertise in the services that organizations provide without much insight into the means by which they provided them. Giddens (1991) argued that professional firms operate as "expert systems" that disembed social relations such that individuals trust the practices used to deliver work without the need to understand them. We seek communicative signals of expertise because in a world of infinite choices relying on expertise gives us the belief we are making the right one. In studying the process by which the communication of expertise is expressed and assessed we can address a number of questions related to why people and organizations chose particular courses of action.

Importantly, viewing expertise through a communicative lens advances our theoretical knowledge by treating expertise as a process that can be studied on multiple dimensions. To understand how expertise relates to organizing requires moving beyond seeing expertise merely as something that one has. Rather, it is critical to study expertise as something that operates in the social world. Each of the chapters in this book treats expertise as something that is real in the sense that it facilitates action, while noting that the meaning of expertise is an emergent product of ongoing interaction—that expertise is communicative. Seeing expertise through this lens allows us to better address questions regarding how and why conceptions of expertise evolve or remain stable, and what individuals and organizations can do to influence these processes. Expertise is a powerful construct, and we need powerful analytical and theoretical tools to study expertise. This book is our attempt to better equip scholars for this task.

Organization of this Book

The book is divided into four sections, each offering a different approach to advancing the study of expertise. The chapters in the first section present different theoretical frameworks for the study of expertise, communication, and organizing. Each chapter presents an ontological discussion of expertise and makes arguments for how to think about the definition and categorization of expertise (and expertises) in ways that make it amenable to study. Of particular importance is that each chapter advocates viewing expertise as multidimensional and dynamic. By dynamic, we mean that expertise is neither objective nor stable across contexts. Rather, the definition of expertise itself is influenced by both the domain of application and the possibilities for communicating that expertise to others. By looking at factors such as the authority, embodiment, and esotericity of expertise, these chapters reveal expertise as both a situated and contingent construct.

In Chapter 2 Kuhn and Rennstam challenge perspectives that view expertise as either an autonomous object or an attributed label and note that these approaches force analysts to treat expertise as something that can exist prior to, and outside of, interaction. They argue that expertise can be best understood as *a claim to knowledgeability* and in doing so they offer a framework for assessing the means by which individuals and organizations might credibly and persuasively enact expertise. Fundamental to this framework is the notion that claims to knowledgeability are evaluated by audiences based on the perceived authority that accompanies communicative acts. The value of this approach is that authority is a contingent construct that can shift over time based on the actions of both humans and non-human actors. Using this model of expertise allows analysts to account for both the stability of claims to expertise in organizational settings with well-established roles and standards, as well as competing claims of expertise in more emergent fields.

The chapter extends the analysis of expertise and authority by considering the role objects have in facilitating and influencing knowledge claims. Specifically, Kuhn and Rennstam contrast technical objects, whose purposes are known, and epistemic objects whose purpose is open to interpretation or contestation. The nature of an object in a context influences the authority of individuals, with technical objects more likely to be associated with authority in practices reflecting use and operation and epistemic objects associated with authority in practices involving decision-making and strategy. Practices also shape the value of claims to knowledgeability in that they include some justification of the worth of expertise, which will differ based on the concerns of individuals in a context, such as price, creativity, efficiency, or other interests. Two cases studies are presented that demonstrate the applicability of this framework for analyzing expertise in organizational settings.

In Chapter 3 Barbour, Sommer, and Gill continue the theme of exploring the relationship between expertise and authority by considering the heterogeneity of expertise present in organizational settings. Like Kuhn and Rennstam they note that expertise should not be treated as an attribute of individuals, and is accomplished through work practices. However, in contrast to a purely practice-based view they also argue that expertise is relational in that it is influenced by what other actors know, and expertise is macromorphic in that it is influenced by elements beyond organizations (e.g. professional certifications, institutional norms) that afford or constrain particular roles and actions.

This understanding of expertise as heterogeneous underpins their taxonomy of expertise, which describes expertise in organizational settings as technical, arcane, interpersonal, and embodied. They propose that understanding the accomplishment of expertise involves analyzing what forms of expertise are meaningful in a particular setting and how these forms interact to facilitate, or restrict, the legitimacy or authority of workers. Each form of expertise is described in detail, and two vignettes are presented to illustrate the ways multiple forms of expertise are at play within work settings. The chapter concludes by looking at how scholars might utilize this framework to study situations in which different forms of expertise might amplify, contradict, or obscure the authority of others.

In Chapter 4 Collins introduces an approach to analyzing expertise that considers the degree to which any particular form of expertise involves exposure to tacit knowledge and is characterized by esotericity. These two factors are integrated with the traditional one-dimensional view of expertise as individual or group accomplishment to develop a three-dimensional model— the expertise-space diagram—that represents the differential nature of expertises within a domain. Critically, this model rejects the assumption that experts are rare individuals, and allows for individuals within a domain to vary in their levels of expertise. Additionally, the model can be used to accommodate any domain of expertise regardless of its ubiquity or perceived value.

One way the model is useful is in considering different horizontal surfaces of an expertise space, in which the esotericity of a domain remains constant but individuals differ in experience or performance. Another way of utilizing the model is to compare different levels of the expertise space to consider differences in specialization, professionalization, or rarity of expertises within a domain. Finally, the expertise-space can be used to trace trajectories of expertises that either follow the progression of individuals and groups or the historical changes in how a domain is structured. An advantage of this model is that is allows for differences in how individuals learn or develop expertise and that these processes may vary across domains. The chapter provides a number of examples of how the model can be applied to different domains and how this framework can be useful for exploring new questions related to expertise.

The second section of the book shifts away from a focus on what constitutes expertise, and instead looks at the processes involved in recognizing, judging, and finding expertise in organizations and groups. These chapters contribute to an understanding of the relationship between communication and expertise by recognizing the role of audiences in observing, interpreting, and attributing expertise. Importantly, each of these examinations considers the role of information and communication technologies (ICTs) in shaping the communication available to individuals assessing the expertise of others and how that communication is perceived. This section is critical to understanding how individuals attempt to effectively utilize expertise in organizations, and why this is such an analytical and practical challenge.

In Chapter 5 Liao, MacDonald, and Yuan provide us with a review of how communication influences processes of expertise recognition in groups. They pay particular attention to how differences in group members' opportunities to communicate, communication styles, and level of communication accommodation relate to the likelihood of group members recognizing each other's respective expertise. Various elements of expectation states theory are discussed in order to demonstrate how individuals form expectations regarding the expertise of others, how communication shapes and reinforces these perceptions, and how attributes of individuals and groups can prompt assumptions about who knows what in a group. This chapter demonstrates the importance of communication in understanding processes of expertise recognition by highlighting the dynamic nature of group interactions and the ways individuals can (or cannot) actively shape the attributions made by group members.

This chapter also highlights how two contemporary trends, the increase of work teams involving intercultural communication and the ubiquity of ICTs in organizations, relate to expertise recognition. Few studies have considered the role of culture and communication styles on expertise recognition, and Liao, MacDonald, and Y. Connie Yuan call attention to ways that differences in individualistic or collectivist orientations, power distance, and communication style can influence judgments about members' expertise in group settings. Noting that intercultural communication is often mediated by technology they examine the various ways that ICTs may facilitate expertise recognition, and possibly neutralize some of the effects of culture. They argue that the use of ICTs may improve expertise recognition in intercultural group settings by limiting the opportunities for, and visibility of, behaviors that would reduce judgments of members' competency. The chapter ends by setting an agenda for how scholars can continue to integrate communication into the study of expertise recognition.

In Chapter 6 Merritt, Ackerman, and Hung provide a historical review of efforts to develop technological systems that help people locate expertise in organizational contexts. Expertise finding is presented as a socio-technical challenge in that it is constituted both by material features of a technology and its associated code and algorithms, and the actions of individuals who design, populate, and appropriate the various technologies. Although the allure of expertise-finding systems is evident—locating individuals who can provide relevant, timely, and trustworthy knowledge—designers have struggled to develop systems that can accurately and reliably find expertise at scale in organizational settings. This chapter addresses both the social and technical challenges associated with expertise finding, and briefly describes the operation of several expertise-finding systems over the past few decades. As organizations continue to invest in knowledge management technologies in an attempt to capture, store, and distribute expertise, recognizing the possibilities and limitations of expertise finding will become increasingly important.

Yoon, Gupta, and Hollingshead broaden the inquiry of assessments of expertise in Chapter 7 and consider how workers judge the competence or the incompetence of other co-workers. They first provide a review of research on competence judgments and note that, though scholars have studied how social stereotypes and communication are associated with attributions of competence, less attention has been paid to what influences judgments of incompetence. Extant research provides little guidance regarding whether individuals use different types of information to make judgments of competence and incompetence, whether those judgments are related to affective dimensions, or how information prompting judgments is gathered.

To further our understanding of competence judgments they present the results of an empirical study regarding how individuals define competence, and how they gather information to make competence judgments of co-workers. The results indicated several differences between the ways individuals evaluate competence and incompetence, suggesting that they may be best viewed as distinct constructs. The differences between competence and incompetence are important because related judgments can apply across task domains and either disqualify or facilitate a worker being viewed as an expert. Furthermore, this framework recognizes the active role that workers can play in attempts to shape judgments of competence and incompetence and the dynamic role communication plays in this process.

In Part III, the focus shifts slightly to the role of expertise in professional contexts. Here, occupations and professional societies become the backdrop for the enactment of expertise, distinct from the organizational influences discussed in the chapters of Part II. Historically, alignment with a profession or professional group signaled that individuals or organizations possessed a specific form of expertise, or had an exclusive claim to knowledge in a specialist domain. The chapters in this section paint a far different picture, and present expertise as something that individuals and organizations enact in efforts to solve emergent problems. This section documents the diverse resources that workers call upon to act as experts and how the communicative acts that constitute expertise also serve to shape processes of identification by organizations and individuals.

In Chapter 8 Lammers, Lambert, Abendschein, Reynolds-Tylus, and Varava examine how expertise operates inside of a hospital emergency department. By situating their analysis in a medical context they are able to consider how expertise is manifest in an institutionalized professional sphere. Whereas previous research has considered contexts where identifying expertise is an ambiguous, contested process (this chapter serves as a counterpoint to Treem, 2012) here the relevant question is how expertise is expressed by established experts. The argument is made that physicians' expertise is a product of both an already recognized and institutionalized attribution that doctors act as experts and active communication present in work interactions.

Lammers et al. present findings from a study involving fieldwork in an emergency department doctors' room, which captured the actions and interactions among physicians and other workers consulting each other on patient care issues. A semantic analysis of the talk of doctors during work, along with an examination of how doctors viewed their own work, revealed both the topics and types of expertise expressed by physicians. The findings demonstrate that physicians' expertise exists both cognitively in the sense they *know* things unique to being a doctor, and communicatively in that they interact with others to apply knowledge and solve emergent problems.

In Chapter 9 Buzzanell and Long consider a paradoxical issue: how can organizations create an environment where it is acceptable for experts to fail? They address this challenge by examining how engineering design teams constitute expertise while sustaining ambiguity around the proper course of action and creating opportunities for learning. Using concepts from organizational communication, professional communication, and engineering education they examine how processes of expertise are constituted by the interplay and overlap of different frames and resources. Specifically, Buzzanell and Long describe how talk enables engineers to express expertise in interaction, texts enable individuals to appear and act as a professional, and design schemas facilitate learning and adaption within ambiguous situations. The usefulness of this three-pronged approach to representing expertise processes is represented through a case study of the work of global engineering design teams. This analysis demonstrates how expertise is generative, and that expertise on project teams involves a continual (re)constitution of expertise based on the varying processes of identification enacted by members.

In Chapter 10 Aakhus, Dadlani, Gigliotti, Goldthwaite, Kosterich, and Sahay discuss expertise as an organizational practice, and apply this perspective by considering organizations that compete to provide *expert communication services*. Using grounded practical theory as a guide the chapter discusses how organizations present the communication expertise they offer, and the ways they design communication services as solutions for the problems other organizations face. An analysis of different organizational types is presented that captures the language and logic used by these organizations to communicate about the respective expertise provided.

The type of expertise presented in this chapter is relational and is manifest in a network of organizational activities and structures that span across local and global contexts. Aakhus et al. note that when organizational expertise is viewed within a network of actors with varying relations and needs analysts should consider the question "when is expertise?" as opposed to asking "where is expertise?" Within this framework communication becomes the means by which organizations operate in an opportunity space, primarily through the establishment of, and interaction within, relationships. The focus is on viewing organizational expertise as practical knowledge and reasoning about both how to design communication services, and how to navigate the market for communication expertise.

Part IV looks at how changes in society and the nature of work may offer new approaches and areas of emphasis for the ongoing study of expertise, communication, and organizing. These chapters recognize that, as work becomes increasingly global, technologically driven, and team-focused, theoretical approaches that see expertise as static and residing in individuals are inadequate to explain how expertise operates in organizational settings. The contributions in this section call attention to the relational nature of expertise and the ways the different configurations and flows of knowledge and actions can amplify the expression of expertise beyond what an individual could do alone.

In Chapter 11 Treem and Barley call on scholars to pay more attention to what they term *process expertise*, a type of expertise that is applicable to managing information and communication both within and across domains, but is not easily aligned with a single specialist domain. They argue that, because people commonly conceptualize expertise in terms of practice in specialist domains, process expertise may be discounted, and process experts marginalized in organizations. The chapter discusses how recognizing the work of process experts can have value for organizations by facilitating the practices of domain experts. Process experts are represented as those who engage in operational processes, curational processes, evaluative processes, and representational processes that manage information in a manner that makes it more useful to others in an organization. This process expertise may be particularly beneficial to individual experts and organizations because it is potentially transferable across contexts in a way that other specialist expertises are not.

In Chapter 12 van den Hooff and Kotlarsky provide a framework for how expertise operates within fluid organizational forms, which are characterized by a dispersed workforce and ambiguous boundaries, and play an increasing role in the economy. These organizations are dynamic in the sense that they rely on rapidly shifting networks of individuals and relationships in order to facilitate innovation and maintain flexibility. While this fluidity makes these organizations more adaptable, it also poses unique challenges regarding the utilization and retention of expertise. To better understand expertise in fluid organizations van den Hooff and Kotlarsky argue we should focus more on knowledge *flows* as opposed to knowledge *stocks*. To emphasize the importance of knowledge flows they explore how processes of coordinating expertise, already a difficult task in organizations with stable roles and structures, becomes even more problematic when the needed expertise is dispersed and dynamic. Specific challenges related to locating, applying, and updating expertise in fluid organizations are discussed, and mechanisms presented that may help overcome obstacles and aid processes of expertise coordination in dynamic environments.

In Chapter 13 Fulk considers whether a collective can enact a form of expertise beyond the expertise of its individual members, and if so, what would this collective expertise look like? The construct of collective expertise is contrasted with approaches that view expertise as a product of individual practices, and instead expertise is considered as a multilevel phenomenon. A number of examples from animal behavior and biological sciences are presented to describe how the expertise of individual actors can be compiled or configured to produce a form of expertise no single group member could enact. Studying collective expertise draws attention to the relationships among organizational members and the ways that the structure and nature of these ties produce a unique form of expertise. Fulk argues that multilevel expertise can emerge from symbiotic relationships in which the actions and knowledge of actors complement each other, or parasitic relations in which some actors exploit the expertise of others. Developing a better understanding of collective expertise will require increased attention to the relations between organizational members, and a discussion of how we might appropriately measure the practice and evolution of collective expertise over time.

On the Future of Expertise: Exploring the Intersection of Technology and Visibility

Taken together, the chapters in this book highlight a number of phenomena that are implicated in the formation, maintenance, and dissolution of expertise, including authority, interdependencies among groups and professions, competence, attributions, signals, sharing, design, culture, and professional norms. To provide some foundations for these common themes, we would like to close by discussing the relationship between visibility and expertise, and the role technology may play influencing these two concepts. Regardless of whether one views expertise as an objective, relational, or situated construct, the question of how expertise is made visible to others is relevant to questions regarding how people locate, assess, value, apply, or even overlook expertise. The centrality of visibility to our understanding of expertise is intriguing for both analytical and practical reasons because there are a number of ways individuals might actively make communication more or less visible to others. In particular, the use of ICT, and their respective features, offer individuals means to broadcast, target, regulate, or restrict communication in ways that are not available in face-to-face settings. As a result the interplay of workplace technologies and the visibility of behavior and work that they enable—or constrain in conspicuous ways—becomes a promising area for inquiry. As we continue our agenda of mapping out a series of phenomena for future research, we would be remiss to leave out a direct discussion of technology and visibility. For while these constructs are not explicitly featured in the chapters presented in this book, a close read will reveal that they lie in the very near background, affecting and influencing each of the phenomena discussed in profound ways.

It is not unknown that computational and mobile technologies are proliferating across organizations (Rice and Leonardi, 2013). Though technology is not the primary focus in this book, each chapter makes clear that technologies have important implications for the enactment of expertise. When one mentions technology in relation to expertise, people's thoughts often go to knowledge management systems, which are communication technologies meant to contain documentation of people's knowledge and, thus, harness expertise and make it available to everyone in an organization. However, the evidence is clear after many years of use that, despite the fact that an increasing number of firms are implementing technologies for knowledge management, few organizations who use them report dramatic improvements in the exploitation of cumulative expertise (Kankanhalli et al., 2005). In recent years, scholars have suggested that many organizations that employ knowledge management systems do not reap the expected benefits because workers do not enter into the technology information that reflects their expertise. Multiple hypotheses exist as to why this might be so, including arguments that people don't know how to use the technology proficiently (Yuan et al., 2005), that electronic documentation has not yet proliferated as a team norm (Walsham, 2002), that people don't think the information they possess is important for others (Cress et al., 2006), or that people don't fully display their individual knowledge for public use because they fear losing status and power (Hollingshead et al., 2002).

All of these explanations share two interdependent assumptions about the relationship between expertise and technology that the chapters of this book largely refute. First, they treat expertise as an objective property of individuals: either a person is an expert or she is not. Second, they treat a person's expertise as a quality that is distinct from his use of the technology: that is, use of a knowledge management system has no effect on whether a person is or is not an objective expert. As the chapters in this book suggest, it may be theoretically problematic and empirically untenable to treat expertise as a stable, individually held attribute that exists independently from the technologies that attempt to harness and disseminate it. Instead, technologies are part and parcel of expertise. They enable individuals to trade certain kinds of knowledge and they provide co-workers and team members a way to view people's actions and make attributions about whether or not someone is an expert.

By enabling a forum for the presentation of task-related and social information in textual, video, or image format, and by allowing people to search and classify those items, nearly all communication technologies provide people with information that can be used as a key proxy to make attributions about the expertise of others. The fact that the information that is entered into or channeled through technologies is visible to a great many organizational members increases the likelihood that such information will be used for attributions of expertise because evaluators will have information to use as a signal for determining what someone knows and will be able to compare information entered by one person with information entered by others. Moreover, as Feldman and March (1981, 178) suggested long ago, "when there is no reliable alternative for assessing a decision maker's knowledge, visible aspects of information gathering and storage are used…as symbols of confidence…and social efficacy." For this reason, individuals may correlate expertise with the length of a contribution in a social text application or the placement of information in particular categories (Adamic et al., 2008). Such information operates as a means for individuals to display what Collins and Evans (2007, 67) call "externally measurable criteria." Because knowledge management technologies are typically networked such that all members of a team have access to the same information at any time, a user can evaluate what information others have entered into the technology, compare those entries, and begin to make attributions of who has expert knowledge. In sum, it becomes both easier and socially legitimate for individuals to rely on visible information communicated through technology when forming attributions about others' expertise.

Attributions of expertise that people make when using technologies are clearly dependent on the nature and quality of the information entered into or communicated through them by others. If a person who has important knowledge on relevant issues does not enter sufficient or detailed information he may not be perceived by others to be an expert, and he will not be called upon to apply his knowledge to a particular problem. Conversely, someone who does not have a great deal of knowledge on a topic but succeeds in entering information into the technology that is seemingly more complete or detailed than information entered by her colleagues may be treated as an expert and given tasks that draw on the expertise people believe she has. In such scenarios, the social construction of expertise is inherently bound up with people's use of a technology. People are treated as having expertise or not depending upon how they use the technology (Treem, 2013).

Because expertise is a valuable personal resource in organizations, determining who has status, who performs what tasks, and who learns what (Wittenbaum, 2000), an individual may be motivated to selectively present information to others that will help those others to form certain perceptions about the nature of his expertise. Such action is likely to be common in situations where individuals believe their personal motivations are more important than, or out of alignment with, the goals of the team (Jarvenpaa and Majchrzak, 2008) and when they believe that becoming known as an expert in the current team will help them to be seen as an expert after they have left the team (Waite et al., 2004). The strategic presentation of information offered for expertise construal should be much easier to accomplish in contexts where knowledge management systems make information immediately and easily accessible to all other members. In these contexts, members can closely monitor whether or not the information they are entering in the technology is producing the desired effect and adjust their actions accordingly. In short, people may use information visibility to strategically reformulate their expertise as opposed to using it in ways that allow others to form accurate directories of their knowledge base.

Interestingly, workplace managers and academics often view communication technologies as passive vehicles for the storage of information. The authors of the chapters in this book would challenge this assumption. Use of a communication technology is much more likely to co-evolve with people's perceptions about who is an expert, as well as the information that people communicate to establish their expertise—or the attributions that people make based on their communications. Researchers who study expertise integration should pay close attention to how and why individuals use technology to share information. If people do use communication technology to share information about who knows what, theories of expertise coordination will need to be specific about how that technology is used and how shifts in the way it is used may enable or constrain the dynamics of expertise coordination over time.

Interestingly, early commentators on technology use in industrial settings argued that computer-controlled manufacturing technologies would strip occupational expertise from workers and encode it in machines (Braverman, 1974; Noble, 1979). In the 1980s, researchers showed that the use of new computerized technologies in knowledge work settings could provide users with new skills and reshape the profile of an occupation's expertise (Barley, 1988; Zuboff, 1988). Today, many researchers combine these de-skilling and re-skilling perspectives to suggest that people make choices about how to use a technology's features. If they use them in ways that allow the technology to automate their work they may lose expertise, but if they reconfigure those features, through redesign or by creating work-arounds, in such a way that they can dramatically alter how the technology works, users may develop new skills and strengthen or change their expert knowledge (Boudreau and Robey, 2005; Majchrzak et al., 2000). This approach proposes that expertise changes when people develop new skills around using a technology—what Black et al. (2004) call "operative" expertise—or when the features of a new technology allow a user to do things she simply could not have done before the technology arrived—what Leonardi and Barley (2008) refer to as "transformational" expertise.

The concept of visibility provides a third way of thinking about how the use of a new technology can lead to changes in expertise. When information that already exists in a social context is invisible to all team members there is little opportunity that any given person will be able to mobilize that information in their work. However, when technologies are used in such a way that information is made visible to everyone in an organization, individuals may use this information to purposefully reshape the distribution of work. If people are assigned to work on different tasks than they had before, or to work on familiar tasks with more concentrated effort, individuals may build new knowledge and skills and hence think of themselves and be thought of by others as experts. In such cases, one's expertise does not derive from knowing how to use the technology (operative expertise) or by using the technology's features to work in radically different ways (transformational expertise). Instead, technologies may simply make information that already existed in the social context visible to everyone and, in so doing, allow people to mobilize it in their actions. In this way, new technologies may lead to the reformulation of expertise in organizations by allowing people to have a fuller view of their information environment. When viewed from this vantage point, technologies that simply make information visible may be powerful agents for change in organizations precisely because they enable users to move information out of the private domain and into public view where the social construction of expertise can occur.

Conclusion

The goal of this book is to better integrate communication into the study of expertise and consider how this can help us explore processes of organizing. We have argued that part of the value of this effort is that invoking, engaging, and expressing expertise provides us with the confidence that we are following an appropriate course of action. Therefore, we present the contributions from our expert colleagues, and say with confidence that the expertise shared in these chapters will provide each of you the requisite expertise to study expertise in the future. Trust us; we're experts!

■ REFERENCES

Adamic, L. A., Zhang, J., Bakshy, E., and Ackerman, M. (2008). Knowledge Sharing and Yahoo Answers: Everyone Knows Something. *WWW2008*. Beijing, China.

Barley, S. R. (1988). Technology, Power, and the Social Organization of Work: Towards a Pragmatic Theory of Skilling and Deskilling. *Research in the Sociology of Organizations*, 6, 33–80.

Black, L. J., Carlile, P. R., and Repenning, N. R. (2004). A Dynamic Theory of Expertise and Occupational Boundaries in New Technology Implementation: Building on Barley's Study of CT Scanning. *Administrative Science Quarterly*, 49, 572–607.

Boudreau, M.-C., and Robey, D. (2005). Enacting Integrated Information Technology: A Human Agency Perspective. *Organization Science*, 16(1), 3–18.

Braverman, H. (1974). *Labor and Monopoly Capital: The Degradation of Work in the Twentieth Century*. New York: Monthly Review Books.

Collins, H., and Evans, R. (2007). *Rethinking Expertise*. Chicago: University of Chicago Press.

Cress, U., Kimmerle, J., and Hesse, F. W. (2006). Information Exchange with Shared Databases as a Social Dilemma: The Effect of Metaknowledge, Bonus Systems, and Costs. *Communication Research*, 33(5), 370–90. doi: 10.1177/0093650206291481

Deetz, S. (1992). *Democracy in an Age of Corporate Colonization: Developments in Communication and the Politics of Everyday Life*. Albany, NY: State University of New York Press.

Feldman, M. S., and March, J. G. (1981). Information in Organizations as Signal and Symbol. *Administrative Science Quarterly*, 26(2), 171–86.

Giddens, A. (1991). *The Consequences of Modernity*. Stanford, CA: Stanford University Press.

Goffman, E. (1959). *The Presentation of Self in Everyday Life*. Garden City, NY: Doubleday Anchor.

Hollingshead, A. B., Fulk, J., and Monge, P. R. (2002). Fostering Intranet Knowledge-Sharing: An Integration of Transactive Memory and Public Goods Approaches. In P. J. Hinds and S. Kiesler (eds), *Distributed Work: New Research on Working across Distance Using Technology* (pp. 335–55). Cambridge, MA: MIT Press.

Jarvenpaa, S. L., and Majchrzak, A. (2008). Knowledge Collaboration among Professionals Protecting National Security: Role of Transactive Memories in Ego-Centered Knowledge Networks. *Organization Science*, 19(2), 260–76.

Kankanhalli, A., Tan, B. C. Y., and Wei, K.-K. (2005). Contributing Knowledge to Electronic Repositories: An Empirical Investigation. *MIS Quarterly*, 29, 113–43.

Kuhn, T., and Jackson, M. H. (2008). Accomplishing Knowledge: A Framework for Investigating Knowing in Organizations. *Management Communication Quarterly*, 21, 454–85. doi: 10.1177/0893318907313710

Leonardi, P. M., and Barley, S. R. (2008). Materiality and Change: Challenges to Building Better Theory about Technology and Organizing. *Information and Organization*, 18, 159–76.

Leonardi, P. M., and Treem, J. W. (2012). Knowledge Management Technology as a Stage for Strategic Self-Presentation: Implications for Knowledge Sharing in Organizations. *Information and Organization*, 22(1), 37–59.

Majchrzak, A., Rice, R. E., Malhotra, A., King, N., and Ba, S. L. (2000). Technology Adaptation: The Case of a Computer-Supported Inter-Organizational Virtual Team. *MIS Quarterly*, 24(4), 569–600.

Mieg, H. A. (2001). *The Social Psychology of Expertise: Case Studies in Research, Professional Domains, and Expert Roles*. Mahwah, NJ: Lawrence Erlbaum Associates.

Noble, D. F. (1979). Social Choice in Machine Design: The Case of Automatically Controlled Machine Tools. In A. Zimbalist (ed.), *Case Studies on the Labor Process* (pp. 18–50). New York: Monthly Review Press.

Rice, R. E., and Leonardi, P. M. (2013). Information and Communication Technologies in Organizations. In L. L. Putnam and D. K. Mumby (eds), *The Sage Handbook of Organizational Communication: Advances in Theory, Research, and Methods* (pp. 425–48). Thousand Oaks, CA: Sage.

Treem, J. W. (2012). Communicating Expertise: Knowledge Performances in Professional-Service Firms. *Communication Monographs,* 79(1), 23–47. doi: 10.1080/03637751.2011.646487

Treem, J. W. (2013). Technology Use as a Status Cue: The Influences of Mundane and Novel Technologies on Knowledge Assessments in Organizations. *Journal of Communication,* 63(6), 1032–53. doi: 10.1111/jcom.12061

Waite, W. M., Jackson, M. H., Diwan, A., and Leonardi, P. M. (2004). Student Culture vs Group Work in Computer Science. *Proceedings of the 35th SIGCSE Technical Symposium on Computer Science Education* (pp. 12–16). New York: ACM.

Walsham, G. (2002). What Can Knowledge Management Systems Deliver? *Management Communication Quarterly,* 16, 267–73.

Wittenbaum, G. M. (2000). The Bias toward Discussing Shared Information: Why are High-Status Group Members Immune? *Communication Research,* 27(3), 379–401.

Yuan, Y., Fulk, J., Shumate, M., Monge, P. R., Bryant, J. A., and Matsaganis, M. (2005). Individual Participation in Organizational Information Commons: The Impact of Team Level Social Influence and Technology-Specific Competence. *Human Communication Research,* 31(2), 212–40. doi: 10.1111/j.1468-2958.2005.tb00870.x

Zuboff, S. (1988). *In the Age of the Smart Machine: The Future of Work and Power.* New York: Basic Books.

Part I

Frameworks for the Study of Expertise and Organizing

2 Expertise as a Practical Accomplishment among Objects and Values

TIMOTHY KUHN AND JENS RENNSTAM

For social scientists, the notion of expertise is fascinating for its slipperiness. Its study has long been marked by a conceptual distinction that illustrates starkly contrasting assumptive grounds. Some conceive of expertise as *autonomous*, such that an expert can be understood as such without validation from others. In this work, the expert is the person who has acquired the relevant training and accumulated the necessary experience within a field to perform some task at a level superior to a novice (Dane, 2010; Day and Lord, 1992; Dreyfus and Dreyfus, 2005). In contrast, others consider expertise to be *attributed*, such that the label is affixed to an actor only by relevant others in (or with reference to) the conduct of practice (see Yoon, Gupta, and Hollingshead, this volume). When expertise is attributed, analytical attention turns not to the contents of the mind, but to actors' abilities to project, often in aesthetic terms, an air of knowledgeability to others through a practice (Alvesson, 2001; Friedson, 2001; Kuhn and Jackson, 2008). From this analytical stance, expertise cannot be determined a priori; instead, the concept is "up for grabs" (Hartelius, 2010, 3) in the sense that participants in a practice seek to persuade audiences of the validity and relevance of their knowledge. Expertise is, accordingly, *a claim to knowledgeability*. In portraying it as a claim, we are suggesting that expertise is best understood as negotiated among actors who always make reference to the situation in which the claim is made.

If expertise is a claim to knowledgeability, the persuasiveness of the claim depends on the *authority* of the claimant. Since its earliest days, organization studies has acknowledged authority as a key element in understanding organizing. The most common starting point is Max Weber (1978), who defined authority as the probability that commands from a given source will be obeyed by a particular group of persons. Authority, then, is *a claim to decidability*, the legitimate right to shape collective decision-making in the service of collectively valued ends; position and expertise are the resources upon which organizational actors typically draw when making such claims on practice (Gilman, 1962; Grimes, 1978; Kahn and Kram, 1994).

The inheritors of Weberian thinking have generally assumed a close association between position and expertise as bases for authority (e.g. Miller, 1970; Simon, 1997). For instance, Barley (1996) suggested that all claims to authority are based either on occupying a particular office in a hierarchy (position) or on the ability to engage in valued skilled practice (expertise)—and that, ideally, position and expertise should correspond. Tellingly, when subordinates in bureaucratic organizations reject the authority of supervisors who have not demonstrated adequate technical skill, or when the subordinates decry the politics that vault non-experts into positions of authority, they are displaying the strong and enduring tension between position and expertise in explaining authority (Sennett, 1980; Taylor and Van Every, 2014). As Barley argues, "insisting on authority of position in the absence of expertise drives a wedge between management and a cadre of employees who are generally committed to the organization's well-being" (1996, 437).

Cases in which the link between expertise and authority is severed are common, as seen in contemporary social debates about climate change, disease control, and disaster preparedness. When those acknowledged to be (or portrayed as) content-area experts are ignored—when they are not recognized as respected and influential voices guiding collective decision-making (i.e. they are not authoritative)—commentators regularly ask why expertise and authority are split. Our response to this question is that they are not really split. Rather, the question arises because we tend to assume that expertise is a static individual capability rather than a practical accomplishment. Experts are not ignored *despite* being experts, but because these actors are not constructed *as* experts by the practice at hand. In other words, who is to be considered an expert and what sorts of knowledge are valued as the basis of expertise depend upon the practice under consideration (see also Barbour, Sommer, and Gill, this volume).

This is a deceptively simple claim, one that becomes more complex as its consequences are interrogated. To engage in this interrogation, we propose a framework for studying expertise that acknowledges its situational and contingent character. We suggest that, because most practices are irredeemably social and material simultaneously (Orlikowski, 2007; Pickering, 1995), the influence of objects of knowledge (Knorr-Cetina, 1997) marking any given practice must occupy a central position in our understandings. And because practices are evaluated by participants with respect to the values they embody and serve, we must also examine the forms of valuation, or "economies of worth" (Boltanski and Thevenot, 2006), upon which practices unfold. In short, starting with the assumption that expertise and authority are neither necessarily connected nor necessarily distinct, we suggest a framework that understands expertise as an accomplishment negotiated in practices informed by objects as well as economies of worth. The framework thus intends to explain *how* expertise is accomplished in practice. In the next section we set out to develop the framework by outlining its main components: objects and economies of worth.

Toward a Framework for Examining the Accomplishment of Expertise and Authority in Organizing

Expertise names the practice of directing skill toward particular problems encountered in practice; those problems emerge from, are recognized in, and are justified through communication. Expertise, as has already been suggested, is a claim to knowledgeability that appeals to an audience engaged in a practice. In turn, authority becomes less about securing others' obedience than about claims to decidability—along with the concomitant promise of value to be produced by the decision advocated by the actor. Claims to authority can be based upon expertise or position and these resources are often in tension in organizing.

In situating both expertise and authority as claims, we are implying that neither is fixed; that both may shift across sites of organizing over time. By way of illustration, Benoit-Barné and Cooren's (2009) study of a conversation associated with Médecins Sans Frontières's operation in the Democratic Republic of the Congo showed how a medical coordinator accomplished authority as she enrolled objects (specifically, a note she had written directing local medical practice) to demonstrate her knowledge about procedure and, more importantly, about the surrounding bureaucratic context. But that authority *shifted* when another participant confronted her in his role as chief technician (his position implicitly granting him the capacity to represent other technicians); he altered the conversation by enrolling objects (a work apron he wore as a symbol of his subject-matter expertise) and by displaying his desire to correct a power imbalance. This case shows that authority and expertise can shift as the basis of the practice at hand shifts over time. It leads us to ask how particular forms of expertise become (ir)relevant in a given situation, along with how it is that the person considered to be an expert can shift during organizing. The framework in this chapter addresses those questions.

Expertise and authority are the products of *claims* that appeal to resources associated with organizational situations. What, then, are the features of situations that lead to potential shifts in authority and expertise? We see two elements that are particularly important: objects of knowledge and conceptions of value. Our framework is described in Figure 2.1, a depiction that we discuss in the following sections.

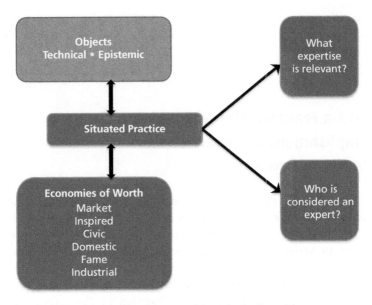

Figure 2.1 Elements of the Accomplishment of Expertise in Organizing

EPISTEMIC AND TECHNICAL OBJECTS

Rather than seeing objects as the inert "stuff" upon which humans work, practice-oriented thinking understands objects as divided into two types: technical and epistemic (Knorr-Cetina, 1997, 1999). Technical objects are instruments, such as a hammer ready at hand to be used by a skilled carpenter. They are taken for granted, their presence and utility are not the subject of interrogation. Epistemic objects, in contrast, are puzzling; they are perpetually unfinished because they call for continued questioning and conceptual effort. Epistemic objects, therefore, are always under construction, such as a cell scrutinized by a biologist, a child taught by a pre-school teacher, or a criminal gang under the surveillance of the police.

The distinction between technical and epistemic objects is well established in organization studies (e.g. Ewenstein and Whyte, 2007; McGivern and Dopson, 2010; Miettinen and Virkkunen, 2005; Rennstam, 2012). The terms have their origin in Heidegger's argument that "equipment" tends to disappear and become invisible when we are using it, but problematic, and no longer just "equipment," when it breaks down (Dreyfus, 1990; Heidegger, 1977; Knorr-Cetina, 1997). Heidegger's "equipment" largely represents a technical object that becomes an epistemic object when it breaks down. A car provides an example. Given that we know how to drive and are driving without paying attention to understanding the car, the car is a technical object while we are driving it. When it breaks down, however, it becomes an epistemic object. Think of a malfunctioning car that puzzles us and needs to be understood and repaired. After repair, it can become a technical object with respect to our use again. Knorr-Cetina (1999, 10) puts this in more Heideggerian terms: technical objects are "available means-to-an-end within a logic of instrumental action," whereas epistemic objects are "continually unready-to-hand, unavailable and problematic." In short, and metaphorically, we may say that a technical object is an instrument, while an epistemic object is a problem.

Objects are not *inherently* either technical or epistemic; the categorization is situated and determined *in practice*. In our car illustration, the vehicle may be a technical object when it is taken as an instrument of transportation, but an epistemic object to someone who is learning how to drive, someone whose car breaks down, or someone who is interested in cars' aesthetic and cultural dimensions. An important outgrowth of this point is that any object can *change* status depending on how it is used. Following this line of thought, technical objects may also *become* epistemic when their technical status is questioned. The argument that practice determines the character of the object is rooted in the literature on hybrid (sociomaterial) agency, which claims that objects gain their role always and only as participants in a network of interactions with humans and/or other objects (e.g. Latour, 2005; Law, 1994; Pickering, 1995). For example, a hammer is likely to be a technical object (instrument) in the practice of carpentry, but an epistemic object (problem) in the practice of designing hammers. Thus, objects do not need to functionally "break down" to be considered epistemic rather than technical.

Moreover, objects can be the sites of struggles over meaning. Epistemic objects are unfinished stabilizers of organization that "interpellate" knowledgeable agents to use their knowledge to make them finished (Rennstam, 2012). Technical objects, in contrast, are understood as storage places for ideology in the sense that they encode naturalized social relationships and discipline action in unreflective ways (Eagleton, 2007). When objects move from epistemic to technical, they become more straightforwardly ideological in this sense: they "disappear" (Dreyfus, 1990), and the individuals interacting with them become subject to different forms of control. Epistemic objects participate in control by eliciting knowledge use, while technical objects participate as taken-for-granted instruments in the "hands" of a user.

The question in understanding whether an object might be understood as technical or epistemic, then, is one of *use*, of practice (see also Buzzanell and Long, this volume). Returning to our interest in expertise, Taylor and Van Every note that expertise might be understood, with respect to technology, "as an *uncovering* of the potentiality of technology; as openness, as learning, as adaptation" (2014, 201; emphasis in original). The intersection of expertise and objects may be most obvious when an actor renders an epistemic object technical or, alternatively, when one applies knowledge to "open up" a previously technical object to new interrogation. Actions such as these are, of course, always accomplished in practice, and therefore imply a set of participants who supply conceptions of value that shape the understandings of objects.

VALUE

Claims to expertise and authority are additionally shaped by the logics that shape the construction of value in a given context. A key element marking discursive moves as locally relevant or irrelevant is whether they provide solutions to organizing problems—and, notably, whether those solutions promise the creation of value. Value production, however, is not a straightforward measurement of benefits and costs expressed by price; it is action that articulates prevailing conceptions of worth—"goods" that can be internal or external to a given practice (McIntyre, 1985). Value, therefore, is a sociocultural construct, a recognition that suggests the presence of multiple value domains (Graeber, 2001, 2005; Harvie and Milburn, 2010).

An account of the multiplicity of value domains that understands them as mere context—in other words, as ontologically distinct containers for practice—would clearly be out of step with the sort of practice-based account we advocate. Therefore, we turn to work by Boltanski and Thevénot (2006), which provides a vocabulary for understanding value as the product of forms of justification (i.e. claims) manifest in practice.

Boltanski and Thevénot characterize six[1] distinct "economies of worth," or "worlds," as models of good (i.e. the valuable) and legitimate action (Boltanski and Thévenot, 2006; Cloutier and Langley, 2013; Jagd, 2011; Patriotta et al., 2011; Stark, 2011). These six worlds are not containers, but *conventions*: practices that generate coordination by channeling uncertainty through chains of events (Thevénot, 2013). The *market* world, first, is that to which most are accustomed: it is where value is measured by price, such that the rare, expensive, and profitable—and, in turn, the accumulation of wealth—is highly valued. Knowledge about the operation of the commercial system and its players (e.g. buyers, sellers, regulators) is esteemed. Second, the *inspired* world is the domain of art and unique, passionate, creative talent. The third realm, the *civic* world, prizes collective welfare and solidarity; here, individual drives are suppressed in the interest of the public good. In the fourth world, the *domestic*, loyal and trustworthy filial ties are prized, as are tradition, hierarchy, and heritage. For the world of *fame*, the fifth world, value is the result of the celebrity; fashionable and renowned elements are considered to

---

[1] Thevénot, Moody, and Lafaye (2000) later added another world they named "green"; we do not include it here both because it has yet to be taken up in the organization studies literature and because its claims are not yet convincingly distinct from the existing orders of worth.

display great value. Sixth is the *industrial* world, where methodical planning and technical efficiency are prized, as are those who can optimize systems through scientific precision.

Analysts seeking to understand valuation as an element of practice should track the justifications for authoritative claims, since those justifications are likely to implicate claims to create worth or value—to create "the good." Acknowledging the simultaneous presence of multiple orders of worth potentially pervading (and emerging from) any practice, what become particularly interesting are the ways in which claims to expertise may encounter conflicting logics, such that a promise to create value through one's application of knowledge may align with one world but interfere with another. Likewise, the possibility of alternative forms of valuation can be resources for struggles over expertise, as actors could draw upon the conception of the good from one domain in arguing against claims based in another. Our attention to multiple economies of worth, therefore, provides an approach for gaining insight into (a) the ways in which claims to expertise and authority receive justification in practice, and (b) how the presence of multiple forms of valuation offer the potential to understand how claims to expertise shift along with changes in a given practice.

SUMMARY

The framework we advocate is intended to foster insight into the practice of organizing. We suggest that bound together are expertise, objects, and value in the accomplishment of authority in organizing—and that these are each to be understood as provisional and ongoing accomplishments generated in practice. Another way of saying this is to suggest that authority is the claim to decidability (and, thus, to the authorship of a collective) created through the alignment of objects, orders of worth, and expertise found in practice—the outcome of the process depicted in Figure 2.1. The status of each element is the result of claims, bids, efforts to persuade, that align and enroll participants in the process of organizing. Although the particular sets of relations among the elements are likely to be empirical questions, the framework leads analysts to examine how claims to expertise enroll (technical and/or epistemic) objects and appeal to particular orders of worth generated in and through the practice.

The value of this framework lies in its heuristic capabilities, its capacity to suggest and frame questions. Based on Figure 2.1 and the preceding discussion, we see two important questions emerging. Specifically, *what expertise is relevant*, and *who is considered an expert?* "Relevant" is a key notion here, as claims to knowledgeability always make reference to the object(s) of knowledge and the forms of valuation marking the practice, such that some forms of knowing and doing are more preferred than others (see Barbour, Sommer, and Gill, this volume). Based on this framework, we might expect to find expertise deployed in the introduction of new objects, in efforts to shift the conception of objects from epistemic to technical (or vice versa), or in the assertion of an alternate conception of value. With this model in place, we turn to two illustrations to explore the analytical purchase of our sensitizing framework.

Illustrations

In the following, we will illustrate how expertise is accomplished in relation to authority, value, and the movement between technical and epistemic objects. In the first example, "the amplifier case," the object has a physical foundation (an amplifier). In the second example, "the diversity management case," the object is abstract, or figurative (diversity management).

THE POWER AMPLIFIER CASE

Our first illustration is taken from a study of engineering work in an organization that develops technology for cellphones (Rennstam, 2012). At one point during the study, the engineers started to talk about exchanging the amplifier of the radio in the phone (all cellphones have a radio that transmits and receives signals, and the radio has an amplifier to amplify the sound), which led to a five-week-long interaction between several actors trying to figure out what to do. The main actors, all engineers, were:

- Harry, a manager who worked with customer relations
- Lars, an engineer who worked with technology development
- Jake, an engineer who worked with technology development and had designed the algorithm of the current amplifier
- Thor, a manager who was previously a project leader
- Fred, an engineer who worked with supplier relations (supplier of components for designing the radio)

The engineers debated what to do at two general work meetings and four meetings dedicated only to discussing the amplifier. The discussions resulted in a decision at the last meeting not to do anything about the amplifier. The question here is this: how did the amplifier move between technical and epistemic status, and how were expertise, authority, and value employed to make the decision?

If we move back to the time before the discussions began, the amplifier was not a problem in the organization. Rather, it was a *technical object*, an instrument that filled the function of amplification in the radio. But then it somehow entered the "epistemic world" of the engineers, that is, it became a problem to be solved in their everyday work. Exactly how this happened is difficult to say, but it seems to have emerged in interaction between Harry and Lars. Harry said that he had talked to customers (producers of cell phones) who indicated that a replaceable amplifier would be desirable (it would enable them to use a cheap and simple amplifier in a basic model, and a more expensive and advanced one in a high-end model, using the same platform technology). Lars, on the other hand, said that he started the whole thing by suggesting that they take out one component in the amplifier design, which would save space and money, but would increase the power consumption. The point here is that there was no single relation between the amplifier and other actors that *changed its status from technical to epistemic* object. Rather, it was a network of actors who represented different knowledge relationships with the object, of which the amplifier vis-à-vis customer relations-knowledge and technology-knowledge (size and power consumption) seemed to be most important.

The amplifier's emergence as a problem in the work of the engineers triggered them to engage in the practice of "knowing" with regard to the amplifier. That is, the amplifier "invited" the engineers to create knowledge about it, to use their knowledge to make sense of it, within the context of their work. This is what epistemic objects do: they are unfinished, puzzling, and problematic (e.g. Knorr-Cetina, 1999) and they *interpellate*, or call upon, knowledgeable people to know more about them (Rennstam, 2012). Within the engineering practice, claims to expertise made bids for how to act with respect to the epistemic object.

The five weeks of debate about the amplifier may thus be understood as a struggle between claims to expertise regarding suppliers, customers, projects, and the technology. Generally, Harry (customer) and Fred (supplier) favored a change in the amplifier, while Thor (project) and Jake (technology) were skeptical. Harry was fascinated by the idea of enabling the customers to decide which amplifier to use, but Thor warned of the problems a new design would create in relation to the rest of the project, and Jake pointed to technological difficulties.

At the last meeting, the claim to expertise regarding the technological capacity of the amplifier "won." Jake argued that the new design would cause too many problems for other components. Based on this claim, the team decided not to pursue a new design. Authority, as an answer to the question about decidability, was accomplished here based not on position, but on a claim regarding what the object would allow—a resource more aligned with Jake's technical knowledge in this instance than others. And the form of value characterizing the practice displayed the dominance of an industrial world, where engineering knowledge and technical efficiency, in the service of system optimization, are prized. After reaching the decision, the amplifier reverted to its previous state as a technical object. It became an instrument for amplification again, and ceased to puzzle, provoke, or interpellate the engineers.

The example thus shows how the amplifier moved from a technical object to an epistemic one, and back again. It also shows how expertise and authority were accomplished, in the sense of being made relevant or present (Cooren, 2006, 83), in relation to the amplifier. If we take seriously that expertise and authority are not actors' possessions but are practical accomplishments, it is only in retrospect that we can establish that the team attributed expertise to Jake. And he accomplished this by drawing on a logic associated with an *industrial* order of worth, a move that "won" over Harry's efforts to enroll a *market*-based conception of value with his attention to the customer. The authority associated with Jake also won over the formal hierarchy: both Harry and Thor were Jake's managers, but their hierarchical position carried less weight than Jake's technical knowledge because of the configuration of claims and participants in the practice. This configuration was not to last, however.

About a year after the engineers decided not to develop a new amplifier design, top management turned the decision around and decided that they should revisit this choice, allegedly because customers had demanded a smaller amplifier. As a result, the amplifier became an epistemic object again, as the engineers were commanded—note the enrollment of the rules of hierarchy as an authoritative resource—to figure out how to fit in a new design. This had consequences for all the relationships just outlined. Technical knowledge with regard to the amplifier was needed, so projects had to be altered to allocate resources to the development of the new design, and suppliers had to be contacted. All this happened abruptly, based on a formal decision from top management—a group which previously had not paid much attention to the amplifier problem, and had not theretofore been a participant in the engineering practice.

The interesting turn of events suggests a different form of expertise was operating in the second episode. The previous situation's industrial version of value benefited Jake, along with the other engineers, as they framed the amplifier as an epistemic object and portrayed their expertise as necessary to determine the trajectory of the amplifier-based engineering practice. But when top management introduced customers' demands as a new epistemic object, it was managerial expertise (in terms of access to, and understanding of, customers) that "won" in this struggle over the trajectory of practice. The shift, then, also evinces a change in valuation in the practice, one that privileged the market world's affinity for the players in commercial affairs over the industrial world's emphasis on efficient technical production.

This sudden turn illustrates not only that the amplifier once again became an epistemic object to the engineers, but also that it became a technical object to top management—one that could be "closed" as they pursued the more important (to top management) epistemic object of customers' demands. The amplifier did not puzzle top management; it did not interpellate them to make sense of it.

Suggesting that expertise shifted to top management in the latter episode is not, of course, to say that engineers suddenly were bereft of knowledge when it came to the design of the amplifier. Rather, the *object of expertise*—as the focal point of competing perspectives—changed, and the enrollment of the market-based logic of the practice enabled a shift in control over the trajectory of practice. From the perspective of this new object of expertise (customers' demands), Jake's time as an expert ended because he was no longer able to *author* amplifier practice. Thinking about our two questions—*what expertise is relevant* and *who is an expert*, the case illustrates not a rejection of Jake or his knowledge, but a recognition that the practice itself changed, and that other objects (customers, as a representation of the market world) became epistemic, carrying with them a basis of valuation that aligned more closely with management. The introduction of an epistemic object, therefore, is instrumental to both locating expertise and to producing value with respect to an economic world.

THE DIVERSITY MANAGEMENT CASE

Our second illustration is similar in that it shows how orders of worth and objects fuel practical negotiations of expertise, and that objects may be understood as technical by some and epistemic by others. But the setting and the nature of the object are different, which indicates a broader relevance of our model. The setting is taken from an ongoing study of the Swedish police by one of the authors, and the object is not physical but the figurative notion of "diversity."

Diversity is a pressing issue to the police, since they are frequently the object of public scrutiny in terms of race, gender, and sexuality. The Swedish police are no exception. From time to time they are accused of being racist, sexist, or homophobic and feel a need to respond to these accusations. One way of responding to the accusations—or to their own insights about diversity-related problems in the organization—is to engage in training of the employees. Our case illustrates such a diversity training program in Skåne, a region in the south of Sweden, and we argue that "diversity" was understood and used by some as a technical object to gain public legitimacy, but by others as an epistemic object to investigate and interrogate in the process of sense-making regarding police work.

As in the case of the amplifier, the origin of the diversity training initiative is difficult to pin down. There were different interpretations as to why the program was undertaken. Many police officers believed that it was a reaction to a number of recent incidents where police officers had expressed themselves in racist and homophobic terms. The program managers, however, pointed to the fact that they had planned for the program before the incidents. Also, they held that the program was the result of instructions from the government (the head of the program said that they were instructed to "do something concrete when it comes to honor violence, domestic violence, and LGBT [lesbian, gay, bisexual, and transgender] issues"). In light of these circumstances, the Skåne police applied for money from the European Social Fund (ESF) to survey the police staff's knowledge of honor violence, domestic violence, and LGBT issues.

The program managers received the ESF grant and conducted a survey in which staff were asked to estimate their personal knowledge of LGBT issues. Sixty percent estimated themselves to have little or no knowledge of LGBT-related issues, 40 percent to have little or no knowledge of hate crime, and 20 percent to have little or no knowledge of domestic violence. Based on this information, the program managers concluded that diversity training was warranted. In other words, "diversity" was constructed as a problem and, specifically, as a problem of a lack of knowledge among police; the solution was understood in terms of information transfer by means of a training program. The program managers, when constructing the need for training, thus understood diversity as an epistemic object, as a problem that could be remedied through the deployment of information.

Shortly afterward, the training program was launched. The majority of the police officers and managers in Skåne went through a facilitated three-hour workshop where they discussed the United Nations Declaration of Human Rights, the Swedish Discrimination Act, key elements of democracy, how power may be exercised in various ways, and the role of the police in relation to the rest of society. They also participated in a role-playing exercise about norms. The last hour of the workshop featured lectures by visitors who each represented a societal minority, including a representative of the Romani in Sweden, a trans-sexual person, and a woman who had been exposed to honor-related violence.

In these sessions, trainers presented diversity as an epistemic object—a feature of social life that held the potential to lead police officers to reconceptualize their understandings of themselves, their work, and the citizens with whom they interacted. The trainers' claims to expertise regarding diversity, claims often based on personal experience, encouraged sense-making about the notion. In the practice of training, experts were those who communicated in a manner that made sense of diversity, who could problematize others' experiences with regard to diversity and encourage reconceptualization. This sort of questioning facilitated a form of exploration that served as a good in itself, separate from any social consequences it might produce. It exemplified the *inspired* world, where work on ideas (via creativity and problematization) rather than economic outcomes is desired.

In these sessions, expert authority did not manifest as one actor determining the collective direction or deciding what diversity "meant." Instead, it looked more like enforced problematization, as trainers' and lecturers' efforts to inspire questioning authored the group practice. Authority of this sort was not questioned in these sessions, perhaps because the trainers and lecturers were invited in for the training, and perhaps because of their professional or personal credentials—in short, their claims to expertise about diversity-related issues.

Among police management, however, diversity was constructed largely as a technical object, an instrument for accomplishing one of the main tasks of the police: to fight crime. Specifically, managers said that the overarching purpose of the diversity training program was to improve the performance of criminal investigations. As Amanda, the project manager, pointed out, "if we have to formulate one single purpose with this project, then it is to prosecute more offenders. That is the absolute goal." Other initiators of the program backed up Amanda's point. For instance, Susan, the gender and diversity coordinator of the Skåne police, said:

This [program] is meant to make us better at what we do, to enable a clearer connection between police and prosecution. [For example k]nowing how to approach girls who have been victims of honor issues, or people who have been victims of hate crime[2]—how do we interact with *them*?

And Ted, the head of education and training:

… the purpose, then, is to produce better investigations that lead to more prosecutions.

Also, the program manual highlighted this instrumental role of diversity, and related it to the importance of public confidence in the police:

[As a method of improving the investigations, it is important to] strengthen the public's confidence in the police's ability to understand the conditions of victims as well as offenders. This is achieved among other things through improved knowledge about different groups in society.

Thus, diversity, as an object, was understood by police as technical in the sense that it was an instrument for increasing the performance of the police. In terms of value produced in this practice, we see evidence of the *industrial* world, where value is measured by efficiency and that which is productive and functional is esteemed. Because diversity could be displayed as a step in the

---

[2] According to *Encyclopedia Britannica*, hate crime pertains to "harassment, intimidation, or physical violence that is motivated by a bias against characteristics of the victim considered integral to his social identity, such as his race, ethnicity, or religion. Some relatively broad hate-crime laws also include sexual orientation and mental or physical disability among the characteristics that define a hate crime."

optimization of the police role in society—a way to improve investigations and prosecute more criminals—the technical object of diversity could be harnessed by experts in producing efficient policing procedures. This accomplishment of expertise enabled management to plan, initiate, and implement "diversity" as an efficacy intervention rather than an intellectual exploration.

Managers of the diversity program therefore closed diversity as an epistemic object. Their appeal to expertise associated with industrial efficiency rendered it technical rather than epistemic as it had been constituted in the training sessions. Managers framed diversity as something that the Skåne police force needs to "have" and something that the officers needed to know more about so that they might prosecute more offenders.

Managers thus established themselves as experts not of diversity but of crime-fighting, a practice in which diversity was seen as an instrument. Put differently, to the managers, crime-fighting was the epistemic object and diversity the technical object. Moreover, management also employed "diversity" as a technical object in the sense that it was an instrument for legitimacy. As noted, the Swedish government wanted the police to "do something concrete" and the training program could be presented to the government as a concrete initiative to improve knowledge about diversity. In this sense, the program created legitimacy and enabled managers to claim responsiveness to the governmental mandate.

Advancing the Study of Expertise

Our examination of expertise and authority, illustrated by these two cases, highlights the need to bring in the additional concepts—technical and epistemic objects, along with economies of worth—presented in this chapter. Our aim is not simply to reframe or complicate understandings of expertise and authority, but to explain how and why organizing in particular settings follows particular trajectories. As illustrated in both of the cases presented in the preceding section, practice could have followed a different path; how particular interests (and the actors associated with them) "won" over others is thus a key issue.

The question now is whether this framework lends itself to the development of analytical insight not available otherwise. We see three primary contributions. First, our framework of expertise rests on a dynamic and processual view of organization where meaning is constantly generated and transformed (Ashcraft et al., 2009; Tsoukas and Chia, 2002). This broadens the understanding of expertise. Not only do we move beyond the simple distinction marking the expertise literature—between seeing expertise as either autonomous or attributed—to instead understand expertise as *accomplished*. We see its accomplishment as always accompanied by two key features of organizing practice: objects and value. Consequently, in cases in which solutions to problems are ambiguous or lacking, when breakdowns occur, or when interests collide, experts are often targets of blame. At the same time experts, by virtue of their authority and knowledge, are central actors in efforts to reconstitute problems as determinate, technical objects. Rather than locate expertise exclusively "in" persons, and rather than relegate objects to a position where they are inert entities at the service of human actors, we suggest that expertise is "up for grabs" in the sense that it is decided in practice just where expertise is to be located, and how it is to be enrolled in problem-solving. Diagnosing difficulties in organizing is not as simple, then, as identifying a person, group, or artifact as deficient. It involves, instead, an understanding of the relationships among expertise, authority, objects, and value as they unfold over time, an exercise that would also be on the lookout for the production of unintended consequences of action.

Second, our framework also provides the possibility of reframing tensions and disorder in organizing. A good deal of scholarship suggests that the normal state of organization is tension and contradiction (Poole and Van de Ven, 1989; Putnam, 1986; Tracy, 2004; Trethewey and Ashcraft, 2004), that organizations operate on a "logic of difference" (Cooper, 1986) instead of demonstrating integration and coherence. From such a vantage point, organizing becomes "an unfolding process of tension between order and disorder that pluralizes and crossconnects artifacts and subjects, human and non-human elements" (Clegg et al., 2005, 154–5). Analysts, in turn, are likely to note "inconsistencies between practices as different economic, social, political and ethical forces shape individual practices and in turn the relationships between practices in an organizational field" (Antonacopoulou, 2008, 122). These inconsistencies are precisely what we have suggested are the sites where the accomplishment of expertise is brought into sharp relief (Kuhn and Porter, 2011). When existing practice is challenged through the assertion of a new logic of valuation (as in the PA case), or when the object of knowledge is transformed (as in the diversity management case), the meaning of expertise can shift. Tracing the resulting struggles over meaning regarding expertise—what expertise is considered relevant, and who is considered an expert—offers the potential to understand how the responses to such tensions participate in the authoring of a collective's trajectory.

A third contribution is methodological, showing the value of analytical distance for making sense of expertise. From a cognitive perspective, expertise is individualized; in other words, the expert is always the expert. From our practice-oriented perspective, expertise becomes contingent on the negotiation between object- and value-informed practice. In order to see how expertise is shifting, the analyst requires distance. For instance, if we only followed the engineers in the engineering case, in our eyes Jake would have remained the expert. We would not have observed the introduction of a new epistemic object, which shifted the relevant expertise toward management. This recognition suggests that the boundaries an analyst establishes around a practice matter, and that focusing on, or following, alternative practices would likely produce different responses to the questions about expertise (see Nicolini, 2012).

Conclusion

The topic addressed in this chapter is important for its breadth and social significance; ours is not merely a question of organizing process. We noted that, in some public controversies—climate change, disease control, disaster preparedness, for instance—those considered "experts" are often ignored in public debates. The framework we developed would explain this by suggesting that ignoring experts is not merely a matter of lacking trust in institutions or of political influence over public discourse (Giddens, 1991; Weber, 2014), but exposes a difference in *practice*. In other words, scientific expertise may well be relevant when the scientists' objects are constructed as epistemic, and when an industrial order of worth is dominant, but when practices alter those features of practice, other forms of expertise ascend to relevance. The response, then, is that in organizing as in public life, expertise and authority are always contingent on the characteristics of situated practice—and our framework provides conceptual and methodological purchase for explaining those contingencies.

▤ REFERENCES

Alvesson, M. (2001). Knowledge Work: Ambiguity, Image, and Identity. *Human Relations*, 54, 863–86. doi:10.1177/0018726701547004

Antonacopoulou, E. P. (2008). On the Practise of Practice: In-tensions and Ex-tensions in the Ongoing Reconfiguration of Practices. *The Sage Handbook of New Approaches in Management and Organization* (pp. 112–31). Los Angeles: Sage.

Ashcraft, K. L., Kuhn, T., and Cooren, F. (2009). Constitutional Amendments: "Materializing" Organizational Communication. In A. Brief and J. Walsh (eds), *The Academy of Management Annals* (vol. 3, pp. 1–64). New York: Routledge.

Barley, S. R. (1996). Technicians in the Workplace: Ethnographic Evidence for Bringing Work into Organizational Studies. *Administrative Science Quarterly*, 41, 404–41. doi: 10.2307/2393937

Benoit-Barné, C., and Cooren, F. (2009). The Accomplishment of Authority through Presentification: How Authority is Distributed among and Negotiated by Organizational Members. *Management Communication Quarterly*, 23, 5–31. doi: 10.1177/0893318909335414

Boltanski, L., and Thévenot, L. (2006). *On Justification: Economies of Worth*, tr. C. Porter. Princeton: Princeton University Press.

Clegg, S. R., Kornberger, M., and Rhodes, C. (2005). Learning/Becoming/Organizing. *Organization*, 12, 147–67. doi: 10.1177/1350508405051186

Cloutier, C., and Langley, A. (2013). The Logic of Institutional Logics: Insights from French Pragmatist Sociology. *Journal of Management Inquiry*, 22, 360–80. doi: 10.1177/1056492612469057

Cooper, R. (1986). Organization/Disorganization. *Social Science Information*, 25, 299–335. doi: 10.1177/053901886025002001

Cooren, F. (2006). The Organizational World as a Plenum of Agencies. In F. Cooren, J. R. Taylor, and E. J. V. Every (eds), *Communication as Organizing: Empirical and Theoretical Explorations in the Dynamic of Text and Conversation* (pp. 81–100). Mahwah, NJ: Lawrence Erlbaum.

Dane, E. (2010). Reconsidering the Trade-Off between Expertise and Flexibility: A Cognitive Entrenchment Perspective. *Academy of Management Review*, 53, 579–603.

Day, D. V., and Lord, R. G. (1992). Expertise and Problem Categorization: The Role of Expert Processing in Organizational Sense-Making. *Journal of Management Studies*, 29, 35–47. doi: 10.5465/amr.2010.53502832

Dreyfus, H. L. (1990). *Being-in-the-World: A Commentary on Heidegger's Being and Time, Division I*. Cambridge, MA: MIT Press.

Dreyfus, H. L., and Dreyfus, S. (2005). Expertise in Real World Contexts. *Organization Studies*, 26, 779–92. doi: 10.1177/0170840605053102

Eagleton, T. (2007). *Ideology: An Introduction* (2nd edn). London: Verso.

Ewenstein, B., and Whyte, J. (2007). Beyond Words: Aesthetic Knowledge and Knowing in Organizations. *Organization Studies*, 28, 689–708.

Friedson, E. (2001). *Professionalism, the Third Logic: On the Practice of Knowledge*. Chicago: University of Chicago Press.

Giddens, A. (1991). *Modernity and Self-Identity: Self and Society in the Late Modern Age*. Stanford, CA: Stanford University Press.

Gilman, G. (1962). An Inquiry into the Nature and Use of Authority. In M. Haire (ed.), *Organizational Theory in Industrial Practice* (pp. 105–42). New York: Wiley.

Graeber, D. (2001). *Towards an Anthropological Theory of Value: The False Coin of our own Dreams*. London: Palgrave.

Graeber, D. (2005). Anthropological Theories of Value. In J. G. Carrier (ed.), *A Handbook of Economic Anthropology* (pp. 439–54). Cheltenham: Edward Elgar.

Grimes, A. J. (1978). Authority, Power, Influence and Social Control: A Theoretical Synthesis. *Academy of Management Review*, 3, 724–35. doi: 10.2307/257928

Hartelius, E. J. (2010). *The Rhetoric of Expertise*. Lanham, MD: Lexington Books.

Harvie, D., and Milburn, K. (2010). How Organizations Value and How Value Organizes. *Organization*, 17, 631–6. doi: 10.1177/1350508410372620

Heidegger, M. (1977). *The Question Concerning Technology and Other Essays*, tr. W. Lovitt. New York: Harper & Row.

Jagd, S. (2011). Pragmatic Sociology and Competing Orders of Worth in Organizations. *European Journal of Social Theory*, 14, 343–59. doi: 10.1177/1368431011412349

Kahn, W. A., and Kram, K. E. (1994). Authority at Work: Internal Models and their Organizational Consequences. *Academy of Management Review,* 19, 17–50. doi: 10.5465/amr.1994.9410122007.

Knorr-Cetina, K. (1997). Sociality with Objects: Social Relations in Postsocial Knowledge Societies. *Theory, Culture and Society,* 14, 1–30. doi: 10.1177/026327697014004001

Knorr-Cetina, K. (1999). *Epistemic Cultures: How the Sciences Make Knowledge.* Cambridge, MA: Harvard University Press.

Kuhn, T., and Jackson, M. (2008). Accomplishing Knowledge: A Framework for Investigating Knowing in Organizations. *Management Communication Quarterly,* 21, 454–85. doi: 10.1177/0893318907313710

Kuhn, T., and Porter, A. J. (2011). Heterogeneity in Knowledge and Knowing: A Social Practice Perspective. In H. Canary and R. D. McPhee (eds), *Communication and Organizational Knowledge: Contemporary Issues for Theory and Practice* (pp. 17–34). New York: Routledge.

Latour, B. (2005). *Reassembling the Social: An Introduction to Actor-Network Theory.* Oxford: Oxford University Press.

Law, J. (1994). Organization, Narrative, and Strategy. In J. Hassard and M. Parker (eds), *Toward a New Theory of Organizations* (pp. 248–68). London: Routledge.

McGivern, G., and Dopson, S. (2010). Inter-Epistemic Power and Transforming Knowledge Objects in a Biomedical Network. *Organization Studies,* 31, 1667–86. doi: 10.1177/0170840610380808

MacIntyre, A. (1985). *After Virtue: A Study in Moral Theory* (2nd edn). London: Duckworth.

Miettinen, R., and Virkkunen, J. (2005). Epistemic Objects, Artefacts, and Organizational Change. *Organization,* 12, 437–56. doi: 10.1177/1350508405051279

Miller, J. P. (1970). Social-Psychological Implications of Weber's Model of Bureaucracy: Relations among Expertise, Control, Authority, and Legitimacy. *Social Forces,* 49, 91–102. doi: 10.1093/sf/49.1.91

Nicolini, D. (2012). *Practice Theory, Work, and Organization: An Introduction.* Oxford: Oxford University Press.

Orlikowski, W. J. (2007). Sociomaterial Practices: Exploring Technology at Work. *Organization Studies,* 28, 1435–48. doi: 10.1177/0170840607081138

Patriotta, G., Gond, J.-P., and Schultz, F. (2011). Maintaining Legitimacy: Controversies, Orders of Worth, and Public Justifications. *Journal of Management Studies,* 48, 1804–36. doi: 10.1111/j.1467-6486.2010.00990.x

Pickering, A. (1995). *The Mangle of Practice: Time, Agency, and Science.* Chicago: University of Chicago Press.

Poole, M. S., and Van de Ven, A. H. (1989). Using Paradox to Build Management and Organization Theories. *Academy of Management Review,* 14, 562–78. doi: 10.5465/amr.1989.4308389

Putnam, L. L. (1986). Contradictions and Paradoxes in Organizations. In L. Thayer (ed.), *Organization<—>Communication: Emerging Perspectives I* (pp. 151–67). Norwood, NJ: Ablex.

Rennstam, J. (2012). Object-Control: A Study of Technologically Dense Knowledge Work. *Organization Studies,* 33, 1071–90. doi: 10.1177/0170840612453527

Sennett, R. (1980). *Authority.* New York: Knopf.

Simon, H. A. (1997). *Administrative Behavior: A Study of Decision-Making Processes in Administrative Organizations* (4th edn). New York: Free Press.

Stark, D. (2011). *The Sense of Dissonance: Accounts of Worth in Economic Life.* Princeton: Princeton University Press.

Taylor, J. R., and Van Every, E. (2014). *When Organization Fails: Why Authority Matters.* New York: Routledge.

Thévenot, L. (2013). Convention School. In B. Jens and M. Zafirovski (eds), *International Encyclopedia of Economic Sociology* (pp. 111–15). London: Routledge.

Thévenot, L., Moody, M., and Lafaye, C. (2000). Forms of Valuing Nature: Arguments and Modes of Justification in French and American Environmental Disputes. In M. Lamont and L. Thévenot (eds), *Rethinking Comparative Cultural Sociology: Repertoires of Evaluation in France and the United States* (pp. 229–72). Cambridge: Cambridge University Press.

Tracy, S. J. (2004). Dialectic, Contradiction, or Double Bind? Analyzing and Theorizing Employee Reactions to Organizational Tension. *Journal of Applied Communication Research*, 32, 119–46. doi: 10.1080/0090988042000210025

Trethewey, A., and Ashcraft, K. L. (2004). Practicing Disorganization: The Development of Applied Perspectives on Living with Tension. *Journal of Applied Communication Research*, 32, 81–8. doi: 10.1080/0090988042000210007

Tsoukas, H., and Chia, R. (2002). On Organizational Becoming: Rethinking Organizational Change. *Organization Science*, 13, 567–82. doi: 10.1287/orsc.13.5.567.7810

Weber, M. (1978). *Economy and Society: An Outline of Interpretive Sociology* (vols 1 and 2). Berkeley, CA: University of California Press.

Weber, P. (2014). America Doesn't Trust its Experts Anymore, *The Week*, Oct. 6. Retrieved from <http://theweek.com/articles/443346/america-doesnt-trust-experts-anymore>.

3 Technical, Arcane, Interpersonal, and Embodied Expertise

JOSHUA B. BARBOUR, PAUL A. SOMMER,
AND REBECCA GILL

Organizational efforts to coordinate expertise or derive and capture value from expertise are famously ineffective and prone to failure (Chua and Lam, 2005; Leonardi and Treem, 2012). Technological interventions aimed at harnessing or supporting the creation, use, and capture of the organizational knowledge held by experts have an especially uneven track record (Flanagin et al., 2009; Huang et al., 2013). Addressing the shortcomings of these efforts depends on conceptualizing expertise and expert knowledge work to account for the emergent and situational character of knowing and the practice of expertise.

Efforts toward such conceptualizations tend to emphasize the problem-centered, situational, and community-driven character of knowing and expertise. Kuhn and Jackson (2008, 473) defined knowledge as having "a capacity to act within a situation," and knowledge work as a communicative accomplishment in the sense that "knowledge in a given context is simply that which enables and sustains problem solving and not necessarily that which can be independently justified as *true*" (p. 456). Experts, then, are those who have a distinctive capacity for solving particular sorts of problems or at least those individuals thought of in organizations as having such capacities (Alvesson, 2001; Treem, 2012).

Given this framing, resources for understanding the variability of knowing and the practice of expertise are key. We seek an understanding of expertise heterogeneity that focuses on differences in the provision of the authority to act or to encumber others to act. Ignoring the heterogeneity of knowing can "oversimplify and sterilize practice" (Kuhn and Jackson, 2008, 473), which may limit efforts to reveal why and when knowing contributes to problem-solving. Problem- and situation-focused frameworks for expertise should be useful *because* they surface difference.

Previous efforts to categorize knowing and expertise have proven useful but not unproblematic (Alvesson, 2001). Research has demonstrated that expertise coordination processes differ depending on knowledge areas or domains

(Boh et al., 2007; Huang et al., 2013; Yuan et al., 2010). In a given situation, individuals may possess and employ similar expertise but to different effects, because of power differences or because the performance of their expertise differs. A focus on expertise heterogeneity brings attention to "why certain forms of expertise become valued in organizational environments whereas others are not" (Treem, 2012, 44).

This may help illuminate how privileged forms of expertise reinforce established knowledge and ways of knowing, which may inhibit innovation (Styhre, 2009) or make more difficult communication among individuals with varying expertise (Barbour and James, 2015). For example, research and theorizing of expertise coordination and knowledge-intensive work tends to focus on the possession and manipulation of cognition in text work such as accounting, lawyering, professing, and engineering, with the focus largely on the production of knowledge in forms decoupled from the individual. This concern with established professional work obscures how expertise in these settings may be different from *and* similar to the knowing in body work or craftwork (Dougherty, 2011; Gherardi and Nicolini, 2002; Gibson and Papa, 2000; Sennett, 2009).

Kuhn and Jackson (2008, 473) argued of their knowledge-accomplishing framework that "diverse or heterogeneous knowledge is key to the conception of episodes and knowledge-accomplishing interaction. As people frame situations, differences in knowledge (e.g., expert/novice) and in approaches to problem solving (i.e., what is considered appropriate) frequently surface" (p. 473). Their efforts to explicate heterogeneity focused on the expert/novice and appropriate/inappropriate distinctions, and they also argued that accounting for interaction of community and difference in knowing is key: "studies of knowing tend to ignore knowledge diversity when they attend to community influences" (p. 473). The goal of this chapter is to conceptualize knowledge heterogeneity as key to understanding expertise power dynamics, which center on perceptions of legitimacy, encumbering other actors, and acting with authority (see also Kuhn and Rennstam, this volume).

Rather than treating expertise as an attribute of an individual, we underpin the chapter with a conceptualization of expertise as relational, practiced, and macromorphic. Expertise is *relational* in the sense that, for example, team members are experts not just because of what they know but because of what the other team members think they know (Hollingshead and Brandon, 2003; Ren and Argote, 2011). Expertise is negotiated in interaction with different audiences (Hollingshead and Brandon, 2003). In these ways, expertise is contingent on the particular problematic situation at hand and the communicators implicated in that situation (Kuhn and Jackson, 2008). In the *practice* of expertise, experts construct and project expertise as part of their identity and impression management (Alvesson, 2001; Leonardi and Treem, 2012). Tsoukas and Vladimirou (2001) argued that the ability to put what we know to use is a matter of socialization, and by extension therefore, its constitutive processes of identity formation and negotiation (see also Gherardi and Nicolini, 2002). The socialization of experts is tied to extra-organizational moorings of what counts as legitimate expertise (Taylor and Van Every, 2014). Expertise is *macromorphic* in the sense that it is entwined with extra-organizational perceptions, certifications, messages, and constellations of beliefs and practices that cast us in particular roles (Barbour, 2010; Lammers and Barbour, 2006). The macromorphic character of expertise is particularly clear in professional contexts (Barbour and Lammers, 2015; Scott, 2008), but it is evident to varying degrees in the practice of expertise generally where systemic, shared beliefs about expert work inform "who has responsibility for what, who is entitled to play which role, and how the resulting outcomes will be distributed" (Taylor and Van Every, 2014, 9).

We focus in this chapter then on how and why expertise has the power to classify, frame problematic situations, and bring interactions to a close through an analysis of particular vignettes or episodes of expertise in practice. We seek to answer the question, *how do different forms of expertise act and interact to accomplish knowledge work?* We first explicate a taxonomy of expertise forms emergent from the vignettes (see Table 3.1). For each episode, we tell the story, then we focus on how those involved framed the problem and deployed or developed knowledge to try and solve the problem (Kuhn and Jackson, 2008). We conclude by returning to the taxonomy to explicate a research agenda for the study of knowing and expertise informed by an understanding of the heterogeneity of expertise.

Table 3.1 Expertise Forms

	Knowledge Work "The performance centers on the ..."	Legitimacy "I judge the performance as legitimate when it ..."	Encumbering "The performance encumbers me because it ..."	Authority "The performance draws force from ..."
Technical	Technical properties of the work	Accurately and correctly yields facts or solutions	Names	Professional acumen, formal education, apprenticeship
Arcane	Policies, standards, and laws that govern the work	Provides a convincing reading per existing conventions	Adjudicates	Law, policy, professional standards
Interpersonal	People involved in the work, relational history of the work	Captures who we are together	Connects	Participation in relationships
Embodied	Physical conduct of the work and the arrangement of the work space	Reads the wisdom in space/material conditions/time with insight	Sees	Consequences of material conditions of work

A Taxonomy of Expertise Forms

Our taxonomy elucidates the heterogeneity of expertise by highlighting the different forms and functions of expertise at work in work (see Table 3.1). Expertise performances—the application of knowing to solve problems— reflect a mix of the *technical, arcane, interpersonal, and embodied*, and particular expertise performances no doubt emphasize particular dimensions. Expertise mobilizes power through the legitimacy it confers, the encumbering of other actors, and a basis in authority that is macromorphic (Alvesson, 2001; Lammers, 2011; Scott, 2008).

Taylor and Van Every (2014, 9) argued that judgments about expertise depend on "thirdness . . . a body of understanding about an object, shared by a community, usually expressed in language, of what the work or other sustained activity they are engaged in means, and how it should be done." Expertise involves authority separate from but related to orthodox organizational hierarchies. Expertise draws its authority from constructed differences in knowing. Experts have disproportional authority to decide—"to author the trajectory of practice" (Kuhn and Rennstam, this volume)—because they have disproportionate claims to knowledge. Expertise is judged as legitimate and therefore has authority to encumber others when it is appropriate and efficacious (i.e. the expertise does what it claims to be able to do, solves the problems it means to in accepted ways). Expertise authority is the power to encumber that is perceived to be legitimate, because it is "in concordance with existing and accepted organizational texts, scripts, or structures" (Kuhn and Rennstam, this volume).

Our taxonomy explores how expertise performances encumber through different sources of legitimacy and authority. The taxonomy is cross-cutting. Whereas research has previously contrasted, for example, implicit/tacit and explicit knowing (Collins, 2011), the technical, arcane, interpersonal, and embodied dimensions of expertise that we frame in our taxonomy each have tacit and explicit elements. Whereas other research looks at expertise specific to knowledge areas (e.g. topics, domains), we expect that any given knowledge area has technical, arcane, interpersonal, and embodied forms. However, we offer the taxonomy not as a replacement for these well-established and insightful conceptualizations of knowing and expertise difference, but rather as another alternative that highlights the differences in legitimacy, authority, and encumbering among expertise forms. The taxonomy is not an end, but is an incomplete list of expertise forms that is useful to the extent it makes these differences clearer. The taxonomy is then less about categorizing expertise functions and more about categorizing the means of the communicative accomplishment of expertise. If we expect (a) any given expertise performance to involve technical, arcane, interpersonal, and embodied expertise, but (b) to varying degrees of salience and importance, then (c) the taxonomy will bring into relief the operation of different means in any given performance. The purpose of the taxonomy is to orient researchers to the interactions among these expertise forms.

When most of us think about expertise, *technical expertise* comes to mind first. Indeed, we developed the taxonomy in part by looking for aspects of expertise performances that were not technical. The technical character of expertise centers on the specific knowledge needed for the work—the "know what." A physician visiting with a patient knows the functioning of the human body. An attorney writing a brief knows the facts of a case. A public relations professional who is preparing a campaign knows the background of the issues at stake. An engineer digging an unconventional natural gas well understands the physical forces in play. Studies of expertise that ask us to describe the people we work with in terms of what they know typically focus on technical forms of expertise. We judge technical expertise as effective and legitimate when it accurately and correctly yields facts or solutions. Technical expertise encumbers other actors, because the names and frames for problems and solutions it offers seem true and legitimate, thereby categorizing organizational activity according to established knowledge. Experts draw technical expertise from professional status earned or indicated through formal study or work experience or apprenticeship.

Arcane expertise focuses on mastery of the rules, laws, and legitimated procedures. A physician knows the privacy rules for interacting with patients and the complex systems of procedures used to bill and pay for care. An attorney writing a brief knows the law. A public relations professional who is preparing a campaign knows the ethical rules for conduct. An engineer digging an unconventional natural gas well understands the regulations governing their work. Our attorney example is particularly useful for drawing the distinction between technical and arcane expertise. An attorney knows the law in the same sense that she or he knows the facts of a case, but the nature of each dimension of expertise is different. Whereas the facts of the case encompass actual happenings, the law reflects a system of rules and procedures. That is, the law, regulations, and ethical codes may have their basis in historical events and technical facts, but knowing them means knowing the codes, rules, and conventions that govern work more broadly. Thus, it is arcane in the sense that it is mysterious, open to only those initiated in the system of meaning. The operation of courtroom rules is specific to particular communities and unwritten depending on apprenticeship in particular courts. To term this expertise "arcane" is to emphasize its obscurity relative to the others. We judge arcane expertise as effective and legitimate when it provides a convincing reading of the situation at hand that fits (or makes it fit) established conventions. Arcane expertise encumbers other actors, because it adjudicates expert conduct and conduct governed by expertise. Experts draw arcane expertise from the law, policy, or professional standards and the force and consequence of those conventions.

Interpersonal expertise focuses on the relationships and relational history implicated in a problematic situation. A physician knows to varying degrees their history with the patients and the nurses involved in providing care. An attorney writing a brief has a sense of her relationships with her clients and the opposing counsel. A public relations professional who is preparing a campaign knows the media professionals to whom he will need to reach out. An engineer digging an unconventional natural gas well knows the other people at the pad.

Put another way, research emphasizes the relational character of expertise without making clear that relationships *themselves* are a domain of expertise. That is, all expertise is to a degree relational; expertise is judged by other experts; experts are defined as such in part by others seeing them as experts; however, our concern for interpersonal expertise focuses in particular on the knowing of those involved in work (not the fact that this knowing is itself relational). Interpersonal expertise focuses on the people involved in the work and their relational histories distinct from the relational character of all aspects of expertise.

Relationships are themselves a subject of expertise that reflects a knowing of the people involved, an understanding of their identities in the context of the state of relationships among them. To offer an oversimplified heuristic, if technical expertise is of facts and arcane expertise of conventions, interpersonal expertise is of relationships between people. We judge interpersonal expertise as effective and legitimate when it captures the relationships among those involved in a given problematic situation (i.e. when it answers "who are they?" "how have they treated us?" "what kind of people are they?" "can they be trusted?"). Interpersonal expertise encumbers other actors because it reflects a useful awareness of how people are connected to one another. Experts draw interpersonal expertise from their history in the relationships and their understanding of who knows whom and how they know them.

Finally, *embodied expertise* exists in the physical conduct of the work and the arrangement of the work space. That is, expertise exists not just in the mind of the expert but also in the disciplined bodies that they use in knowledge work. A physician has a gut feeling about a patient's overall health before consulting a specific diagnostic tool. An attorney working on a brief is spurred on by a visualization and felt understanding of the space and interactions in a courtroom. A public relations campaigner has an instinctual read of the tone of an interaction with a journalist. An engineer experiences a visceral sense of the state of drilling at the pad. In other words, expertise is as much about the lived, embodied experience of knowing and knowledge as it is about the cognitive constructs and schema we typically associate with being an expert. Embodied expertise focuses on the physical conduct of the work and the arrangement of the space of work over time. We judge the performance of embodied expertise by the wisdom exercised in particular spaces, the reading of the material conditions, and the insight about the timing of work. Embodied expertise encumbers other actors because it sees, hears, smells, feels, or tastes an aspect of the work that others cannot, because it can perform an action with greater skill, or because it controls the physical space with greater force. The authority of embodied expertise centers on the material conditions of the work itself.

Narrative Interrogation of the Taxonomy

Having unpacked the taxonomy, we turn now to a pair of vignettes. The goal of these narratives is to provide extended examples that may be used to interrogate the boundaries of the taxonomy and to explore the interactions among different forms of expertise. The narratives, which focus on resident inspectors and construction project managers, are derived from the authors' research in nuclear power plants (Barbour and Gill, 2014; Gill et al., 2014) and on construction sites, but we offer them not so much as empirical data but as examples that are useful on their face (Jacobs, 1986). The narratives were selected from the authors' experiences as exemplary problematic situations (Kuhn and Jackson, 2008), and they are described here as vignettes to capture the use of different forms of expertise to solve a problem.

As coherent examples, they offer space to explore the taxonomy to the extent that they are plausible (Jacobs, 1986). Stories taken from these two occupational areas are especially useful because they reflect hybrids of body and text work (Dougherty, 2011; Marvin, 1994). Construction work is physical, but it also involves knowledge-intensive decision-making (Bartholomew, 2008; Egbu and Robinson, 2005), and expertise recognition is established through knowledge in physical work and learning-by-doing (Styhre, 2008). The regulation of complex industrial systems such as nuclear power plants involves knowledge of engineering, craft, procedure, and law, and the work takes place in a physical plant as well as orthodox office settings (Barbour and Gill, 2014). We proceed by telling the stories and highlighting the technical, arcane, interpersonal, and embodied expertise therein.

STEEL REINFORCEMENT

As a concrete contractor, after the major pours were complete, I worked a strike list, fixing issues in the construction. Finishing the items on time was essential, because the work could hold up other trades working in the space. I parked, walked into work, and after our morning briefing, we divided up to work on particular projects throughout the site. The architect had noticed a change in the placement of windows that was not consistent with the original design. To address this, concrete support beams (approximately 2.5 by 2.5 feet in size) running between the windows needed to be cut to make room for the new window placement. The engineer on the site called for additional reinforcement in the form of steel plates that could help carry the load across the modified beams. These supports ran above and below the concrete floor between the first and second floor, and needed to be connected with vertical steel plates that had to pass through the floor where it intersected with the exterior concrete wall. Post-tension cables ran through the floor to provide structural support and prevent cracking. We could not rip up the entire floor to attach one steel plate; we could not see exactly where the post-tension cables were either. Once the concrete floor had been poured, the cables had been put under extreme pressure by stretching them from the outside, hence "post-tension." Severing one might cause it to tear out of the floor like a rubber band snapping. We needed to remove part of the floor next to the wall to insert the steel support without disturbing a cable.

The blueprints and specifications for post-tension cable installation indicated in general terms the number of cables and how far apart they should have been placed, but not the exact locations. A certain amount of flexibility was needed during the pouring process. The only way to proceed was to chip into the floor from above and below, feeling our way through and hoping we picked the right spot. We chipped away at the floor along the wall with a hammer drill fitted with a spade bit. The two of us who were chipping were told that if we struck a post-tension cable with our hammer drill, there was a chance it could snap up and out of the concrete floor. The foreman warned, "If you hit something that feels like metal, stop."

I chipped away concrete from the floor while another team member chipped away from the floor below. I made contact with metal. The vibration changed. I could feel it in my hands, and I could see some rusty steel through the dust and chunks of concrete. It was rebar used to strengthen the concrete, and not a plastic wrapped steel cable. We eventually created a hole big enough for the additional support without encountering a post-tension cable.

We had to attend to the architect and engineer, because of their credentials and the building contracts and legal frameworks that give them the authority to make decisions on the project. But on the job site, problems were going to be addressed using knowledge that came not just from books and the office, but from years of hands-on work. The blueprints may say one thing, but I know what is and what is not going to work in the space. I had to satisfy the engineer and do the work nonetheless, and I had to do it with the materials and physical access I had.

This vignette involves multiple expertise interactions. Technical expertise included the knowledge of forces involved and how materials will respond to those forces as hammer drills were used to chip away at the concrete (i.e. choosing the right tool for the job). The architect wielded technical expertise in his recognition of the need to address the window location in the first place, and the engineer did as well in the design of the reinforcements that were to be used to accommodate the modified exterior structure. Yet the technical mastery of the engineer and architect were in direct conflict with the embodied and arcane expertise of the concrete contractor who knew the time, money, and potential safety risks involved with such a complex solution. The contractor had a gut-level sense of the time and financial realities at the site, which drew legitimacy from his experience on jobs past. Arcane expertise included myriad relevant but conflicting safety regulations and building codes. The contractors had to make the building safer (e.g. with the steel plate) while creating hazards for themselves (e.g. "if you hit something that feels like metal, stop"). The hierarchy of the job site dictated, by virtue of the arcane, that if an architect asked for a change, the engineer was required to provide a solution in accordance with the laws and regulations which governed the modification of structural concrete and steel, as long as that request fell within the powers afforded to the architect within their contract.

The contractor also trusted the embodied expertise of the other person doing the drilling. He was confident that the other person would not put his safety in danger by trying to chip away at a post-tension cable from below. The two performing the work had done work together before, understood that each other would know what it would feel like to strike a steel cable during the process. The embodied expertise was particularly important, because of the physical realities of the site. The contractors could not get access to where they needed to place the plate, and they could not rip up the entire floor. Although the project manager was present when they poured the floor, he could not be sure exactly where the cables were located. They had to act by feel—an embodied knowing of the work (Sennett, 2009), and they knew they could do so because they knew that the feel of the cable would be different, and that they could stop before damaging a cable.

The contractor drew on his interpersonal expertise as well. He asked if this was an engineer he trusted. He was asking, in other words, if the reinforcement was completely necessary, or just "over-engineering." He used what he knew of the people and the physical site to negotiate competing implications of expertise forms.

WALKING DOWN THE CONTROL ROOM

A visit to the control room is a typical, day-to-day activity of resident inspectors at nuclear power plants. Walking into the control rooms with the inspectors, I noticed a quiet hum, the armed guards doing their rounds, and the walls of lights, screens, instrumentation, switches, and handles. The beige and black boards held analog dials with indicators and plastic, color-coded lighted switches. Plastic signs labeling the different parts of the plant organized the boards into sections. A few monitors had been replaced with digital screens. A glass wall surrounded the boards, separating the disciplined space from the quiet offices surrounding it. We stopped and talked to a manager about the previous night's logs and a few ongoing issues. Before even coming to the room, he had skimmed the log.

We stepped to the opening of the control room, and we asked permission to enter. The operator turned to us, and replied we could. We walked along, stopping for whispered questions and explanations. I asked if the inspector knew what all the switches meant and what the indicators should read. He pointed to the stacks of binders under the boards—instruction manuals, explaining that he knew much of the boards. He told the story of being visited by leaders who would quiz him. He shared that knowing the boards was less about memorizing the meaning of every indicator, although knowing that was important too. Instead, as he walks through he can take in the board as a whole.

He explained that he has to know both. He has to know the look of the boards. He also has to know the meaning behind all the board's indicators, but he can find that information if he needs it. A person can sit at the office and memorize the details of the boards, but it takes time at a plant in the space of control room to develop a sense of the board. That sense can be useful, but he warned that inspectors have to be careful they do not confuse what is normal with what ought to be or what is.

This narrative reflects the technical expertise needed for "walking down the boards," including the engineering knowledge about the reactors and the systems that support them. The inspector's expertise was legitimate, because of his training and mastery of the documentation of the technical specifications of this plant and others. Being in the space also meant knowing the arcane, such as the rules that governed the room (e.g. the control room log, the rules for shifts, the legal and policy control of the space). His knowledge of the arcane empowered him to be in the space at all, and to translate his understanding of problems (if any) into action.

Later, the inspector reflected on his history with the particular manager to whom we spoke—interpersonal expertise in the history of past interactions and experiences with particular reactor staff. His interpersonal expertise could influence his work because he could use what he knew to make judgments about the information he was gathering. It could influence with legitimacy, because of the history he had accrued with that person and who they were in relationship to each other (inspector–manager). But the practice of walking down the boards was as much about the look of the board, the gestalt of what it ought to be, as it was about tracking down a particular issue in the boards. His embodied expertise was useful for action and legitimate, because of all of the times he had walked down the boards in the past. However, the inspectors' warning also demonstrates that one form of expertise operating in a space can obscure others. The embodied sense of what the boards ought to look like captures what is normal but not, per se, what they ought to look like when the plant was operating properly.

Advancing the Study of Expertise

By surfacing the heterogeneity of expertise, the taxonomy raises questions about how these forms interact. This taxonomy of different forms of expertise is valuable, because it enriches our understanding of the relational character of expertise and existing models of expertise coordination. We argue that the study of expertise should integrate a focus on (a) interaction among forms of expertise with a particular concern for how differences in knowing (b) are negotiated in relationships (c) with differing implications for expertise coordination.

INTERACTION OF EXPERTISE FORMS

In the stories in this chapter, expertise amplified, contradicted, negotiated, and obscured other forms of expertise. Answering why and how particular forms of expertise have authority and encumber others in organizing means understanding those interactions. In situations where forms of expertise agree, we would expect them to *amplify* each other, meaning that the framing of the problem should be even clearer, the encumbering even stronger, the legitimacy of a particular take more supported than would be expected otherwise, because a particular reading of the situation draws on multiple forms of authority. In the vignettes, the inspectors hoped their technical and embodied expertise would work together to make clearer what was happening in the control room. In other words, the knowledge of the appropriate settings for each switch bolstered the inspectors' internal feeling that everything was operating well at the time. Research informed by an interest in expertise heterogeneity should look for how different forms of expertise may build on each other to offer more and more forceful interpretations and decisions.

When expertise forms disagree or *contradict* each other, researchers should be prompted to ask how and why particular forms of expertise are ascendant in a given situation. In the stories, the embodied expertise of the concrete contractor drilling into a building's support structure was ascendant. It allowed those involved to solve the problem at hand despite the concerns raised by relevant arcane expertise (i.e. safety regulations) and in service of other arcane expertise (i.e. the requirements of building code). The contractors' embodied expertise addressed shortcomings in technical expertise (i.e. the lack of knowledge about the exact locations of post-tension cables).

As contradiction points to questions about the relative power of expertise forms, we expect the struggle over the framing of problematic situations to draw on the authority of expertise judged the most efficacious (problem-solving), where efficacy depends on the particular situation. The notion of contradictory expertise might prompt researchers to make predictions about the contingent authority of expertise. However, instead of trying only to predict which aspect of expertise will rule the day when they conflict, the taxonomy orients the analyst to how actors draw on different forms of expertise to classify problems, make arguments about appropriate solutions, and, in the end, act. The struggle among competing expertise forms implicates not only the struggle to act in problematic situations, but also the competition among experts for the legitimacy of particular readings of situations over others, which is at the heart of collective expert identity negotiation (Barbour and James, forthcoming). These struggles for legitimacy (and in turn authority and encumbering) are evident too when experts challenge each other's judgment, decide what information to share and what not, and negotiate technological and organizational change (Barbour, 2010).

Expertise forms may also not agree without necessarily contradicting either. A given expertise may offer an ambiguous reading of or be unable to resolve the uncertainty in a situation. In such circumstances, the other forms of expertise may help *negotiate* that ambiguity. In the story focused on drilling the floor and cutting the concrete wall, actors drew on embodied and interpersonal expertise to manage the contradictions in the arcane and the ambiguities in the technical. Arcane expertise offered competing courses (drill and do not drill), and the technical expertise in the situation could not identify with certainty the location of the post-tension cables. The contractor was able to feel for the cables by virtue of embodied expertise gained through experience with the impact drill. The embodied expertise allowed the contractors to act despite the uncertainty of the location of the cables. Research informed by a conceptualization of expertise heterogeneity should consider how expertise forms work in concert to negotiate uncertain or ambiguous situations to enable action.

Expertise may clarify in that sense, but a particular form of expertise may also *obscure* alternative meanings. That is, a particular aspect of expertise may be so salient that others are not considered or not understood as relevant. As the inspector walked down the boards, he expressed concern that, instead of amplifying his awareness of the state of the plant, his embodied expertise might obscure a technical reading of the panels and indicators.

Future research focused on how expertise may obscure should be of particular interest in studies of embodied expertise. In the study of knowledge work, concern for technical, arcane, and interpersonal forms of expertise has overshadowed embodied expertise (Collins, 2011; Gherardi and Nicolini, 2002). All work involves a material, physical understanding of the confluence of bodies, the situation, and what is or is not possible (Sennett, 2009). The embodied character of expertise is particularly clear in the trades and craft work, where capacity to act typically involves body work. Embodied expertise may be the most easily obscured, because it is vested not in the mind of the surgeon but in her hands, not in the argumentation of the attorney but in his eye for the face of a confused client, not in the Rolodex of the public relations professional but in his ear for the tone of a conversation, not in the technical specifications of the engineer but in her feel for a building in progress. The taxonomy should be useful for future research in part as a tool for revealing expertise that may otherwise be obscured or unapparent even to those who wield it.

In sum, the taxonomy offers a framework for considering how expertise amplifies, contradicts, negotiates, and obscures expertise. The interaction among these forms of expertise center on the differing authority conferred by expertise, authority tied to systems of understanding, to macromorphic structures, to "thirdness." Taylor and Van Every argued for the importance of expertise negotiation in organizing itself, "The thirdness has been translated into a property, not of individuals, or pairs of individuals, or even of groups, but of the community as a whole. It is a system" (2014, 197). A key implication of the systemic, macromorphic character of expertise (see Fulk, this volume) is that these different forms of expertise are not just vested in the individual but in organizational and institutional structures. Though it may be useful to conflate particular experts with expertise (e.g. common in studies of particular professions, Barbour and Lammers, 2015), research concerned with expertise heterogeneity should not do so. Instead, the taxonomy prompts us to ask how, for example, engineering *and* crafting are technical and embodied, arcane and interpersonal.

RELATIONAL EXPERTISE

A focus on interaction among these forms of expertise may also enrich theorizing in this domain, by nuancing a key insight of communicative approaches to expertise: that it is constructed and judged in relationships (Huang et al., 2013; Ren and Argote, 2011). The taxonomy underscores that expertise is also relational in the sense that our expertise can focus on the interpersonal. Relationships *themselves* and the history and tenor of relationships involved in problematic situations are the subject of expertise. Expertise is *in* and *about* relationships. Research should consider not only the relational negotiation of expertise, but also relationships as an object of expertise. Research could consider, for example, how generating technical, arcane, and embodied expertise produces concomitant interpersonal expertise.

EXPERTISE COORDINATION

The taxonomy also speaks to another key question in the communicative study of expertise and knowledge work. Scholars and practitioners have an overriding concern for understanding how expertise coordination systems work and how to make them work more effectively (e.g. more creatively, more quickly, Hollingshead and Brandon, 2003). The material and discursive maps of expertise, of who knows who knows what, form differently (e.g. experience, word of mouth, credentials, role). Additional research should consider how different forms of expertise complicate the creation and use of material and discursive maps of expertise. For example, expertise is attended to differently—it is salient in different ways. The forms of expertise in the taxonomy look different in practice. They involve different tools. Teams may specialize not only by knowledge domain, but also expertise form. These forms involve different trust criteria, and they are coordinated differently. Interaction among expertise forms may generate new knowledge as well when, for example, the clarification of ambiguous problematic situations creates a new useful knowledge for action (Kuhn and Jackson, 2008).

Conclusion

Although our conceptualization of expertise and knowledge encompasses more than the attributes of an individual, it is nonetheless focused on how individuals use what they know. How that something differs is the key to our taxonomy, but expertise is still herein something mobilized by the individual. Expertise is not just an attribute, but it is a capacity for action—a capacity that reflects different authority, and therefore different legitimacy criteria and different encumbering. Therefore, we locate expertise in the action of those individuals—not a characteristic but a socially constructed, shared sense of what the expert can or cannot do. Expertise and communication are related in that experts employ and develop different forms of what they know in and through communication. Expertise is organizational in the sense that it is embedded in networks of relationships emergent in organizing (see Fulk, this volume), and it is extra-organizational in that expertise authority depends not just on the understandings of the local others' judgments about the expert. Experts draw legitimacy, their capacity to encumber others, and their authority from sources in and outside the organization.

Recognizing these distinctions is essential in the face of the profound technological change that characterize (post)modern life. Taylor and Van Every argued "changes in technology necessitate a rethinking of management practice: literally how to organize—and how to establish authority in the new assemblies of organizing" (2014, 199). The stories in this chapter demonstrated the fundamental entwining of technology (broadly defined) and expertise, including how the very technologies designed and utilized by experts can ultimately undermine and subvert knowledge. Understanding technological change therefore necessitates understanding how knowledge, knowing, and expertise are bound up in and by technologies (Sennett, 2009). Importantly, our taxonomy of expertise and knowledge work focuses analysis on expertise heterogeneity, recognizing that expertise operates in nuanced ways in the relationship between technology and organization. The taxonomy, in particular, illuminates diverse resources for accomplishing knowledge work, incorporates varying relational dynamics, and complicates expertise coordination in necessary ways.

■ REFERENCES

Alvesson, M. (2001). Knowledge Work: Ambiguity, Image, and Identity. *Human Relations*, 54, 863–86. doi: 10.1177/0018726701547004

Barbour, J. B. (2010). On the Institutional Moorings of Talk in Health Care. *Management Communication Quarterly*, 24, 449–56.

Barbour, J. B., and Gill, R. (2014). Designing Communication for the Day-to-Day Safety Oversight of Nuclear Power Plants. *Journal of Applied Communication Research*, 42, 168–89.

Barbour, J. B., and James, E. P. (2015). Collaboration for Compliance: Identity Tensions in the Interorganizational Regulation of a Toxic Waste Facility. *Journal of Applied Communication Research*, 43, 363–84.

Barbour, J. B., and Lammers, J. C. (2015). Measuring Professional Identity: A Review of the Literature and a Multilevel Confirmatory Factor Analysis of Professional Identity Constructs. *Journal of Professions and Organization*, 2, 38–60. doi: 10.1093/jpo/jou009

Bartholomew, D. (2008). *Building on Knowledge: Developing Expertise, Creativity and Intellectual Capital in the Construction Professions*. Oxford: Blackwell.

Boh, W. F., Ren, Y., Kiesler, S., and Bussjaeger, R. (2007). Expertise and Collaboration in the Geographically Dispersed Organization. *Organization Science*, 18, 595–612.

Chua, A., and Lam, W. (2005). Why KM Projects Fail: A Multi-Case Analysis. *Journal of Knowledge Management*, 9, 6–17.

Collins, H. (2011). Three Dimensions of Expertise. *Phenomenology and the Cognitive Sciences*, 12, 1–21. doi: 10.1007/s11097-011-9203-5

Dougherty, D. J. (2011). *The Reluctant Farmer: An Exploration of Work, Social Class and the Production of Food*. Leicester: Troubador Publishing.

Egbu, C. O., and Robinson, H. S. (2005). Construction as a Knowledge-Based Industry. In C. J. Anumba, C. O. Egbu, and P. M. Carrillo (eds), *Knowledge Management in Construction* (pp. 31–49). Oxford: Blackwell.

Flanagin, A. J., Pearce, K., and Bondad-Brown, B. (2009). The Destructive Potential of Electronic Communication Technologies in Organizations. In P. Lutgen-Sandvik and B. Davenport-Sypher (eds), *The Destructive Side of Organizational Communication: Processes, Consequences, and Constructive Ways of Organizing* (pp. 229–51). Mahwah, NJ: Routledge.

Gherardi, S., and Nicolini, D. (2002). Learning the Trade: A Culture of Safety in Practice. *Organization*, 9, 191–223. doi: 10.1177/1350508402009002264

Gibson, M. K., and Papa, M. J. (2000). The Mud, the Blood, and the Beer Guys: Organizational Osmosis in Blue-Collar Work Groups. *Journal of Applied Communication Research*, 28, 68–88.

Gill, R., Barbour, J. B., and Dean, M. (2014). Shadowing in/as Work: Ten Recommendations for Shadowing Fieldwork Practice. *Qualitative Research in Organizations and Management*, 9, 69–89.

Hollingshead, A. B., and Brandon, D. P. (2003). Potential Benefits of Communication in Transactive Memory Systems. *Human Communication Research*, 29, 607–15.

Huang, M., Barbour, J. B., Su, C., and Contractor, N. (2013). Why do Group Members Provide Information to Digital Knowledge Repositories? A Multilevel Application of Transactive Memory Theory. *Journal of the American Society for Information Science*, 64, 540–57.

Jacobs, S. (1986). How to Make an Argument from Example in Discourse Analysis. In D. G. Ellis and W. A. Donohue (eds), *Contemporary Issues in Language and Discourse Processes* (pp. 149–67). Hillsdale, NJ: Erlbaum.

Kuhn, T., and Jackson, M. (2008). Accomplishing Knowledge: A Framework for Investigating Knowing in Organizations. *Management Communication Quarterly*, 21, 454–85.

Lammers, J. C. (2011). How Institutions Communicate: Institutional Messages, Institutional Logics, and Organizational Communication. *Management Communication Quarterly*, 25, 154–82.

Lammers, J. C., and Barbour, J. B. (2006). An Institutional Theory of Organizational Communication. *Communication Theory*, 16, 356–77.

Leonardi, P. M., and Treem, J. W. (2012). Knowledge Management Technology as a Stage for Strategic Self-Presentation: Implications for Knowledge Sharing in Organizations. *Information and Organization*, 22, 37–59.

Marvin, C. (1994). The Body of the Text: Literacy's Corporeal Constant. *Quarterly Journal of Speech*, 80, 129–49.

Ren, Y., and Argote, L. (2011). Transactive Memory Systems 1985–2010: An Integrative Framework of Key Dimensions, Antecedents, and Consequences. *Academy of Management Annals*, 5, 189–229.

Scott, W. R. (2008). Lords of the Dance: Professionals as Institutional Agents. *Organization Studies*, 29, 219–38.

Sennett, R. (2009). *The Craftsman*. New Haven: Yale University Press.

Styhre, A. (2008). The Role of Social Capital in Knowledge Sharing: The Case of a Specialist Rock Construction Company. *Construction Management and Economics*, 26, 941–51.

Styhre, A. (2009). *Managing Knowledge in the Construction Industry*. New York: Routledge.

Taylor, J. R., and Van Every, E. J. (2014). *When Organization Fails: Why Authority Matters*. New York: Routledge.

Treem, J. W. (2012). Communicating Expertise: Knowledge Performances in Professional-Service Firms. *Communication Monographs*, 79, 23–47.

Tsoukas, H., and Vladimirou, E. (2001). What is Organizational Knowledge? *Journal of Management Studies*, 38, 973–93.

Yuan, Y. C., Fulk, J., Monge, P. R., and Contractor, N. (2010). Expertise Directory Development, Shared Task Interdependence, and Strength of Communication Network Ties as Multilevel Predictors of Expertise Exchange in Transactive Memory Work Groups. *Communication Research*, 37, 20–47.

4 Three Dimensions of Expertise

HARRY COLLINS

The argument presented here is that traditional philosophical and psychological analyses are mainly concerned with, or at least emphasize, the development of expertise in individuals.[1] Doing some violence to psychology, which, after all, does look at group practices such as education, and perhaps doing a little less violence to philosophy, I am going to say that both disciplines treat expertise "one-dimensionally." Typical of their results are "stage theories." The psychologist Chi (2006) says that individuals go through six stages of increasing sophistication as they become expert while the philosophers, Stuart and Hubert Dreyfus (1986), have a very influential "five-stage model" of the development of expertise.[2]

The Periodic Table of Expertises (Figure 4.1) must now be briefly introduced. The Periodic Table is at the heart of a program of research called "SEE," which stands for "Studies of Expertise and Experience."[3] For the purposes at hand, we need concentrate on only a couple of lines of the table. The line labeled "Dispositions," which describes certain individual abilities, can be ignored for current purposes. "Meta-expertises" are expertises we use to judge other experts and that line can also be ignored along with "meta-credentials," which are self-explanatory. The crucial lines for the current exercise are "Specialist Expertises" and "Ubiquitous Expertises."

The underlying idea of the Periodic Table is that the acquisition of nearly every expertise, if not all of them, depends on the acquisition of the tacit knowledge pertaining to the expert domain in question. Tacit knowledge can be acquired only by immersion in the society of those who already possess it. Therefore, the process of moving to the right-hand end of the Specialist Expertise line depends on becoming socially embedded in the appropriate groups of experts so that one can acquire "specialist tacit knowledge"

[1] This is an abridged and edited version of a paper first published in *Phenomenology and the Cognitive Sciences*: Harry Collins, 'Three Dimensions of Expertise', *Phenomenology and the Cognitive Sciences*, 12(2) (2013), 253–73, doi: 10.1007/s11097-011-9203-5. We thank the editor of the journal and publisher for their cooperation. The editors of this volume have been especially helpful in adding cross-references to other chapters in the volume and in suggesting the substitution of professional socialization for general educational trajectories in one section of the paper; these changes improve the fit with the theme of the book.

[2] Thanks to Greg Feist for the reference to Chi.

[3] References to work pertaining to SEE will be found throughout this text.

UBIQUITOUS EXPERTISES					
DISPOSITIONS				Interactive Ability / Reflective Ability	
SPECIALIST	*UBIQUITOUS TACIT KNOWLEDGE*			*SPECIALIST TACIT KNOWLEDGE*	
EXPERTISES	Beer-mat Knowledge	Popular Understanding	Primary Source Knowledge	Interactional Expertise	Contributory Expertise
				Polimorphic / Mimeomorph	
META-	*EXTERNAL (Transmuted expertises)*		*INTERNAL (Non-transmuted expertises)*		
EXPERTISES	Ubiquitous Discrimination	Local Discrimination	Technical Connoisseurship	Downward Discrimination	Referred Expertise
META-CRITERIA	Credentials		Experience		Track Record

Figure 4.1 The Periodic Table of Expertises

(as indicated in the heading). The process is social though the outcome is real—an ability to do and understand things that one could not do and understand before.

The two right-hand categories of the Specialist Expertise line indicate that there are two kinds of socialization that can lead to two kinds of specialist expertise. The rightmost category—contributory expertise—is what is normally thought of as an expertise, and it is the practical expertise that enables one to contribute to a domain of practice. To acquire contributory expertise one must work within the expert domain. Interactional expertise, on the other hand, can be acquired by deep immersion in the linguistic discourse of the domain alone. At first thought of as a kind of subsidiary expertise, interactional expertise is now seen, at least by some such as the author, as more and more the essence of human collective practices and social life in general. For example, it has been argued that, without interactional expertise, we would all live isolated lives, our understanding bounded by just those things we had practiced ourselves in the way that a chihuahua knows nothing, and can know nothing, of the practical world of the foxhound or sheepdog. It follows that we would be unable to cooperate and build common understandings and there would be no possibility of a sophisticated division of labor anywhere in society. Animals have little in the way of division of labor because they do not have the language-based understanding of each others' discrete practical competences that is needed. Furthermore, it has also been argued that, for humans, by far the larger part of acquiring even a practical, contributory expertise is the acquisition of interactional expertise because the language of an expert domain provides the meaning of those narrow physical practices—our specialties—which we contribute to the domain as a whole.[4] Whether any of this is true, it remains that one can acquire neither interactional nor contributory expertise without prolonged social contact with the specialists.

The three leftmost categories of the specialist line are different. They are not really specialist expertises at all but examples of specialist knowledge ("information" would have been better). This is because they are acquired through reading or the like without contact with specialists. What happens in the left-hand categories is the acquisition of some "explicit knowledge." But, as Polanyi puts it: "all knowledge is either tacit or rooted in tacit knowledge. A wholly explicit knowledge is unthinkable" (Grene, 1969, 144). Thus, as the heading indicates, to acquire explicit knowledge one needs "ubiquitous tacit knowledge." Ubiquitous tacit knowledge is all the things we come to learn as we become members of our native society. Ubiquitous expertises include how close to others to walk on a sidewalk, when to talk and when to shout, how to dress, and so on and so on, but more germane for the purposes at hand, they include fluency in our native language, literacy, knowing what books and other written sources are, and how they are to be obtained and used. It is these latter examples of ubiquitous expertise that enable one to attain the three leftmost kinds of specialist knowledge. The first kind can be acquired by reading things like beer-mats (coasters) in pubs and the resulting knowledge isn't much use except for playing "Trivial Pursuit" and the like; the second kind comes from reading popular science books and articles; the third kind comes from struggling through original research papers or textbooks, or perhaps from technical material found on the internet. In Collins and Evans (2007), it is argued that even the third of these can be very misleading and is not to be compared with the real specialist expertises that can only be acquired from immersion in the society of specialists.

From Line to Space

That brief description of the Periodic Table is sufficient to bring out the two dimensions that, it is argued, should be added to the standard psychological and philosophical approach. These are: (a) degree of exposure to tacit knowledge—the more exposure the more potential expertise—and (b) what may or may not be a neologism, the "esotericity" of the expertise. While traditional analyses take the word "expert" to refer only to rare, high-level, specialists, SEE considers that ordinary language-speaking, literacy, and the

---

[4] For the latest and most radical version of this position, see Collins (2011b).

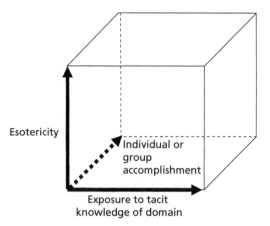

Figure 4.2 Expertise-Space Diagram

like exhibit a high degree of expertise even though everyone has them—they are ubiquitous. This is, perhaps, one of the most radical contributions of SEE to the analysis of expertise as indicated by the initial strong opposition to the idea of "ubiquitous expertise" from philosophers and psychologists. Part of the task of this chapter will be to try to make it obvious that the idea of ubiquitous expertise is a necessity if we are to avoid confusion.

The three-dimensional model, which will be referred to as the "Expertise-Space Diagram" (ESD), is shown in Figure 4.2.[5] In the figure, the depth dimension is what used to be the (mostly) single-dimensional model of expertise but now refers to groups and domains as well as individuals. The horizontal dimension is the extent of exposure to tacit knowledge, once more, referring to either groups or individuals, depending on how the diagram is used. The vertical dimension is the extent to which the domain is esoteric with

---

[5] I originally called it the "Expertise Phase Diagram" as it was inspired by chemical phase diagrams that I remember from (high) school. The idea of phases suggests sudden transitions. The existing analysis of expertise is, of course, filled with such discontinuities. There are the stage theories that have already been mentioned. There are the discontinuities in child development discussed by Shrager. There is a lingering notion that, stages aside, something special happens as you move up the vertical axis. There is the discontinuity between mimeomorphic and polymorphic actions (Collins and Kusch, 1998) and the difference between Relational, Somatic, and Collective tacit knowledge (Collins, 2010). The difference between interactional and contributory expertise is central (with what Ribeiro calls, "physical contiguity" located in-between) and the entire Periodic Table of Expertises is full of classes and therefore discontinuities. Also, the Imitation Game idea (Collins and Evans, 2007) has some sense of discontinuity about it when we speak, in certain special circumstances, of people "passing" or "failing." There is, therefore, too much to represent on the diagram and it seems better to think of all three axes as continuous. It may be that the table is seriously flawed in not recognizing some important discontinuities at the outset. But, to move from this default position and establish that some unrepresented boundary has vital analytical significance and/or renders the table incoherent requires argument and justification.

ubiquitous domains, such as language-speaking or literacy at the bottom and things like gravitational wave (GW) physics at the top.

A "domain" is to be understood as consisting of the individuals within it rather than by reference to the topic. Thus, the domain of GW physicists extends to all those who have significant social contact with the professional world of GW physicists but not those who know something about the topic from their reading.[6] When I am reading a book on GW physics, I am not, by that fact, in the domain of gravitational physics. If I have no social contact with GW physicists but am reading such a book, I am in the domain of either "popular understanding" of GW physics or "primary source knowledge" depending on what sort of book it is. These domains are found in the middling regions of the vertical dimension. With the three dimensions in mind, we now have an "expertise-space" instead of an "expertise line." All three scales run from zero at the origin so that, for example, instead of asking whether this or that person is an expert in such and such, one asks for their degree of expertise and one possible answer is "zero."

Putting the Space Diagram to Use: Mode 1—Surfaces

The ESD encompasses psychology and philosophy but may shed new light on some of their conclusions. For example, some existing analyses may appear more narrowly focused than had been thought, and some claims or assumptions—for example, that a one-dimensional analysis exhausts the domain of expertise in general—will be seen to be incorrect. Furthermore, simply making use of the ESD seems to transform or make redundant certain previously fixed ideas about the notion of expertise.

Consider, for example, the idea that experts are necessarily rare people— unusual individuals who have self-consciously devoted many hours of their lives to gaining a special ability. It is certainly true that this is how the term "expert" is regularly used in many societies but, in so far as we want to understand and analyze expertise, the ESD seems to suggest that the common use prevents clear thinking. Once it was believed that burning could be fully understood by what appeared to be going on: the expulsion of one substance from another. But, weigh the burned material and it turns out to be heavier than before, and this did not make sense without new ways of thinking about it. The idea that the only experts are rare individuals seems like the same kind

[6] GW physics is regularly used as an example since the author of this paper has spent nearly forty years immersed in the field on and off. See Collins (2004, 2011a).

of mistake as was once made in the case of burning. Putting the matter in terms of the ESD may help to show why.

GRAVITATIONAL WAVE PHYSICS

Figure 4.3 shows one of at least three ways in which the ESD can be used. The dark "surface" shown on the leftmost version of Figure 4.3 represents a domain such as GW physics which is located at the top level of the space because it is highly esoteric. It takes on its strange shape for the following reasons. At the left front corner are located novices newly entering the field—they have minimal accomplishments in the domain and have had little exposure to its tacit knowledge, but they are in the domain because they have social contact with its practitioners. As they learn, and their exposure to tacit knowledge builds, they will move toward the right, and sooner or later, they will become maximally competent or a little less than maximally competent—hence there is some depth to the surface at the right-hand edge.

The back left-hand corner is empty because it is impossible to be competent in GW physics without exposure to the tacit knowledge, so while the back boundary of the dark surface may not be the straight line that has been drawn, there will certainly be no one found on the back edge who is not also on the right edge. This empty space is called the "epistemological void" and will always be found where tacit knowledge is integral to an expertise.[7] The more a

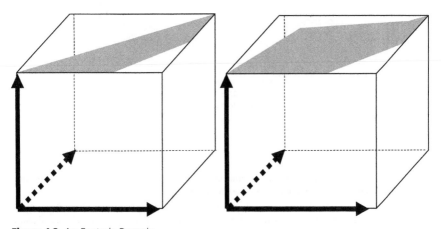

Figure 4.3 An Esoteric Domain

---

[7] Theresa Schilhab continues to press upon me that the acquisition of "Somatic Tacit Knowledge," which, to simplify, is sets of physical procedures embedded in body and nerve pathways such as that required to balance on a bicycle (Collins, 2010), is less dependent on immersion in a culture. You can, as it were, learn to balance on a bike all by yourself. There may be some truth in this, but I prefer to

formal component is important to an expertise the more the line that links the front left-hand corner and the back right-hand corner, and comprises the rear bound of the expertise surface, will curve toward the back line—because competence can increase by gaining formal knowledge as well as tacit knowledge so you can move back a bit without always moving rightwards. This is illustrated in the rightmost version of Figure 4.3.[8]

The front right-hand empty space, called the "sociological void," is there because, if one has some exposure to the tacit knowledge of the domain but fails to make progress, one is likely to be expelled from the community of those who have it.[9]

CAR-DRIVING

Figure 4.4 shows the domain of car-driving in a modern developed society. It is not quite on the floor of the diagram because not everyone can drive a car, but it is near the bottom. The car-driving surface has the same shape as the

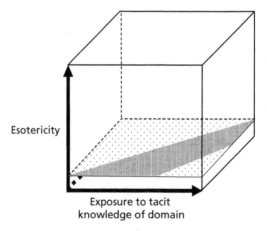

Esotericity

Exposure to tacit
knowledge of domain

Figure 4.4 A Near-Ubiquitous Domain

concentrate on the fact that you would be unlikely to know what a bike was for if you were truly isolated. Schilhab's point should not be forgotten nevertheless.

[8] For those who might like to work with these surfaces but don't know how draw them, go to "autoshapes," "lines," and then choose the closed irregular loop. Click on a point in the original figure and then go the next point and click again. Go from point to point until the loop is closed and then doubleclick. This creates a straight-edged figure that can be colored, shaded, etc. Right-click within this figure (usually once, but sometimes one seems to need to do it twice), and choose "edit points." The corners of the figure can then be dragged into the exactly right places so as to fine-tune the shape. Clicking anywhere on a straight edge generates a new "point" which can be dragged to create a more complicated shape. The same method is used to create areas of shading (choose "no lines") that are used to fill existing features such as the domain "floors."

[9] Rob Evans worked out the meaning of the two voids.

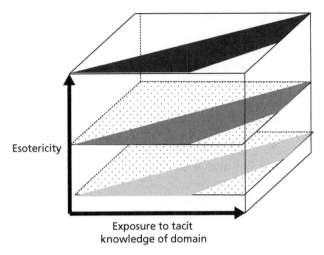

Figure 4.5 Historic or Location Change in Car-Driving

GW domain surface for the same reasons. (Thus, though it is stretching the point a little, if you cannot pass your test, you are eventually excluded from the community of drivers, and hence there is a sociological void.)

Figure 4.5 shows car-driving once more but includes a middle level which could represent either car-driving at the beginning of the twentieth century or car-driving in some rural location in a developing society. In either case, driving would be thought of as the domain of specialists. This demonstrates the confusion that is caused by insisting that experts can only be found in esoteric domains. Car-driving is a ubiquitous domain, but if one insists that, by that fact, it cannot really be an expertise, then pretty well the same activity must have been an expertise at one time and not at another or must be an expertise at one place and not another. The top level of Figure 4.5 shows racing-car-driving, the position of which will not change over time or place— it is always esoteric.[10]

COMPUTER USE

A still more striking example of a historical change, which has happened in the lifetime of some us, is ability to use a computer. Not so long ago, this was the

---

[10] It is surely worth recounting that, at the Berkeley meeting, one delegate insisted that only esoteric expertises counted as expertises and that car-driving was not one of them. He insisted that the Dreyfuses' analysis (Dreyfus and Dreyfus, 1986) showed this clearly. Bert Dreyfus, however, attended the workshop on the crucial morning and, as when Woody Allen brought Marshall McLuhan to the cinema queue, Dreyfus was able to deny in person that he thought it might be better to think of ubiquitous expertises as expertises proper and that car-driving was certainly a case in point and had been treated as such in his own works.

preserve of a small elite—now, young schoolchildren have it. Changing technology may have been the driver of this trend up to about the late 1970s, but since the introduction of desk computers, it has been much more about the changing "idea" of what a computer is. Thus, I began to word-process in around 1980 on a Tandy TRS 80 model II, with an 8-inch floppy disc, when there was only one in the entire School of Humanities and Social Sciences at Bath University, and I was thought to be pretty smart because I was one of only two people who could use it—the other being the statistical economist who had ordered it. Later, becoming Head of the School, I introduced word processors to the administrative staff who resisted, saying that computers could be used only by clever people such as academics and not by them. I argued that within a few months they would be the experts on word processing and the academic staff would be coming to them for lessons— and so it turned out.

NATURAL LANGUAGE AND FOREIGN LANGUAGE

Figure 4.6 makes the point about changing location in a still more striking way.[11] The bottom shape represents the natural language spoken in a society and is about as ubiquitous as anything can be. This time, the sociological void has disappeared because even those who cannot master language tend not to be excluded from language-using communities. The dark shape above, however, represents the very same language but spoken fluently in a foreign

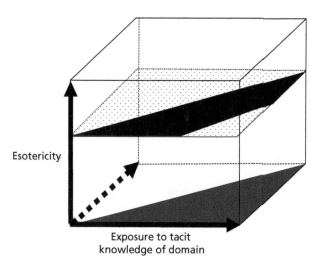

Figure 4.6 Language and Location

---

[11] The language point is also made in Collins and Evans (2007, 3).

country. This renders the person an expert, able to command a salary and honor as a result of possessing an esoteric ability. Here, there is a sociological void—in the long term, you can't associate much with foreign-language speakers if you cannot speak the language. Once more, if one cannot accept that the light grey surface represents an expertise, then the very same ability undergoes a transmutation as soon as someone travels from their native country to a foreign country. This feels like a very bad basis for a coherent understanding of expertise.

Figures 4.5 and 4.6 seem to make it obvious that there must be ubiquitous expertises and that to deny it invites confusion and confounded analysis. It has certainly caused trouble in the past, for example, when we were told over and over that natural-language-speaking computers would be with us in a year or two. The "boosters" believed that, because natural-language-speaking was something that anyone could do—"even little children can speak"—it must be easy. It is, of course, very far from easy and natural-language-handling computers are as far away as ever.[12]

Of course, it just might be that there really is a difference between "the same" activity when it is a ubiquitous expertise and when it is not. It is certainly the case that the experience of learning a second language is not the same as learning a first language, so that, even if the end-point is fluency in both, the apparent similarity may mask a deep and interesting difference. It may even be that speaking one's native language in a foreign land is a different activity from speaking one's native language in one's own land in some non-obvious way. It may be that ordinary car-driving when acquired as an esoteric skill, as in some rural part of a developing country, is by that fact different from ordinary car-driving when acquired as an everyday skill, and so on. But the advantage of the ESD is that it invites this kind of question. Furthermore, it insists, if a diagrammatic convention can "insist," that the default position is that the same expertise is the same expertise when esoteric at one time or place and ubiquitous at another time and place, so that any differences have to be understood, argued for, and justified. Under the old "all expertise is esoteric" fiat, the question would never be asked, leave alone researched.

Space Diagram Mode 2—Levels

CAR-DRIVING REVISITED

Figure 4.7 also represents car-driving but in a different way. Figure 4.5 represented historical changes in the perceived degree of expertise involved in

---

[12] See Collins and Kusch (1998) and Collins (2010) for more extended discussions of why this is so.

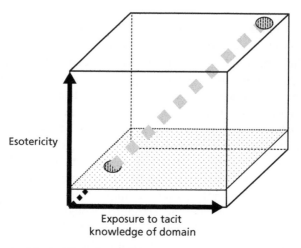

Esotericity

Exposure to tacit
knowledge of domain

Figure 4.7 Levels of Esotericity in One Activity

car-driving and the continued esoteric position of racing-car-driving. Figure 4.7 takes car-driving as the activity and implies a progression through discrete levels (hence, the broken line) from ordinary car-driving at the bottom to racing-car-driving at the top. How to represent driving is purely a matter of two different conventions: Figure 4.5 treats racing-car-driving as discontinuous with street driving—a different activity; Figure 4.7 treats them as instances of the same thing—driving.[13] It treats the gaining of lots of experience of driving in different countries, practicing controlled skids and handbrake turns, rally-driving, go-karting, Formula Ford, Formulas 3, 2, and 1, and so forth, as also instances of the same thing, and imagines them arranged on a line representing some kind of ordered sequence. The steadily decreasing numbers of drivers involved at each level is indicated by the vertical movement while the left–right diagonal movement indicates the extra tacit knowledge that must be acquired as one goes upwards, culminating with the racing driver. There is no absolute right or wrong about it; the choice of Figures 4.5 or 4.7 depends on the analytical purpose at hand.

It may be that some drivers progress through all or many of these stages in a driving career. In that case, the "trajectory" (see Figure 4.9) from street driver to racing driver might well follow the path of the broken line. It is important to notice that progression through the Dreyfus five-stage model of skill acquisition would already have been completed for street driving at the lowest level. It could be said to reapply all over again for racing-driving or any of the other levels, but this is better handled by thinking in terms of different activities as represented by the surfaces of Figure 4.5.

---

[13] If I was forced to choose between the two, I would say that driving a Formula 1 car is a completely different activity to street driving.

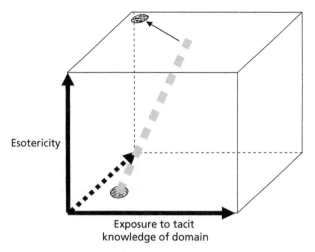

Esotericity

Exposure to tacit
knowledge of domain

Figure 4.8 Expertise (or is it Information?) without Tacit Knowledge

EXPERTISE WITHOUT TACIT KNOWLEDGE

Figure 4.8 shows the pattern of an expertise that, at the highest level, does not depend on tacit knowledge. As already explained, in such cases, individual or group competence can be high even though little tacit knowledge has been acquired so the "epistemological void" may be occupied. Figure 4.8 is meant to represent the relationship between ordinary performance in arithmetical or memory tasks typical of the general population, progressing upward through increasing development of skills, including the associated tacit knowledge, as far as the abilities of stage performers such as "Mr. Memory" and the like. Then, the line jerks left to represent the prodigious feats of autistic savants. Savants appear to manage the extraordinary performances in the absence of tacit knowledge, at least, in the absence of collective tacit knowledge, which absence appears to be a principal feature of their special way of being in the world. Unlike the case of car-driving, there is no individual "trajectory" along this line. Those who achieve the upper level and those who achieve the lower level are not the same people but two groups doing different kinds of things.

Space Diagram Mode 3—Trajectories and Locations

PROFESSIONAL DEVELOPMENT AND ORGANIZATIONAL ENTRY

Figure 4.9 shows how the ESD can be used to represent the trajectories or locations of individuals or groups—block arrows are used. In this case, the

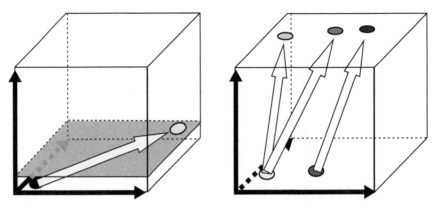

Figure 4.9 Professional Development Trajectories

example is the attempt to provide a trajectory for groups of professionals under four kinds of regime.[14]

The left-hand diagram shows early formal education in a professional domain. This is largely a matter of socialization into a large subset of the ubiquitous expertises—teaching the tacit knowledge of simple transactions, the idea of books, basic literacy, instructions, relevant procedural information. The right-hand figure is meant to illustrate three aspects of professional development a worker, or groups of workers, might develop upon joining an organization.

The leftmost line of the right-hand figure represents the kind of professional development that is informed by the same basic philosophy as distance learning—that is, it is largely a matter of absorbing facts and formulae that could be as well delivered via manuals, PowerPoint presentations, or online modules as on-site at the organization. Note its broad similarity in end-point, or at least aspiration, to that of the autistic savants represented in Figure 4.8!

The middle line is meant to represent a more traditional worker orientation program which is primarily on-site, with other new employees, and is designed to include an element of socialization into ways of thinking associated with an organization and brought about by close contact with active and experienced organizational members. Here, a little more in the way of tacit knowledge pertaining to the domain is intended to be transferred.

The rightmost line is meant to represent the established professional, beginning roughly where initial organizational orientation ended but involving more exposure to a richer socialization process. Perhaps, these kinds of figures could be used in thinking about different modes of professional

---

[14] This is the section that Treem and Leonardi have adapted from the original that dealt with educational trajectories from kindergarten to Ph.D. As author I have not changed what they have done. I think what they have done is entirely proper and nicely demonstrates that the Expertise Space Diagram is a general way of thinking that can be applied in many ways.

development. Importantly, the figure presents a model whereby professional expertise exists on a continuum across the ESD, and expertise is not understood as a specific state of level that one reaches (see Buzzanell and Long, this volume, for additional discussion regarding professional development). The diagram should discourage short-cuts which inadvertently concentrate on delivery of information as opposed to tacit knowledge.

Advancing the Study of Expertise

The space diagram, it has to be admitted, was originally conceived as a way of showing psychologists that the way they analyzed expertise was radically different to the way it was analyzed under SEE: "You are on the depth axis, we are interested only in the front face." Working with the diagram soon revealed, however, that the best kind of analysis combined all three axes. One does not have to use the ESD to see that it is useful and that it is especially useful because it is a space rather than a surface or a line. The ways of using the ESD set out here—the surfaces, levels, and trajectories—may not be the best ones, or there may be additional ones and the examples might not be the most revealing, but none of this may matter (see Barbour, Sommer, and Gill, this volume, for other ways to characterize expertise). The uses of the ESD as presented in this chapter have been primarily intended to establish that it is coherent and meaningful, on the principle that if one is in doubt about meanings one should try some uses and if there are uses, there must be meanings. Even if those who work with expertise do not want to draw diagrams, the convention should still be valuable as a continual reminder that the analysis of expertise must be three-dimensional and that the idea of expertise is not exhausted by exploring individual development. The investigation of expertise might proceed through joint introspection or through measurements of performance, but whatever the preferred method the location of the expertise in three dimensions needs to be borne in mind if we are properly to understand the reach of the conclusions. The ESD can also be used to ask new questions, set new research agendas, and position different disciplines' contributions to the expertise problem in respect of one another. One hopes, of course, that at least some analysts may use it in a more direct way.

METHODOLOGICAL INTERACTIONALISM
AND EDUCATIONAL PRACTICES

As explained, SEE emphasizes more and more that language has a central role in learning even in the case of practical expertises. The most extreme expression of this is a rule of thumb called "methodological interactionalism" (Collins, 2011b). Methodological interactionalism posits that the study of the acquisition of practical expertise should work on the initial assumption that it is entirely a matter of language. Thus, while we know that practical expertises are acquired much more rapidly through engaging with them in a practical way, methodological interactionalism would insist that one starts by assuming that this is because engaging with some practical expertise in a practical way is the best way to maximize the time one spends in discourse with other practitioners—practicing automatically maximizes the hours spent in co-location, and therefore relevant discourse. That is almost certainly not the whole story but it forces one to justify the specific role of physical practice rather than simply assuming at the outset that learning a practice is all about practicing.

The study of different educational practices and styles of apprenticeship must bear on the relative role of language and physical practice. For example, I am told that certain Japanese pottery apprentices are never spoken to by their masters (they have to "steal" their secrets). It would be interesting to compare apprenticeship regimes in which talk is central feature and those in which it is not. Does the absence of talk slow the apprenticeship process and would the introduction of talk to an otherwise silent regime speed it up?

THE NOTION OF A "PRIVATE EXPERTISE"

One kind of question that seems very much in the SEE/philosophy overlap is the extent to which the idea of expertise is bound to the idea of language. Can there be a private expertise? For example, if I become extremely skilled at some private activity such as clicking my big toes together and I do not tell anyone about it, is that an expertise? Is lying in bed in the morning, which does not have a literature or a discourse, an expertise? Also, immanent in the text is the question of whether expertises which belong in the top back left-hand corner of the ESD—those which are based largely on information—are really expertises at all.[15]

THE DISTINCTION BETWEEN INTERACTIONAL
AND CONTRIBUTORY EXPERTISE

There is a sort of question which is specific to the idea of interactional expertise and its relationship to contributory expertise (see Treem and Barley, this volume, for additional discussion of contributory expertise). From the beginning, SEE has been troubled by questions such whether the distinction between

---

[15] This relates to the earlier question raised by Schilhab (n. 7).

contributory and interactional holds in the case of various activities such as literary analysis where the contributory part of it appears to be interactional. Likewise, we might ask what is contributory and what is interactional in mathematics and other domains in which it is not so clear where the boundary between physical practice and linguistic practice should be drawn.

If there is a pattern in the nature of these questions and future directions it is that they are fundamentally communicative. Each deals with how language and discourse might serve both as a means of acquiring expertise and exhibiting expertise to others. Though the ESD provides a framework to classify the nature of expertise it also provokes questions related to visibility and acceptance of this expertise in particular social contexts. In the cases of methodological interactionism and private expertise there is the question of whether expertise can exist at all without communication. With interactional expertise, there is the question of when communication itself constitutes the practice and substance of the domain expertise. Focusing more directly on the communicative practices associated with expertise offers a helpful bridge between philosophical and psychological approaches to the study of expertise, and other disciplines interested in the operation of expertise.[16]

Summary and Final Remarks

The argument put forward here is that a much richer and much more interdisciplinary approach to expertise is possible if expertise is treated as three-dimensional rather than one-dimensional. An attempt has been made to show how a three-dimensional model would operate. All this has been worked out in a matter of a few weeks, the initial foray being intended to show how different the disciplines are rather than to show how they can be melded together. Perhaps the fact that the internal logic of the exercise pushed it toward interdisciplinarity is telling us something important.

On the grandest scale, the conception of expertise immanent in the arguments in this chapter seems different to what has gone before. Many studies of expertise take it to be something that is coextensive with personal development and can only be studied through personal accounts. Here, on the other hand, expertise is treated as "stuff" rather than process. You can have an expertise or not have it, and it can be passed between people, sometimes in the form of the explicit and sometimes the tacit—like red and white blood corpuscles. When it passes, the recipient can do something new or can understand something new. Thinking in terms of expertise-stuff allows for a certain freedom: of course, we are bound to remain interested in accounts of

---

[16] This paragraph added by the editors.

how the stuff was transferred—the accounts of those who have acquired an esoteric skill but also the accounts of anthropologists and other "participant comprehenders" who have acquired a strange people's native expertise. And it allows us to be interested in the expertise-stuff of natives in our own society who cannot provide accounts of its acquisition because it all happened when they were too young and too unreflective. It allows us to ask whether cats and dogs and machines, from which we can obtain no accounts, have expertise-stuff in the same sense as humans. It might seem that they have because they sometimes do the same things as humans can do, such as hunt or calculate. But then, we have to ask whether their expertise-stuff is the same as ours or do they have different "blood groups." As intimated, I am sure that machines do have different stuff even if they appear to be able to do some of the things we do, and I think the best way to think of animals is as them having a different blood group, and there is also no possibility of blood transfusion between animals because they do not have language. Doubtless, what has been set out in this chapter merely scrapes the surface of the possibilities.

REFERENCES

Chi, M. T. H. (2006). Two Approaches to the Study of Experts' Characteristics. In K. A. Ericsson, N. Charness, P. J. Feltovich, and R. R. Hoffman (eds), *The Cambridge Handbook of Expertise and Expert Performance* (pp. 21–30). New York: Cambridge University Press.

Collins, H. (2004). *Gravity's Shadow: The Search for Gravitational Waves.* Chicago: University of Chicago Press.

Collins, H. (2010). *Tacit and Explicit Knowledge.* Chicago: University of Chicago Press.

Collins, H. (2011a). *Gravity's Ghost: Scientific Discovery in the Twenty-First Century* Chicago: University of Chicago Press.

Collins, H. (2011b). Language and Practice. *Social Studies of Science*, 41, 271–300. doi: 10.1177/0306312711399665

Collins, H., and Evans, R. (2007). *Rethinking Expertise.* Chicago: University of Chicago Press.

Collins, H. M., and Kusch, M. (1998). *The Shape of Actions: What Humans and Machines Can Do.* Cambridge, MA: MIT Press.

Dreyfus, H. L., and Dreyfus, Stuart E. (1986). *Mind over Machine: The Power of Human Intuition and Expertise in the Era of the Computer.* New York: Free Press.

Grene, Marjorie (1969). *Knowing and Being: Essays by Michael Polanyi.* London: Routledge & Kegan Paul.

Part II
Reviewing Dimensions of Expertise in Organizational Contexts

5 The Impact of Communication Behaviors on Expertise Recognition in Intercultural Collaboration

WANG LIAO, PATRICK MacDONALD, AND Y. CONNIE YUAN

Accuracy in expertise recognition[1] is crucial for successful group collaboration (Austin, 2003). The reason is that groups are more likely to make better decisions and thereby obtain better performance when experts are given the opportunity to fully apply their knowledge (Einhorn et al., 1977; Libby et al., 1987). Yet group members often fail to recognize each other's expertise (Littlepage et al., 1995). As a result, the whole group may perform worse than its best member. Hence expertise recognition deserves more research attention because misjudgment of expertise can lead to under-utilization of a group's intellectual resources.

While management scholars have carried out some interesting studies on expertise recognition in group collaboration (Baumann and Bonner, 2004; Bonner et al., 2007; Bunderson, 2003; Littlepage and Mueller, 1997; Littlepage et al., 1995; Thomas-Hunt and Phillips, 2004), few communication scholars have paid much attention to this issue. For communication scholars, we believe that this is not only an area that is worthy of further research attention, but also an opportunity to make major contributions to small group research. The reasons are twofold. First, expertise needs to be communicated (Treem, 2012; Yuan et al., 2013). Treem (2012, 25) proposed to approach expertise as "an attribution that emerges through social inter-action and is communicated to others through the process of organizing."

---

[1] When reviewing related literature, we found two terms tend to be used interchangeably: expertise recognition and expertise/competence judgment. The former requires a benchmark against which to evaluate accuracy in expertise judgment, while the later can be purely perceptual regardless of accuracy in perception. Although the same psychological and cognitive mechanisms may be at work influencing the formation of the judgment, we want to point out such differences because the two terms have been operationalized differently in empirical research, which may cause differences in the results of hypothesis testing across studies.

Van den Hoff and Kotlarsky (in this volume) also emphasized the need to take a more dynamic approach to study expertise, as organizations become more "fluid" with a higher degree of globalization and more extensive outsourcing activities. Furthermore, expertise is invisible, and hence relies on communication to be externalized for others to identify and utilize. When not communicated appropriately, expertise may not give its holders actual influence in group decision-making (Bottger, 1984; Littlepage and Mueller, 1997; Littlepage et al., 1995), thus preventing the value of expertise from being fully utilized (Yuan et al., 2013). Second, communication behaviors can be important heuristic cues for people to infer other's expertise. In contemporary society, cross-functional, interdisciplinary collaboration has become a typical way for structuring organizational work (Ford and Randolph, 1992; Keller, 2001). When group members come from different functional backgrounds, they may lack the needed knowledge to judge each other's expertise (Berger, 1974). Dual-information processing theory (Chaiken and Trope, 1999) predicts that when people lack the ability to systematically process expert information they resort to heuristic cues, such as characteristics of a person's communication styles. Given these reasons, we believe that findings from communication research can provide valuable insights into expertise recognition.

The goal of this chapter is therefore to provide an overview of existing research on how communication may influence expertise recognition. We focus on three aspects of communication behaviors, including communication opportunities, communication styles, and communication accommodation as an organizing schema because they are tightly connected to expectation states (ES) theory (Berger, 1974)—a widely adopted framework by studies of expertise judgment (Bunderson, 2003; Bunderson and Barton, 2011). Special attention is given to the impact of culture because intercultural collaboration has become more common in an ever-globalizing economy, and cultural differences can significantly influence how people communicate and perceive communication (Gudykunst et al., 2005). The impact of technology is also considered because much intercultural collaboration in contemporary organizations happens in distributed teams, supported by information and communication technology (ICT; van den Hoff and Kotlarsky, this volume). They can exert significant contextual influence on communication effectiveness and expertise emergence in communication (Maruping and Agarwal, 2004; Treem, 2013).

In the following sections, we will first review several branches of ES theory that are closely related to communication opportunities, styles, and accommodation. Findings from relevant empirical studies will also be discussed. We then review literature on how national culture may influence communication behaviors in these three aspects, which in turn influence people's expertise recognition. The impact of ICT will also be discussed. The chapter ends with a discussion on directions for future research.

Expectations, Expertise Recognition, and Communication

Expertise recognition is a status-organizing process (Bunderson, 2003; Bunderson and Barton, 2011). Many extant studies that examined the effects of communication on expertise recognition (Bazarova and Yuan, 2013; Bunderson, 2003; Bunderson and Barton, 2011; Littlepage and Mueller, 1997; Thomas-Hunt and Phillips, 2004; Yuan et al., 2013) are based on ES theory. As a research program, ES theory comprises several branches that examine conditions, processes, and consequences of the emergence of status in a task group (Berger, 1974). A comprehensive review of ES theory is beyond the scope of this chapter, and can be found elsewhere (Berger, 1974; Berger et al., 1985; Correll and Ridgeway, 2006; Wagner and Berger, 2002). Here we focus on the major branches of the theory that can inform studies on the impact of communication opportunities, styles, and accommodation on expertise recognition.

PERFORMANCE EXPECTATION AND COMMUNICATION OPPORTUNITIES

Power and prestige theory (Berger and Conner, 1974), which is the original and core branch of ES theory, maintains that power and prestige orders in a task group emerge as each member forms a stable and consistent *performance expectation* of each other. Performance expectation refers to "a generalized belief that an actor holds about the capacity of himself or others to contribute to task completion" (p. 87). In the process of developing such a belief, group members observe the distribution of contribution opportunities, reactions to others' contributions, and subsequent behavioral changes in the group. When group members set higher performance expectations for a recognized expert, the expert is often given more opportunities to perform, and is also more likely to be evaluated positively in subsequent interactions. Because such emergent performance expectations can affect performance opportunities and competence evaluations, the resulting power and prestige orders become self-sustaining (Berger and Conner, 1974).

Opportunities to perform are closely related to opportunities to communicate. Berger and Conner (1974) argued that if group members have equal probabilities to perform, to receive feedback, or to be influenced by others, they should gain identical performance expectations. Holding these probabilities constant, a talkative member has a higher probability to receive a better performance expectation than a silent member because the talkative member has a greater probability to initiate interactions (p. 101). Studies have confirmed this prediction that indeed talkative members were more likely to be identified as experts, despite their actual expertise (Bottger, 1984; Littlepage and Mueller, 1997; Littlepage et al., 1995). An important implication is that, although people of higher social status may have higher probabilities to dominate communication, pre-existing status is not the only factor that can influence communication opportunities in group collaboration. Low-status group members can boost their rankings and even break a pre-existing order of status hierarchy if they are given or have the drive to create more opportunities for themselves to participate in group discussions.

A noteworthy difference existed in the measurement of talkativeness, however. While some scholars measured this concept as the amount of communication opportunities across group members, using such objective measures as word counts (Bottger, 1984), thought-unit counts (Bazarova and Yuan, 2013; Yuan et al., 2013), or turn-taking (Li et al., 2015; Woolley et al., 2010); others measured it using subjective perceptions of one another (Littlepage and Mueller, 1997; Littlepage et al., 1995). Despite such differences in the empirical operationalization of the concept, the results are consistent across studies when the research samples contained people from Western cultural backgrounds only. Taken together, the results seem to suggest that opportunities to participate in discussions matter for expertise recognition, regardless of whether they are actual opportunities or perceived ones.

STATUS CHARACTERISTICS/CUES AND COMMUNICATION STYLES

A second branch of ES theory that can be used to study how communication may influence expertise recognition is *theory of status characteristics and expectation states* (Berger and Fisek, 1974). This branch of ES theory was originally proposed to explain differential performance expectations by *status characteristics*. Status characteristics can be classified into two types (p. 173). The first one is *diffuse* status characteristics, such as gender, race, and age, because such characteristics are often tied to stereotypes of general aptitude and performance expectations, including those that may be irrelevant to a focal task. The second one is *specific* status characteristics, such as experience and amount of training, among others, because this type of characteristics leads to specific performance expectations. Social categories (e.g. "democrats" and "republicans") that are relevant neither to a focal task nor to general aptitude can also become status characteristics when they are associated with differential control of resources (e.g. rewards) or pre-accepted status characteristics (Berger and Fisek, 2006; Ridgeway, 1991). Using a similar concept, *status cues*, Berger et al. (1986) extended this branch of ES theory and proposed that status cues can be further classified into *indicative* versus *expressive* ones. While the former refers to those cues that become immediately observable with the group members' presence, the latter refers to those emergent cues observable only during group interactions.

Expressive cues focus exclusively on characteristics of communication, including both the content and paralanguage of social interactions (Berger et al., 1986; Bunderson and Barton, 2011). Expressive cues can be further classified into speech-based cues, such as speed, loudness, and fluency; as well as gesture-based cues, such as eye contact or seat choice in a conversation. All these expressive cues can have direct impact on performance expectations (see Berger et al., 1986; Ridgeway et al., 1985). Furthermore, because expressive cues, such as gestures and language styles, can also convey information about a person's social categories (e.g. gender, ethnicity, and race), these cues can have additional indirect effect on performance expectations via stereotypes attached to these social categories (Berger et al., 1986).

In parallel to sociologists' investigation of expressive cues for expertise judgment under the ES framework, communication scholars examined how they may influence the credibility of an information source. These cues are referred to as *communication styles* in the field of communication. In addition to those expressive cues investigated under the ES framework, scholars found that other communication styles, for example, dominance, confidence, and openness in communication (Bonner et al., 2007; Littlepage and Mueller, 1997; Yuan et al., 2013) can all boost one's perceived expertise and/or influence. Similarly, linguistic styles, such as the use of jargon or long words, were also found to relate to perception of higher expertise (Toma and D'Angelo, 2014). While these styles can be conceived as trait-like individual properties, they are also communicative in nature. As a result, they provide people an opportunity to break away from pre-existing status, and makes expertise evaluation more relational, contextualized, and reflective of changes in group interactive dynamics (Treem, 2012). In short, we believe that more exciting findings can emerge when research on ES theory and communication styles is more systematically integrated.

BEHAVIORAL INTERCHANGE PATTERNS AND COMMUNICATION ACCOMMODATION

Theory of evaluation and expectation is a third branch of ES theory that can be used to explain the impact of communication on expertise recognition. This branch of ES theory argues that performance expectations can be affected by behavioral interchange patterns, which refers to repeated interaction cycles among group members (Fisek et al., 1991, 1995; Fisek et al., 2002). In such interactions, some group members may behave in accordance with high-status manners, while others behave in low-status manners (Fisek et al., 1991). When such "leader–follower" behavioral cycles emerge and repeat in group interactions, members form shared beliefs about the power and prestige orders in the group. They would also treat these ordered positions as concrete social roles and then perform per the role enacted in the pattern (Fisek et al., 2002).

While status characteristics/cues (e.g. confidence) are considered to be properties of individual group members (Berger et al., 1986; Ridgeway et al., 1985), behavioral interchange patterns emerge from the interactions between two or more members. Similar to status characteristics/cues, behavioral interchange patterns are communicative. Moreover, they also capture the emergent nature of expertise judgment. Such patterns are self-maintaining through the enactment of the expert vs. non-expert roles. While we agree that expertise is essentially a form of human capital (e.g. intelligence, knowledge, and skills), we also believe that expertise is inherently coupled with role relations, which are actualized through behavioral interchange patterns. Given the dynamic and relational nature of expertise in contemporary organizations (Treem, 2012; van den Hooff and Kotlarsky, this volume), behavioral interchange patterns and their revelations in communication can be an important place where expertise can be inferred and enacted.

One frequently studied type of behavioral interchange pattern in the field of communication is *communication accommodation*, which has been found to capture power and status dynamics implicated in communications (Gregory and Webster, 1996). Communication accommodation refers to a process through which people "reduce or magnify communicative differences" in interpersonal communications (Giles, 2008, 163). Accommodation happens when group members converge in communication behaviors along various dimensions, including characteristics of speech (e.g. utterance length, speech rate, and response latency), gestures (see Giles et al., 1991), linguistic styles (Niederhoffer and Pennebaker, 2002; Liao et al., in press), and nonverbal vocal signals (Gregory and Webster, 1996), among others.

Communication accommodation is associated with expertise recognition for two reasons. First, task group members often have an internal drive to gain acceptance by the other group members, particularly those with higher status (Shepperd, 1993). To seek social approval (Gallois et al., 2005; Giles, 2008), group members can be motivated to accommodate to the communication features of others who appear to be competent. Second, people are attentive to other group members' accommodating/non-accommodating communication behaviors (Gallois et al., 2005; Giles, 2008; Giles and Gasiorek, 2014). While being accommodated can increase liking and understanding (Giles, 2008, 36), it may also suggest status differences. In task groups, an accommodator can be interpreted as possessing a lower status than the accommodated. Given the central role of competence in status organizing in task groups, the asymmetric pattern of communication accommodation can enact the roles of expert and non-expert between the accommodator and the accommodated, reinforcing group members' perceptions and rank-ordering of each other's expertise (Liao et al., in press).

In sum, ES theory (Berger et al., 1986; Bunderson and Barton, 2011) suggests that communication can influence expertise recognition because opportunities to communicate, styles of communication, and accommodation in communication behaviors, can indicate a person's competence level. To better understand how communication affects expertise judgment in multinational teams, the next section will discuss the impact of national culture on how people communicate and how they perceive communication.

Impacts of National Culture on Communication and Expertise Recognition

Culture is usually defined as a shared system of ideas, meanings, manners, rituals, and values that are acquired and enacted through interactions with others (Swidler, 1986). National differences in culture have been repeatedly observed in organizational behaviors (see, for a overview, Hofstede et al., 2010). When people from different countries differ in how they communicate and how they interpret other's communication, intercultural collaboration can be challenging; and inaccurate expertise recognition is one of the potential issues. As detailed in this section, the cultural relevancies of communication opportunities, styles, and accommodation across societies can cause problems for developing consistent expertise judgments in multinational teams.

CULTURE AND COMMUNICATION OPPORTUNITIES

Two dimensions of national culture, that is, individualism versus collectivism, and masculine versus feminine orientation in Hofstede's (1983, 1998) terms, can explain people's differential willingness to engage in a group discussion and to use the discussion as an opportunity to influence group decisions. Collectivist versus individualist societies differ in how much they expect individuals to value in-groups (Hofstede, 1983). For example, people from an individualistic society are more likely to pursue their individual goals even if those goals are contrary to the goals of the groups that they belong to (Hofstede, 1983). In contrast, people from collectivistic societies tend to supplant their own goals for the goals of their in-groups (Triandis et al., 1988). Given that collectivistic societies advocate conformism to in-groups more than individualistic societies (Bond and Smith, 1996), it can be anticipated that people from collectivist societies are more likely to suppress expressions of ideas that could conflict with or diverge from those held by in-groups (Goncalo and Staw, 2006).

Masculine and feminine orientation can also influence the willingness to speak out because the two orientations differently emphasize task perform-ance and relational harmony (Hofstede, 1998). Driven by the concern for top task performance, individuals from societies with a masculine orientation are expected to stand up for themselves, begin and disengage from conversa-tions, and express their own beliefs (Richmond and McCroskey, 1989). Conversely, societies with a feminine orientation promote sensitivity toward others, helpfulness, and friendliness (Hofstede, 1998). If speaking out for task performance is perceived as threatening to relational harmony, individuals from societies with a feminine orientation may refrain from doing so. In addition, these individuals may even utilize silence as a way of participation because in societies with a feminine orientation silence can be used to show agreement, lack of interest, or even contempt, depending on the context; this is not often the case in societies with a masculine orientation such as Germany or Great Britain where silence is much less meaningful (Giri, 2006).

Therefore, communication opportunities can be unevenly distributed in a team comprising members from mixed cultural backgrounds across the spec-trum of individualism–collectivism and/or masculine–feminine orientation. It is particularly true when members stick to their cultural norms about speaking out. As ES theory has suggested, one's expertise/competence level can be underestimated when s/he speaks less, even if s/he is willing to participate in a group discussion through meaningful silence. As members of a multinational team hold different understandings of the meaning of silence, the uneven distribution of communication opportunities can intro-duce more inaccuracies in the team's expertise recognition.

CULTURE AND COMMUNICATION STYLES

Differences in national culture are also reflected in direct versus indirect, and dominant versus submissive communication styles, which, as already dis-cussed, are particularly relevant to expertise judgment. Direct versus indirect communication styles are often associated with low- versus high-context cultures defined by Hall (1976). The low and high contexts capture how message meaning is transmitted, and to what extent people need to refer to social contexts to gain appropriate interpretation of social interactions (Hall, 1976). Although all societies utilize both, East Asian societies predominantly use high-context communication such that the communication styles of people from these societies tend to be indirect, less contentious, and less dramatic (Gudykunst and Lee, 2002). Conversely, people from North America and Europe are more likely to use precise and less ambiguous communication styles given the predominant low-context communication in these societies (Park and Kim, 2008).

Power distance, another dimension of national culture (Hofstede, 1983; Hofstede et al., 1983), can also influence people's communication styles, for instance, dominance and submissiveness. Power distance refers to the dependency of relationships within a society (Hofstede et al., 2010). Societies with smaller power distances (e.g. Israel and Sweden) tend to advocate easily approachable supervisors and the ability for subordinates to contradict their supervisors (Hofstede et al., 2010). This tendency can attenuate both dominant and submissive communication styles in task groups (Tiedens et al., 2007). Conversely, societies with greater power distances (e.g. Mexico and the Philippines) display either large dependences between supervisors and subordinates or counterdependence (Hofstede et al., 2010, 61). As a result, dominant and submissive communication styles can be more prevalent in these societies.

As discussed earlier, ES theory suggests that direct and dominant communication styles are often associated with one's perceived competence level. As a result, members from high-context societies are more likely to be judged as less competent than people from low-context societies. However, studies of dominant communication styles and expertise judgment yielded inconsistent evidence, especially in multinational teams (Littlepage and Mueller, 1997; Yuan et al., 2013). Cultural difference in power distance may be a possible explanation as people with different levels of power distance treat dominance differently as a status cue. They may also weigh the formal hierarchy in a task group differently when judging each other's expertise.

CULTURE AND COMMUNICATION ACCOMMODATION

As cultures differentially conceive power distance, individuals with different cultural backgrounds can further differ regarding their tendency to accommodate to others' communication. Communication accommodation can be associated with interpersonal hierarchy (Giles, 2008). Within a society with larger power distances, a subordinate is expected to respect the power difference and is unlikely to contradict his or her supervisor. Instead, he or she may accommodate to the supervisor's communication. This is because subordinates from high-power-distance societies often possess a greater desire for social approval, which can motivate communication accommodation (Gregory and Webster, 1996). In a complementary manner, a supervisor with a similarly high level of power distance can refrain from accommodating his/her subordinates in order to maintain the power distance. Ironically, subordinates from larger power-distance societies may also experience greater feelings of communication apprehension when interacting with their supervisors (Madlock, 2012). To overcome onset apprehension, subordinates may refrain from approaching their supervisors, and thus avoid accommodation. Such non-accommodation may be perceived as appropriate or unrelated to incompetence by high-power-distance supervisors because this kind of behavior preserves the status quo of power hierarchy.

In sum, we reviewed how national cultures may differentiate people's likelihood to speak out, their communication styles, and also their likelihood to accommodate to others' communication behaviors. Generally, cultural differences can be a challenge to accurate expertise recognition in multinational teams, as suggested in recent studies (Bazarova and Yuan, 2013; Li et al., 2015; Yuan et al., 2013, 2016). However, a more encouraging finding of these studies is that ICTs, which are frequently used to support collaboration across national/cultural boundaries, can to some extent mitigate the negative influence of intercultural communication on group outcomes, as has been confirmed in other studies (e.g. Shachaf, 2008). In the next section we discuss why ICTs can have such an impact. Suffice to say here is that intercultural collaboration can present some difficulties for group members if people are not cognizant of the difference in values and perceptions of others. Knowing when to use humility in communication, when to be assertive, or even when to be silent is vital to a person's expertise being adequately recognized in cross-cultural interaction.

The Impact of Information and Communication Technology

As reviewed in the earlier section of this chapter, people from different cultural backgrounds communicate differently (Gudykunst et al., 1996), and have different views about which characteristics of communication behaviors are indicative of a person's expertise (Yuan et al., 2013). As intercultural collaboration frequently involves using ICT to connect people from different corners of the world, it is important to gain a better understanding about how ICT may influence the collaboration process. While a plethora of studies have been published on the broad issue of collaboration, there is a dearth of research that specifically examines how ICT-enacted differences in communication behaviors can influence expertise recognition in intercultural collaboration. Bazarova and Yuan (2013) have conducted one of the first studies on this topic. They found that, despite having comparable actual expertise, American group members were perceived as more competent and influential than their Chinese counterparts in face-to-face (FtF) groups; however, the significant gaps in expertise perception and in influence between the two ethnic groups narrowed or became insignificant in the computer-mediated-communication (CMC) groups. The results seem to suggest that ICT may function as a leveling ground for people to have their expertise appropriately recognized despite characteristics of their communication behaviors. We believe that this topic is definitely worthy of further exploration. Moreover, as the authors acknowledged, their initial study could not answer the question about what exactly caused the disappearance of these differences between the two ethnic groups in the two communication settings. To answer this question, it may be helpful to take into account the effects of ICT on communication opportunities, styles, and accommodation.

ICT AND COMMUNICATION OPPORTUNITIES

Existing theories characterizing ICTs may provide some interesting insights to explain Bazarova and Yuan's (2013) findings about more equal distribution of communication opportunities between native and non-native speakers in text-based CMC settings. For instance, media synchronicity theory proposes that features of ICT can be evaluated along the following five dimensions (Dennis et al., 2008; Maruping and Agarwal, 2004). *Immediacy of feedback* evaluates whether the communication medium allows delay in responding. *Symbol variety* describes co-presence of verbal and non-verbal communication cues. *Parallelism* evaluates whether the medium allows simultaneous conversations. *Rehearsability* is centered on how the medium allows more time for people to think through their messages. Finally, *reprocessability* describes whether the medium records previous communication, to allow reprocessing information at a later time. Media synchronicity theory provides some valuable insights to explain Bazarova and Yuan's (2013) findings. About communication opportunities, CMC provides more communication opportunities to non-native speakers than FtF settings for the following reasons. First, while immediate feedback is anticipated in FtF communications, it is not required in text-based CMC settings. This means that non-native speakers will have more chance to provide feedback in CMC settings, as compared to FtF settings, because finding their turns to speak up in a FtF discussion is more challenging (Li et al., 2015). This is of direct importance for expertise recognition because, as predicted by ES theory, more communication opportunities implicate more cues for positive expertise evaluation. Second, related to immediacy of feedback, ICT allows parallel conversations. As a result, non-native speakers have a higher chance of having their thoughts conveyed in text-based CMC because they face less pressure to move along with the fast flow of FtF conversation. This again implicates more communication opportunities for non-native speakers, and thereby more expressive cues for others to more positively evaluate their expertise. Third, non-native speakers have more time to rehearse and edit their conversation in text-based CMC than in FtF settings. This will reduce the number of negative competence cues (e.g. accent, grammar mistakes) communicated to others. Fourth, ICT gives non-native speakers more time to process and reprocess the conversation at their own speed. As they gain a better understanding of the content of the group discussion, they are more likely to give informed, thoughtful responses, which again can generate more communicative cues that contribute positively to others' evaluations of their expertise.

To date, only sporadic evidence has been collected supporting these propositions as to why CMC can provide a leveling ground for equal communication opportunities in intercultural collaboration. For instance, related to having parallel conversations, Li et al. (2015) found that a large difference in turn-taking in conversation between native and non-native speakers could cause less accuracy in expertise recognition and thereby lower performance at the group level; however, the gap in conversational turn-taking between native and non-native speakers was substantially reduced in text-based CMC groups in comparison to FtF groups. To our limited knowledge, there do not exist other studies that have examined all the dimensions of media synchronicity theory in intercultural collaboration. More systematic investigation of each technological dimension of ICT is certainly warranted so that more targeted intervention programs can be developed to support effective expertise recognition. For instance, upon finding that allowing parallel conversation could significantly reduce gaps in turn-taking in intercultural collaboration, a behavioral intervention, such as an explicit reminder of equal contribution from all members, may be sufficient to reduce a huge dispersion of turn-taking in group discussion.

ICT AND COMMUNICATION STYLES

While numerous studies have examined how ICT usage could influence group collaboration, few explicitly examined how ICT can influence communication styles, especially those closely related to expertise judgment in intercultural collaboration. In one of the initial studies on this topic, Yuan et al. (2013) found that the difference between FtF and CMC indeed moderated perceptions of several communication styles in intercultural collaboration (see Figure 5.1). However, the pattern is not consistent. For example, CMC reduced differences in perceived confidence, tenseness, and communication competence between American and Chinese participants, yet CMC exaggerated differences in perceived contentious, frank/directness, and task-related communication between the two types of participants.

To address these questions about how and why ICT can influence actual and perceived communication styles in intercultural collaboration, and how such changes can influence expertise judgment in ICT-supported collaboration, a series of studies need to be done in a more systematic fashion. First, researchers need to know how people form different opinions about a person's communication styles. Take assertiveness as an example. Researchers need to know what verbal and nonverbal, or linguistic and paralinguistic, cues are

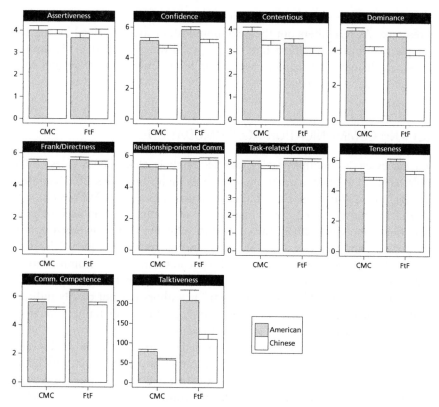

Figure 5.1 Means and 95% Confidence Intervals of Members' Communication Styles Rated by Each Other in 51 Four-Person Multinational Groups (each group comprises two Chinese and two Americans, and was randomly assigned to use FtF or CMC)

indicative of such a communication style. Next, researchers also need to find out among these different cues which ones are more likely to be filtered out or enhanced per characteristics of ICT. Only then can we explain why communication styles can change from one setting to another.

Nevertheless, we believe that ICT's influence on communication styles can benefit expertise recognition because ICT can filter out negative competence cues. Although other cues that are indicative of the status of non-native speakers still exist in CMC settings (e.g. grammatical mistakes), reduction in the number of such cues can provide a better chance for non-native speakers' true expertise to be judged appropriately. For instance, ICT can remove nervous mannerisms, which are typically viewed unfavorably in expertise judgment. ICT can further benefit intercultural collaboration because many negative competence cues represented in communication styles are associated with cultural differences. For example, Americans and Europeans may be judged as overly confident by East Asians when cues of confidence are presented. As ICT filters out these communication styles ascribed by culture, people may put more effort into judging each other's expertise via limited cues, which may lead to more systematic information processing and thus greater objective judgment.

ICT AND COMMUNICATION ACCOMMODATION

As discussed in multiple review articles (Gallois et al., 2005; Giles, 2008; Giles et al., 1991) and a recent meta-analysis (Soliz and Giles, 2013), context can significantly influence communication accommodation. While culture is one of the most studied contextual factors of communication accommodation (Soliz and Giles, 2013), the contextual influence of ICT is much underexplored. Soliz and Giles (2013) systematically reviewed 149 articles that spanned nearly forty years of research on communication accommodation. Among the seventy-six empirical studies eligible for meta-analysis, only seven included a CMC context. Though the authors did not clearly indicate which seven studies included a CMC setting, based on our limited literature search, most of these studies examined communication accommodation in CMC only (e.g. accommodation in email conversation as in Colley and Todd, 2002). In the absence of a FtF comparison group, it is difficult to evaluate how ICTs have functioned as a contextual factor influencing communication accommodation in different contexts. Liao et al. (in press) explored this issue tentatively and found a positive effect of differences in self-confidence on group members' communication accommodation, which was measured as convergence in linguistic styles, but the effect was significant in FtF only. They also found that communication accommodation could lower others' evaluation of the focal person's expertise, but the effect was significant in text-based CMC only. While their findings have offered some preliminary evidence that ICT can function as a moderating contextual factor, much more can be done to explore why such moderation effects can happen.

It is possible that different characteristics of ICT, for instance, reprocessability and symbol variety of the medium, can significantly influence which communication cues are filtered out or highlighted in different communication media. Consequently, differential accommodation may happen either because there are less decipherable cues to trigger accommodation or more exaggerated cues that can set accommodation in a different direction. Regardless, we believe that more empirical studies that compare communication accommodation in different communication channels, in addition to those studies that examine accommodation in only CMC, are warranted to gain a better understanding of the impact of ICT usage on this process.

Taken together, we believe that, because of the characteristics of ICT (as those suggested by media synchronicity theory), CMC settings can reduce differences in communication behaviors between people with different cultural backgrounds. As discussed earlier, ES studies have repeatedly found that people rely on diverse social cues to infer others' expertise, and that these cues can significantly bias people's judgment. As CMC filters out certain cues that tend to link non-native speakers with incompetence, and gives non-native speakers more opportunities to generate cues that can better demonstrate their true knowledge, higher accuracy in expertise recognition may happen even for people who might otherwise appear incompetent outside of a CMC setting. Although no empirical study has been conducted to test these propositions, we believe that the value of using ICT to level the ground between native and non-native speakers, or amongst people with varying degree of competence in FtF communication, cannot be overlooked, and is worthy of further empirical investigation.

Advancing the Study of Expertise

In the previous sections, we reviewed relevant theories and studies that examined how communication behaviors, in particular communication opportunities, styles, and accommodation, may influence expertise recognition in group collaboration. The review focused on different branches of ES theory because this theory has been used most frequently in management research on this topic. While doing the review, we have also pointed out possible contributions that communication research can make to help enrich this endeavor. For instance, research on communication styles can inform ES studies on what additional expressive cues can influence status/competence judgment. Furthermore, focusing on communication dynamics complements existing ES studies and social judgment research (see Yoon, Gupta, and Hollingshead, this volume, for more detailed discussion) in that this approach can better capture the fluid, emergent nature of expertise (Treem, 2012; van den Hoff and Kotlarsky, in this volume), and explore how people can break away from pre-existing power and prestige orders that are based on such fixed characteristics as race and gender, among others. Communication research on ICT usage provides additional insight on how technology can be a contextual factor of expertise emergence, especially when cultural differences impose difficulties in communication and expertise recognition. The ultimate goal is to help people achieve better accuracy in expertise recognition regardless of their cultural backgrounds, language proficiency, and intercultural communication competence. To achieve this goal, we have shown existing connections between communication research and ES research on competence/expertise judgment. We will highlight next a couple more topics that are worthy of further exploration.

DIRECTIONS FOR FUTURE RESEARCH

Another area of communication research that may help inform expertise recognition research is persuasion, particularly those studies that examined the issue of source credibility in message design. Source credibility has been defined as the ability of a source to "inspire belief in their representations" (Beaulieu, 2001, 85). When making a decision based on some information presented, the credibility judgment of the source becomes of great importance (Gordon and Spears, 2012). When a person is interacting in areas outside of their own expertise, it is more difficult yet equally important to be able to trust another person's information and judge the credibility of that information. A listener determines the credibility of a speaker by perceiving the speaker's expertness, trustworthiness, attractiveness (Giffin, 1967; Lafferty et al., 2002; Ohanian, 1990), and likeability (Clow et al., 2006). Additionally, perceptions of speaker credibility can be affected by the social influence of a group (Giffin, 1967). We believe that future research on expertise recognition can benefit from a more systematic integration of those communication studies on source credibility.

A second area of research that we think can expand existing ES theory on expertise recognition is a better integration of ES theory and social role theory. The social role theory postulates that individuals construct social roles for people, including themselves. These social roles are important to the recognition of expertise because culture affects perceptions of individual differences based on gender roles (Eagly and Karau, 1991; Eagly et al., 1992; Joshi, 2014; Reskin et al., 1999) and ethnicity (Bazarova and Yuan, 2013; Yuan et al., 2013). Take gender as an example. Thomas-Hunt and Phillips (2004) found that women were judged to be less of an expert than men in their group, and that women were less able to influence the group and felt like they were having less of an impact. With decreased ability to influence the group, as compared to men, women received lower performance ratings, including their ratings of themselves. Because socially constructed roles can influence people's judgment of typical and atypical behaviors, expectations derived from social role can affect the perception of expertise and competence (Koenig and Eagly, 2014). Therefore, when examining how social cues may influence competence/expertise judgment per ES theory, it is also important to take into consideration the different roles that people perform in their daily work. It is also of interest to investigate how communication dynamics help people overcome prescribed social orders of competence and status, and recognize expertise in a manner more reflective of actual interactive dynamics within group discussions.

▨ REFERENCES

Austin, J. R. (2003). Transactive Memory in Organizational Groups: The Effects of Content, Consensus, Specialization, and Accuracy on Group Performance. *Journal of Applied Psychology*, 88(5), 866–78. doi: 10.1037/0021-9010.88.5.866

Baumann, M. R., and Bonner, B. L. (2004). The Effects of Variability and Expectations on Utilization of Member Expertise and Group Performance. *Organizational Behavior and Human Decision Processes*, 93(2), 89–101. doi: 10.1016/j.obhdp.2003.12.004

Bazarova, N. N., and Yuan, Y. C. (2013). Expertise Recognition and Influence in Intercultural Groups: Differences between Face-to-Face and Computer-Mediated Communication. *Journal of Computer-Mediated Communication*, 18(4), 437–53. doi: 10.1111/jcc4.12018

Beaulieu, P. R. (2001). The Effects of Judgments of New Clients' Integrity upon Risk Judgments, Audit Evidence, and Fees. *Auditing: A Journal of Practice and Theory*, 20(2), 85–99. doi: 10.2308/aud.2001.20.2.85

Berger, J. (1974). Expectation States Theory: A Theoretical Research Program. In J. Berger, T. L. Conner, and M. H. Fisek (eds), *Expectation States Theory: A Theoretical Research Program* (pp. 3–22). Cambridge, MA: Winthrop.

Berger, J., and Conner, T. L. (1974). Performance Expectations and Behavior in Small Groups: A Revised Formulation. In J. Berger, T. L. Conner, and M. H. Fisek (eds), *Expectation States Theory: A Theoretical Research Program* (pp. 85–109). Cambridge, MA: Winthrop.

Berger, J., and Fisek, M. H. (1974). A Generalization of the Theory of Status Characteristics and Expectation States. In J. Berger, T. L. Conner, and M. H. Fisek (eds), *Expectation States Theory: A Theoretical Research Program* (pp. 163–205). Cambridge, MA: Winthrop.

Berger, J., and Fisek, M. H. (2006). Diffuse Status Characteristics and the Spread of Status Value: A Formal Theory. *American Journal of Sociology*, 111(4), 1038–79. doi: 10.1086/498633

Berger, J., Wagner, D. G., and Zelditch, M. J. (1985). Expectation States Theory: Review and Assessment. In J. Berger and M. Zelditch Jr. (eds), *Status, Rewards, and Influence: How Expectations Organize Behavior* (pp. 1–73). San Francisco: Jossey-Bass.

Berger, J., Webster, M. J., Ridgeway, C. L., and Rosenholtz, S. J. (1986). Status Cues, Expectations, and Behavior. In E. J. Lawler (ed.), *Advances in Group Processes* (vol. 3, pp. 1–22). Greenwich, CT: JAI Press.

Bond, R., and Smith, P. B. (1996). Culture and Conformity: A Meta-Analysis of Studies Using Asch's (1952b, 1956) Line Judgment Task. *Psychological Bulletin*, 119(1), 111–37. doi: 10.1037/0033-2909.119.1.111

Bonner, B. L., Sillito, S. D., and Baumann, M. R. (2007). Collective Estimation: Accuracy, Expertise, and Extroversion as Sources of Intra-Group Influence. *Organizational Behavior and Human Decision Processes*, 103(1), 121–33. doi: 10.1016/j.obhdp.2006.05.001

Bottger, P. C. (1984). Expertise and Air Time as Bases of Actual and Perceived Influence in Problem-Solving Groups. *Journal of Applied Psychology*, 69(2), 214–21. doi: 10.1037/0021-9010.69.2.214

Bunderson, J. S. (2003). Recognizing and Utilizing Expertise in Work Groups: A Status Characteristics Perspective. *Administrative Science Quarterly*, 48(4), 557–91. doi: 10.2307/3556637

Bunderson, J. S., and Barton, M. A. (2011). Status Cues and Expertise Assessment in Groups: How Group Members Size One Another Up...and Why it Matters. In J. I. Pearce (ed.), *Status in Management and Organizations* (pp. 215–37). New York: Cambridge University Press.

Chaiken, S., and Trope, Y. (1999). *Dual-Process Theories in Social Psychology*. New York: Guilford Press.

Clow, K. E., James, K. E., Kranenburg, K. E., and Berry, C. T. (2006). The Relationship of the Visual Element of an Advertisement to Service Quality Expectations and Source Credibility. *Journal of Services Marketing*, 20(6), 404–11. doi: 10.1108/08876040610691293

Colley, A., and Todd, Z. (2002). Gender-Linked Differences in the Style and Content of E-Mails to Friends. *Journal of Language and Social Psychology*, 21(4), 380–92. doi: 10.1177/026192702237955

Correll, S. J., and Ridgeway, C. L. (2006). Expectation States Theory. In J. Delamater (ed.), *Handbook of Social Psychology* (pp. 29–51). New York: Springer.

Dennis, A. R., Fuller, R. M., and Valacich, J. S. (2008). Media, Tasks, and Communication Processes: A Theory of Media Synchronicity. *MIS Quarterly*, 32(3), 575–600. Retrieved from <http://misq.org>.

Eagly, A. H., and Karau, S. J. (1991). Gender and the Emergence of Leaders: A Meta-Analysis. *Journal of Personality and Social Psychology*, 60(5), 685–710. doi: 10.1037/0022-3514.60.5.685

Eagly, A. H., Makhijani, M. G., and Klonsky, B. G. (1992). Gender and the Evaluation of Leaders: A Meta-Analysis. *Psychological Bulletin*, 111(1), 3–22. doi: 10.1037/0033-2909.111.1.3

Einhorn, H. J., Hogarth, R. M., and Klempner, E. (1977). Quality of Group Judgment. *Psychological Bulletin*, 84(1), 158–72. doi: 10.1037/0033-2909.84.1.158

Fisek, M. H., Berger, J., and Moore, J. C. J. (2002). Evaluations, Enactment, and Expectations. *Social Psychology Quarterly*, 65(4), 329–45. doi: 10.2307/3090106

Fisek, M. H., Berger, J., and Norman, R. Z. (1991). Participation in Heterogeneous and Homogeneous Groups: A Theoretical Integration. *American Journal of Sociology*, 97(1), 114–42. doi: 10.1086/229742

Fisek, M. H., Berger, J., and Norman, R. Z. (1995). Evaluations and the Formation of Expectations. *American Journal of Sociology*, 101(3), 721–46. doi: 10.1086/230758

Ford, R. C., and Randolph, W. A. (1992). Cross-Functional Structures: A Review and Integration of Matrix Organization and Project Management. *Journal of Management*, 18(2), 267–94. doi: 10.1177/014920639201800204

Gallois, C., Ogay, T., and Giles, H. (2005). Communication Accommodation Theory: A Look Back and a Look Ahead. In W. B. Gudykunst (ed.), *Theorizing about Intercultural Communication* (pp. 121–48). Thousand Oaks, CA: Sage.

Giffin, K. (1967). The Contribution of Studies of Source Credibility to a Theory of Interpersonal Trust in the Communication Process. *Psychological Bulletin*, 68(2), 104–20. doi: 10.1037/h0024833

Giles, H. (2008). Communication Accommodation Theory. In L. A. Baxter (ed.), *Engaging Theories in Interpersonal Communication: Multiple Perspectives* (pp. 161–73). Thousand Oaks, CA: Sage.

Giles, H., and Gasiorek, J. (2014). Parameters of Non-Accommodation: Refining and Elaborating Communication Accommodation Theory. In J. P. Forgas, O. Vincze, and J. László (eds), *Social Cognition and Communication* (pp. 155–72). New York: Psychology Press.

Giles, H., Coupland, J., and Coupland, N. (1991). *Contexts of Accommodation: Developments in Applied Sociolinguistics*. New York: Cambridge University Press.

Giri, V. N. (2006). Culture and Communication Style. *Review of Communication*, 6 (1–2), 124–30. doi: 10.1080/15358590600763391

Goncalo, J. A., and Staw, B. M. (2006). Individualism–Collectivism and Group Creativity. *Organizational Behavior and Human Decision Processes*, 100(1), 96–109. doi: 10.1016/j.obhdp.2005.11.003

Gordon, R., and Spears, K. (2012). You Don't Act like You Trust Me: Dissociations between Behavioural and Explicit Measures of Source Credibility Judgement. *Quarterly Journal of Experimental Psychology*, 65(1), 121–34. doi: 10.1080/17470218.2011.591534

Gregory, S. W., and Webster, S. (1996). A Nonverbal Signal in Voices of Interview Partners Effectively Predicts Communication Accommodation and Social Status Perceptions. *Journal of Personality and Social Psychology*, 70(6), 1231–40. doi: 10.1037/0022-3514.70.6.1231

Gudykunst, W. B., and Lee, C. M. (2002). Cross-Cultural Communication Theory. In W. B. Gudykunst and B. Mody (eds), *Handbook of International and Intercultural Communication* (2nd edn, pp. 25–50). Thousand Oaks, CA: Sage.

Gudykunst, W. B., Lee, C. M., Nishida, T., and Ogawa, N. (2005). Theorizing about Intercultural Communication: An Introduction. In W. B. Gudykunst (ed.), *Theorizing about Intercultural Communication* (pp. 3–32). Thousand Oaks, CA: Sage.

Gudykunst, W. B., Matsumoto, Y., Ting-Toomey, S., Nishida, T., Kim, K., and Heyman, S. (1996). The Influence of Cultural Individualism–Collectivism, Self Construals, and Individual Values on Communication Styles across Cultures. *Human Communication Research*, 22(4), 510–43. doi: 10.1111/j.1468-2958.1996.tb00377

Hall, E. T. (1976). *Beyond Culture*. Garden City, NY: Anchor Press.

Hofstede, G. H. (1983). The Cultural Relativity of Organizational Practices and Theories. *Journal of International Business Studies*, 14(2), 75–89. doi: 10.1057/palgrave.jibs.8490867

Hofstede, G. H. (1998). *Masculinity and Femininity: The Taboo Dimension of National Cultures*. Thousand Oaks, CA: Sage.

Hofstede, G. H., Hofstede, G. J., and Minkov, M. (2010). *Cultures and Organizations: Software of the Mind* (3rd edn). New York: McGraw-Hill.

Joshi, A. (2014). By Whom and When is Women's Expertise Recognized? The Interactive Effects of Gender and Education in Science and Engineering Teams. *Administrative Science Quarterly*, 59(2), 202–39. doi: 10.1177/0001839214528331

Keller, R. T. (2001). Cross-Functional Project Groups in Research and New Product Development: Diversity, Communications, Job Stress, and Outcomes. *Academy of Management Journal*, 44(3), 547–55. doi: 10.2307/3069369

Koenig, A. M., and Eagly, A. H. (2014). Evidence for the Social Role Theory of Stereotype Content: Observations of Groups' Roles Shape Stereotypes. *Journal of Personality and Social Psychology*, 107(3), 371–92. doi: 10.1037/a0037215

Lafferty, B. A., Goldsmith, R. E., and Newell, S. J. (2002). The Dual Credibility Model: The Influence of Corporate and Endorser Credibility on Attitudes and Purchase Intentions. *Journal of Marketing Theory and Practice*, 10(3), 1–12. Retrieved from <http://www.jmtp-online.org>.

Li, H., Yuan, Y. C., Bazarova, N. N., and Bell, B. (2015). Talk and Let Talk: The Effects of Language Proficiency on Speaking up and Expertise Recognition in Multinational Teams. Paper presented at the 75th Annual Meeting of the Academy of Management, Vancouver, British Columbia, Canada, Aug.

Liao, W., Bazarova, N. N., and Yuan, Y. C. (in press). Expertise Perception and Communication Accommodation in Linguistic Styles in Computer-Mediated and Face-to-Face Groups. *Communication Research*. doi: 10.1177/0093650215626974

Libby, R., Trotman, K. T., and Zimmer, I. (1987). Member Variation, Recognition of Expertise, and Group Performance. *Journal of Applied Psychology*, 72(1), 81–7. doi: 10.1037/0021-9010.72.1.81

Littlepage, G. E., and Mueller, A. L. (1997). Recognition and Utilization of Expertise in Problem-Solving Groups: Expert Characteristics and Behavior. *Group Dynamics: Theory, Research, and Practice*, 1(4), 324–8. doi: 10.1037/1089-2699.1.4.324

Littlepage, G. E., Schmidt, G. W., Whisler, E. W., and Frost, A. G. (1995). An Input-Process-Output Analysis of Influence and Performance in Problem-Solving Groups. *Journal of Personality and Social Psychology*, 69(5), 877–89. doi: 10.1037/0022-3514.69.5.877

Madlock, P. E. (2012). The Influence of Power Distance and Communication on Mexican Workers. *Journal of Business Communication*, 49(2), 169–84. doi: 10.1177/0021943612436973

Maruping, L. M., and Agarwal, R. (2004). Managing Team Interpersonal Processes through Technology: A Task-Technology Fit Perspective. *Journal of Applied Psychology*, 89(6), 975–90. doi: 10.1037/0021-9010.89.6.975

Niederhoffer, K. G., and Pennebaker, J. W. (2002). Linguistic Style Matching in Social Interaction. *Journal of Language and Social Psychology*, 21(4), 337–60. doi: 10.1177/026192702237953

Ohanian, R. (1990). Construction and Validation of a Scale to Measure Celebrity Endorsers' Perceived Expertise, Trustworthiness and Attractiveness. *Journal of Advertising*, 19(3), 39–52. Retrieved from <http://www.jstor.org/stable/4188769>.

Park, Y. S., and Kim, B. S. K. (2008). Asian and European American Cultural Values and Communication Styles among Asian American and European American College Students. *Cultural Diversity and Ethnic Minority Psychology*, 14(1), 47–56. doi: 10.1037/1099-9809.14.1.47

Reskin, B. F., McBrier, D. B., and Kmec, J. A. (1999). The Determinants and Consequences of Workplace Sex and Race Composition. *Annual Review of Sociology*, 25(1), 335–61. doi: 10.1146/annurev.soc.25.1.335

Richmond, V. P., and McCroskey, J. (1989). *Communication: Apprehension, Avoidance, and Effectiveness* (2nd edn). Scottsdale, AZ: Gorsuch Scarisbrick.

Ridgeway, C. L. (1991). The Social Construction of Status Value: Gender and Other Nominal Characteristics. *Social Forces*, 70(2), 367–86. doi: 10.1093/sf/70.2.367

Ridgeway, C. L., Berger, J., and Smith, L. (1985). Nonverbal Cues and Status: An Expectation States Approach. *American Journal of Sociology*, 90(5), 955–78. doi: 10.1086/228172

Shachaf, P. (2008). Cultural Diversity and Information and Communication Technology Impacts on Global Virtual Teams: An Exploratory Study. *Information and Management*, 45(2), 131–42. doi: 10.1016/j.im.2007.12.003

Shepperd, J. A. (1993). Productivity Loss in Performance Groups: A Motivation Analysis. *Psychological Bulletin*, 113(1), 67–81. doi: 10.1037/0033-2909.113.1.67

Soliz, J., and Giles, H. (2013). Relational and Identity Processes in Communication: A Contextual and Meta-Analytical Review of Communication Accommodation Theory. In E. L. Cohen (ed.), *Communication Yearbook* (vol. 38, pp. 1–62). New York: Routledge.

Swidler, A. (1986). Culture in Action: Symbols and Strategies. *American Sociological Review*, 51(2), 273–86. doi: 10.2307/2095521

Thomas-Hunt, M. C., and Phillips, K. W. (2004). When What you Know is Not Enough: Expertise and Gender Dynamics in Task Groups. *Personality and Social Psychology Bulletin*, 30(12), 1585–98. doi: 10.1177/0146167204271186

Tiedens, L. Z., Unzueta, M. M., and Young, M. J. (2007). An Unconscious Desire for Hierarchy? The Motivated Perception of Dominance Complementarity in Task Partners. *Journal of Personality and Social Psychology*, 93(3), 402–14. doi: 10.1037/0022-3514.93.3.402

Toma, C. L., and D'Angelo, J. D. (2014). Tell-Tale Words: Linguistic Cues Used to Infer the Expertise of Online Medical Advice. *Journal of Language and Social Psychology*, 34(1), 25–45. doi: 10.1177/0261927X14554484

Treem, J. W. (2012). Communicating Expertise: Knowledge Performances in Professional-Service Firms. *Communication Monographs*, 79(1), 23–47. doi: 10.1080/03637751.2011.646487

Treem, J. W. (2013). Technology Use as a Status Cue: The Influences of Mundane and Novel Technologies on Knowledge Assessments in Organizations. *Journal of Communication*, 63(6), 1032–53. doi: 10.1111/jcom.12061

Triandis, H. C., Bontempo, R., Villareal, M. J., Asai, M., and Lucca, N. (1988). Individualism and Collectivism: Cross-Cultural Perspectives on Self-Ingroup Relationships. *Journal of Personality and Social Psychology*, 54(2), 323–38. doi: 10.1037/0022-3514.54.2.323

Wagner, D. G., and Berger, J. (2002). Expectation States Theory: An Evolving Research Program. In J. Berger and M. J. Zelditch (eds), *New Directions in Contemporary Sociological Theory* (pp. 41–76). Lanham, MD: Rowman & Littlefield.

Woolley, A. W., Chabris, C. F., Pentland, A., Hashmi, N., and Malone, T. W. (2010). Evidence for a Collective Intelligence Factor in the Performance of Human Groups. *Science*, 330(6004), 686–8. doi: 10.1126/science.1193147

Yuan, Y. C., Bazarova, N. N., Fulk, J., and Zhang, Z.-X. (2013). Recognition of Expertise and Perceived Influence in Intercultural Collaboration: A Study of Mixed American and Chinese Groups. *Journal of Communication*, 63(3), 476–97. doi: 10.1111/jcom.12026

Yuan, Y. C., Liao, W., and Bazarova, N. N. (2016). Expertise Judgments per Communication Styles: A China–US Comparative Study. Paper presented at the 66th International Communication Association Annual Conference, Fukuoka, Japan, Jun.

6 Expertise Finding

DAVID T. MERRITT, MARK S. ACKERMAN,
AND PEI-YAO HUNG

The vision of expertise finding through technical systems is alluring. Organizationally, being able to easily find the requisite expertise whenever required would create a far more efficient organization. Finding the right person to answer a question, whether because of the required arcane knowledge or the complexity of the inquiry, would prevent those asking from being stuck and those asked from being unnecessarily bothered. Knowledge processes could be sped up and improved. Organizational members would not only be able to do their jobs more effectively by getting the help they need, they would also learn from one another, creating meaningful communities of practice (CoP) (Lave and Wenger, 1991; Wenger, 1999) and learning organizations (Cohen and Sproull, 1996; Senge, 2006). Using the same mechanisms, managers would be able to more carefully monitor how well expertise was disseminated and used and to more effectively determine where an organization needed to grow its expertise in the topics required for further growth (Fulk, this volume).

Expertise finder systems (EFs) help people locate required expertise in organizations and online communities. This is a meaningful and valued new socio-technical functionality that is attractive to organizations hoping to better utilize the expertise of workers. EF systems have evolved substantially over the last twenty years, as organizations and designers have developed a better understanding of the problems associated with the use of these technologies. What one can see is the slow but steady evolution of expertise finding in terms of both its technical and social mechanisms, as one might expect from the changes observed over time with other successful technologies (Petroski, 1994). Nonetheless, only part of the vision of expertise finding has been realized, and an understanding of the inherent limitations and constraints is important in developing a better understanding of the interaction between technology use and the utilization of expertise in organizations.

This evolution began in the 1990s, when the view that substantial efficiencies could be gained by properly using organizational knowledge was heavily promoted. Stewart (1991, 44) spoke for many others when he wrote, "Such collective knowledge is hard to identify and harder still to deploy effectively. But once you find it and exploit it, you win."

However, after early failures in knowledge management (e.g. Cohen and Prusak, 2001; Davenport and Prusak, 1998) where people tried to externalize organizational members' knowledge into databases and other repositories, interest turned to expertise sharing—tying *people* together in better ways to garner the desired efficiencies (Stewart, 1991).

A great deal of research and commercial products quickly followed based on the idea of connecting those with expertise with others seeking that form of expertise. Knowledge management efforts quickly found that asking others what expertise they have or seek is an excellent way to transfer knowledge as needed (Cohen and Prusak, 2001; Hinds and Pfeffer, 2003; Pipek et al., 2003). Often, asking others is better than trying to use final project reports or other decontextualized information to infer expertise. Individuals can have contextualized knowledge, such as understanding important features about the people involved in a project, their location in the organization, the quality of the work and products produced, and so on (Fitzpatrick, 2003). People also have very situated knowledge, such as knowing what kinds of resources are available internally or the kinds of solutions that might work best within the organization. In asking others, those people can abstract and decontextualize that situated and contextualized knowledge as needed so it will be useful to the asker. Moreover, asking people not only provides for interactive dialogue and diagnosis, it also leads to social interaction which can facilitate and encourage expertise sharing more broadly.

Over the last twenty years, significant strides have been made in expertise finding. We can now find expertise, at least some kinds, at organizational scales beyond work groups. While people in a small social setting often know who knows what at a very specific level of detail, and they know whom to approach for a friendly response, this socially nuanced knowledge does not scale easily as organizations grow in size, and people can no longer find the required knowledge from others in a local environment. EF systems are therefore particularly useful in large organizations to mechanize the processes of finding the expertise necessary in the organization's activities. EFs are also used between networks of companies (e.g. Pipek et al., 2003 and Reichling et al., 2007) and in internet-scale social computing and social network systems (e.g. Horowitz and Kamvar, 2010).

However, several critical factors limit the capabilities of EFs. First, expertise finding is a socio-technical problem with a symbiosis among organizational requirements, technical possibilities, and available data. These three aspects must co-evolve together for the EF system to operate optimally. There has been a successive introduction over the last twenty years of better technical mechanisms, such as matching algorithms and heuristics, as well as new types of data. In turn, as new data have become available, new algorithms and heuristics have been developed. Yet these algorithms and heuristics are always limited, as will be discussed in this chapter, and will always be pushing for new types of data. EFs also have evolved to include new forms of technical architectures, making the introduction of new technical mechanisms and new kinds of applications possible.

Concomitantly, as the technology improved, the organizational require-ments and possibilities, as well as the processes surrounding expertise finding, also grew, and these steps in understanding have led to further technical and social innovation. As the nature of the problem of expertise finding has become more salient for contemporary organizations and the gap between organizational visions and technical capabilities more understood over time, there has been a growing appreciation that expertise finding is hard, much harder than was naively assumed at first.

Indeed, socio-technical systems often have trade-offs or even gaps between social requirements and technical capabilities (Ackerman, 2000). In the case of EFs, not only are the social issues not yet completely understood, but also the translation from organizational and social practices and requirements to technical mechanisms is not straightforward and often inherently constrained by the technology itself.

This chapter examines the socio-technical characteristics of EFs and their capabilities to interrogate the complex interplay of the social and the technical in considering the location, recognition, and utilization of organiza-tional expertise. We start with the most important social requirements seen in EF in practice, and note that they actually result in socio-technical trade-offs. We follow with a description of how the basic technical capabilities have co-evolved with the uses of data. The explication of how the social, technical and data are intertwined will demonstrate the current state-of-the-art capabilities as well as the inherent trade-offs and constraints in EFs.

Social Requirements and Socio-Technical Trade-Offs in Expertise Finding

The requirements for EFs are bound into their socio-technical nature. The obvious beginning place in designing an EF is that it finds expertise. To do this, the aim is to target specific people with expertise in specific topics. The aim is to have a question or information request answered or to find the right person without bothering others. Zhang and Ackerman (2005) detail the social costs of targeting larger groups of people with questions: they include flooding organizational members with questions or other requests for information, creating distractions, and interrupting people's work. This query overload becomes a disincentive to pay attention to requests. Therefore, the ideal is to target specific individuals if possible instead of broadcasting requests. The best case is that one would find exactly the right person in a large organization to satisfy an information need, and do so on the first try. Even the ability to definitely find a small set of potential candidates with suitable expertise in a specific and narrowly defined topic would be better than broadcasting.

However, the technical mechanisms rely on a set of representations of human capabilities and activities; these representations necessarily translate human capabilities and activities in a way that computational systems can handle. At their most basic, the technical mechanisms for assessing expertise and topic are extremely limited, as are the technical mechanisms for determining the user's information need. Text as a surrogate for information need and expertise topic is necessarily limited. The terms from a document are an inherently incomplete representation of the knowledge in that document, and a set of terms, or dimensionally reduced set of terms, is an incomplete representation of the knowledge in a document collection. This creates problems in matching queries (which are also an inherently incomplete representation of a user's information need) with the document set (which is a representation of organizational knowledge).

The representation of expertise is even more of a problem than is the topic because the system must use an assessment of the relative strength of knowledge or understanding for an individual. Not only are the data for expertise noisy and incomplete, the measurements of expertise are limited. What people know, and what people want to know, is often very nuanced and fine-grained, and a search for information or an answer may be ambiguous or ill-formed when it starts. Systems make expertise judgments quite differently than humans (e.g. Liao, MacDonald, and Yuan, this volume). Furthermore, expertise must be distinguished from being merely interested in a topic. This difficulty in assessing expertise leads to a necessarily limited and incomplete representation of someone's expertise; this is a major obstacle in the work of recognizing expertise.

Furthermore, the determination of expertise is constrained by the types of topics the EF can handle. As a single topic becomes more broadly defined, the ability to assess who has knowledge of that topic becomes easier, although certainly not perfect. For example, it is substantially easier to determine from the data currently available who has knowledge of a technical matter in general (say, the Java programming language) than a single issue (say, a specific application programming interface (API) function call or even multimedia support). The broader the definition of a topic, the more data can be brought to bear on the assessment, and the more reliable that assessment will be. On the other hand, a broad topic is less optimal because potentially many more people will be contacted and bothered by an inappropriate question.

Thus, current systems do not attempt to narrowly define either topic or relative expertise. This does not fulfill the initial set of social requirements, and creates the requirement that the users either help narrow the candidate set or bother others. For example, in current EFs, users can view a candidate set, and they can judge for themselves the suitability of any given candidate for the specific information need they have, the availability of that potential information source, and even the likelihood of trust and helpfulness. Often, using an EF, the individual must then select which of the identified candidates to approach in a selection step. However, people have different communication styles and comfort levels in approaching others in organizational settings (Yoon, Gupta, and Hollingshead, this volume). Past information research, dating back to at least Allen (1977), has shown that information seekers carefully weigh the psychological and social costs of asking others for information in organizations. One must face the possibility of loss of face in not knowing something, being chastised for asking the wrong person, or owing someone reciprocally for help. This can be harrowing for some people, and the social costs can make expertise finding less optimal than one might prefer. The social costs of asking an inappropriate person and broadcasting a query are organizational and social issues that have not yet been resolved. While separating the identification and selection stage can make EF design easier, it can cause a disruption to users' social processes of expertise finding; newer EFs attempt to ease the separation.

In addition to finding people through technical means, it is important to note that an organization or other collectivity must find suitable motivations for people to answer queries. Orlikowski (1992) discovered the importance of finding suitable reward systems to facilitate technology use, and this dynamic is a challenge in a number of organizational contexts (Davenport and Prusak, 1998). Only some EFs have explored incentives, primarily those at internet-scale rather than within organizations.

In summary, expertise finding is a standard socio-technical problem (Ackerman, 2000). Human social activity is nuanced and heavily situated and contextualized; systems lack this capacity (Ackerman, 2000). This creates what Ackerman (2000) calls the social-technical gap, and this gap between technically working and organizationally (or socially) workable creates inherent limitations, as well as new possibilities, in the use of systems. Although EFs have evolved substantially over the past two decades it is important to recognize that they cannot currently meet the social requirements of expertise finding perfectly. The chapter next turns to some reasonable approximations based on our limited representational capabilities.

Technical Capabilities in Expertise Finding

To explicate how and why EFs, even while inherently constrained, open great new possibilities for organizations, we walk through how EFs have been forced to evolve. While this is an overview of the history of the technical capabilities, the reader should focus on how the technical capabilities co-evolved with the social requirements of EFs.

The history of EFs shows three basic technical problems being worked out, all of which gradually became clearer in their requirements. First, as mentioned, for an EF to narrowly target people with the requisite expertise so as not to distract, annoy, or flood others in the organization (Zhang and Ackerman, 2005), the EF must have a detailed representation, or profile, of users. The more detailed the profile is, the better. Profiles suffer from the so-called "sparse data" problem of recommender systems (Jannach et al., 2010; Konstan and Riedl, 2012). That is, compared to the kinds of detailed expertise one might want, EFs lack the highly detailed data that would be required. The history of EFs show representations getting better over time and using better data in more advanced ways to identify expertise.

Second, profiles have to come from somewhere. As with recommender systems' cold start problem with new users, a user's profile must start with something. People commonly will not provide data for themselves generally, and in any case, self-reports are notoriously unreliable (Bernard, 2012). Therefore, the history of EFs shows considerable effort placed in creating profiles automatically, using existing data. Using automatically generated profiles also allows for better maintenance of those profiles over time.

Finally, unlike with general recommendation systems where a desired object should be in inventory, EFs must deal with whether the identified person is actually available and suitable. This selection step was separated from the identification problems as part of the EF history (McDonald and Ackerman, 1998). Selection includes further refinement of a candidate pool of individuals based on a more detailed understanding of the people or their context. EFs have also tackled the issue of motivating the selected individual to answer queries.

Ackerman et al. (2013) surveys at length EFs and expertise sharing systems. Here we describe seven representative systems that display the range of functionality and data used in EFs in roughly chronological order.

WHO KNOWS—THE START

The Who Knows system (Streeter and Lochbaum, 1988) was one of earliest EFs. The goal of Who Knows was to connect a user's request for technical information with the relevant suborganization in a very large company (8,000 people in the described implementation). Who Knows aimed at contributing to our understanding of how to facilitate information retrieval. Earlier information retrieval systems used matching based on term vectors (i.e. the words contained in a document), but Who Knows used a new technique, singular value decomposition (now called latent semantic analysis, LSA), that mapped terms so as to reduce the dimensionality of the query and document collection. LSA not only obtained better results for documents, it also provided suitable profiles for people. People are not well represented by bags of words, even as much as documents. Instead, Who Knows allowed large vocabularies of words to be mapped to a much smaller number of terms. This provided matching for potential people, or in this case, groups of people, to contact.

To do this, Who Knows used specially selected data, which were organization-specific collections of project documents, such as technical memoranda and project descriptions. In Streeter and Lochbaum's evaluation, Who Knows was able to consistently rank the correct suborganization in the top eight out of 104 suborganizations.

Who Knows, while largely an information retrieval system, was the first system, to our knowledge, that also considered people as information objects that could be identified and retrieved. Individual expertise was not assessed; suborganizations were assumed to be expert on a topic if they had produced suitable documents.

YENTA—EF IN EMAIL NETWORKS

While Who Knows focused on finding people, Yenta (Foner 1997; Foner and Crabtree, 1997) focused on introducing people with *similar interests*. Finding similarity of interests creates a partial EF, because a similarity of interests can imply a similarity of expertise but does not always do so.

Nonetheless, Yenta had some major innovations for EFs. Yenta built profiles for people based on personal data that Yenta kept private (the profiles were also private), and the system provided a way to refer people to one another based on these profiles. Thereby, Yenta could tie together people who were not publicly known, such as users who had no publicly accessible data like email exchanges or public postings in forums or newsgroups. To do this, Yenta used a decentralized, peer-to-peer architecture that was very innovative for the time to connect all Yenta users. This carefully protected users' privacy. Foner (1997) did not describe the implementation in detail, but without releasing data, a Yenta agent (user-facing client) could accept referrals from and send referrals to other Yenta agents based on the users' profiles.

Yenta matched people with similar interests (with admittedly unknown expertise) *without* waiting for a human request to do so. A user's Yenta agent searched for interests represented by other agents, and attempted to form clusters of users with similar interests. Yenta had a user join or create a cluster when the similarity measure exceeded a threshold; the specificity of data and topics were not described. A simulation demonstrated Yenta's efficacy in creating convergent clusters on topics.

Yenta added a decentralized, distributed architecture to EF functionality. Its use of data was still that of an information retrieval system (i.e. based on documents, email, and posts), but its architecture allowed privacy protection as well as the automatic clustering of similar users.

EXPERTISE RECOMMENDER—AN ARCHITECTURE FOR THE EF SOCIAL PROCESS

Both Who Knows and Yenta used standardized types of data. McDonald and Ackerman's (2000) Expertise Recommender (ER) also focused on locating expertise within an organization, but it offered a flexible software architecture that could support a range of expertise finding and recommendation models using different types of data. ER not only could automatically generate profiles from documents and communications, it also added the use of organization- or context-specific data and heuristics for matching. In McDonald (2001), which studied ER use in a software company, ER used a heuristic based on customer support activity data to find people who could help with technical support. It also used a second heuristic based on software change data to weigh who would be the best developers to ask about the software's functionality.

ER added several innovations to EFs. First, ER assumed that organizations and suborganizations differed, and so it allowed an organization to add multiple heuristics in addition to the standard methods for building user profiles and making recommendations. The underlying conceptual model of differing organizational expertise structures, data, and incentives distinguished it from earlier work, arguing for a more nuanced view of expertise finding over that of previous systems, such as Who Knows and Yenta. Second, the work (including the field study reported in McDonald and Ackerman, 1998) separated three common social behaviors in expertise finding activities: expertise identification, expertise selection, and expertise escalation. While these were merely analytically separable (often occurring together in real behavior in the field), the three behaviors offered useful abstractions for constructing EF systems, and ER extended previous work to consider additional factors, such as suitability and availability. ER, in addition to multiple heuristics for expertise identification, had separate methods for expertise selection. It also allowed users to interactively examine potential candidates, using a number of criteria including their position in the organizational structure (McDonald, 2001).

EXPERTISEFINDING FRAMEWORK—BRIDGING ORGANIZATIONS AND BUILDING SOCIAL CAPITAL

The ExpertFinding Framework (Becks et al., 2004), and its successor TABUMA (Reichling et al., 2005), in addition to providing an extensible architecture and strict privacy controls, approached EF by considering the role that social capital plays. This greatly expanded the understanding of EFs as learning and exploratory mechanisms in organizations. That is, in addition to finding people, the ExpertFinding Framework expanded expert finding to let users find suitable candidates in an explicitly more exploratory manner. The ExpertFinding Framework specifically targeted a type of social capital needed to link members in different communities (or interests), which they termed "bridging" social capital. The ExpertFinding Framework was used within a regional industrial network of companies. In the initial ExpertFinding Framework prototype, user profiles were built from very specific personal data from an e-learning application, and users were able to modify the matching process by adjusting the weights of the numerous matching criteria. Users could match not only user profiles (user's education and experience) but also user (learning) histories.

SMALLBLUE—HYBRID ARCHITECTURES FOR EF

SmallBlue (Lin et al., 2008; Yarosh et al., 2012) shows the current state of the art for EFs. SmallBlue, meant for large organizations, was implemented by and used daily within IBM. Its data included users' communication (emails and chat), content from the company intranet (blogs, wikis, and enterprise directories), as well as user-defined profiles. It then added social network-based data, "whom people know," to profiles with "what people know." SmallBlue's expertise identification algorithm consisted of the standard information retrieval term vector matching. However, it also considered social distance, defined as the social proximity between two people in a social network.

As well as determining a candidate set as earlier systems did, SmallBlue also contributed to exploration in the selection phase of EF. It placed the ranked candidates in context by providing organizational information about each one. Data included the candidate's interests and activities compiled from the company's numerous internal sources (e.g., social networking software, company directory, geographic location, shared documents) and LinkedIn if candidates had an account. Yarosh et al. (2012) showed this additional information reduced the "strikeouts" that occurred when a contacted candidate was not sufficiently knowledgeable to meet the seeker's needs or when the candidate was not available to answer. The map of social connections between seeker and answerers was often cited as the most helpful information in the SmallBlue system.

SmallBlue made several important contributions to expert finding. As mentioned, it more deeply explored expertise selection as a focus area within EFs. It also showed that social network position ("who knows whom") was important for EF. Finally, SmallBlue's framework, including its hybrid heuristics and algorithms, was proven to be effective for daily use within a very large organization (approximately 150,000 people).

EF IN Q&A COMMUNITIES

The previous EFs were organizational; however, by the early 2000s, online communities were becoming increasingly important. Zhang et al. (2007) examined a way to measure expertise by focusing on the social network in online question-and-answer communities to rank the expertise of users. By assuming question answerers are likely to have more expertise than question askers, the authors used a simple z-score measure, the deviation from the behavior of a "random" user who would post an equal number of questions and answers. They assessed their metric using data from a question-and-answer (Q&A) community, Java Forum (with over 330,000 messages). Comparing z-score against human raters and the Hyperlink-Induced Topic Search (HITS) and PageRank algorithms, they showed the z-score doing as well as human raters and slightly outperforming HITS and PageRank. This work was followed by QuME (Zhang et al., 2007), which used the z-score to route questions within a Q&A community, validating the potential of EF for Q&A communities.

Other work in this area includes Kao et al. (2010), which combined a user's knowledge, reputation, and authority into an expertise metric. Their metric is the weighted sum of a user's knowledge score, derived from knowledge profiles and reputation, as well as an authority score from HITS or PageRank. One knowledge profile is created for each topic of interest, and a user's reputation is the ratio of best answers (voted on by question asker) to answers provided by the user. The metric was tested on a small dataset from Yahoo! Answers in Taiwan.

Munger and Zhao (2014) extended this work by introducing an unsupervised learning method for automatically identifying experts in Q&A communities, based on a forum post's helpfulness and sentiment. A post's sentiment is measured by performing a sentiment analysis on the post content, where higher occurrences of positive sentiment keywords indicate a favorable sentiment. Combining this with a post's rating and length, as well as the answerer's responsiveness, provided additional metrics for an EF.

SOCIAL SEARCH

Finally, as the societal use of social network systems (SNS), such as Facebook or Twitter, became standard, individuals turned to them to answer questions and seek expertise. Within large organizations, people used proprietary versions of EFs, such as Yammer or SmallBlue, to find expertise. However, social search, or asking questions and getting answers, occurs frequently on all SNS systems.

There has been increasing interest in adding more formal Q&A to SNS so that they may operate as more robust EF systems. Bozzon et al. (2013) reported a prototype EF system, which was the first, to our knowledge, designed exclusively for public SNS. Their approach used Facebook, Twitter, and LinkedIn data, and they found that the inclusion of *indirectly* related resources (posts not made by the candidate expert) made the system significantly more accurate. However, even though informal social search is used widely by individuals, no formal system using SNS only (such as Facebook Questions) has been successful to date.

In addition to attempts to add in social search to SNS, more specialized EFs have been constructed. While SmallBlue added social network data to candidates' descriptions, Aardvark (Horowitz and Kamvar, 2010) further refined this by improving routing queries to a relevant and available set of candidates using social network data. Aardvark aimed at solving issues of motivation in answering by routing questions to people "nearby" in the social network. Similarly, it aimed to provide high-reliability information through the social intimacy and trust of people "nearby."

Aardvark incorporated social network content as primary data in addition to its use of expertise profiles. As did previous EFs, Aardvark indexed people based on the topics for which they had some expertise. Topic expertise was constructed from users' self-reports, friends' reports, structured profile pages (e.g. Facebook profiles), and unstructured text content (e.g. Facebook news feed, Twitter messages, Aardvark messages). As far as we know, this was the first time a user's feedback was used in EFs.

In addition to expertise measures, Aardvark also calculated how connected a user was to other Aardvark users. Aardvark's measures of social connectedness were quite sophisticated. Social connectedness was based on a variety of social measures: social network distance between users, commonality of social connections, and similarities between individuals, such as demographics, profiles, vocabulary, chattiness (frequency of messaging), verbosity (length of messages), politeness, and speed (how fast in responding to questions).

By having these two profiles (expertise and social network position), Aardvark could calculate at query time the probability that a user would successfully answer a question based on their expertise as well as the social connectedness between individuals. Aardvark grew from about 2,000 users in the first month to over 90,000 users after six months of public use. This impressive rate of adoption verified the design goal of helping humans reach out in their immediate social vicinity for "hypercustomized" answers to unique information needs.

In summary, there has been an expanding understanding of the technical mechanisms required to support the organizational and social requirements in expertise finding. EFs' history shows an increasing scope of available data and the technical capabilities to handle those data in order to find others, and help the user select a suitable person. Not only have the technical capabilities increased over time, the EFs' architectures have grown to handle an increasing number of rating schemes, matching algorithms and heuristics, and selection criteria.

We should note that EFs are not the only technical solution for organizations that wish to support finding specific people. Instead, another way to find expertise and share knowledge is to have online places where people with expertise might "hang out" and others with information needs could find them (Ackerman and Halverson, 2004). Within organizations, CoP, small online groups where people could obtain information or discuss things of interest (Wenger, 1999), became important. One such CoP, along with the organizational challenges, was described in Haas et al. (2003). EADS Airbus established a CoP to allow engineers and others to talk with one another about specific topics, such as avionics, and to create and store documents such as Lessons Learned. A CoP for Siemens is described in Davenport and Probst (2002). Additionally, as already noted, in the early 2000s, online communities became increasingly important for individuals in organizations as well as societally. They served a similar function as CoPs did, but for wider interests.

Data Required to Assess Expertise

As this history of EFs shows, EFs' technical capabilities and their ability to resolve organizational and social requirements are completely dependent on the available data. The difficulties in creating suitable profiles, especially with the additional problem of limited or reduced data (such as the email logs or hand-coded expertise maps used in the first EFs), led to the use of more and more kinds of data. The addition of new kinds of data led to better retrieval of suitable candidates. (We do not separate the use of new kinds of data from using multiple kinds of data here. In Information Retrieval studies, however, it has been shown that multiple methods lead to better results than the use of any single method.) Next, we survey the kinds of data available and used, including their limitations. The discussion of available data must be inherently limited, as availability is ever-changing as more and more digital traces become available.

Table 6.1 shows the kinds of data used in the exemplar systems discussed. We categorize data sources into classes based on whether they directly or indirectly capture "artifactual" or "interactional" indicators of expertise. Data used directly do not have to be converted to or reconstructed from other data before it is used in an expertise measurement.

Direct artifactual indicators are explicit statements of expertise, and they are commonly found in self-disclosures, like someone declaring "I'm an expert in Java programming," or a credential on someone's résumé, such as a Professional Engineer license. As an example, Ackerman et al. (2003) proposed the Knowledge Mapping Instrument (KMI) to estimate people's expertise where

Table 6.1 Expertise Finder Systems, Data Used, and Expertise Identification Algorithms/Metrics Used

System	Who users are	What data is used	How expertise is identified
1988 *Who Knows* (Streeter & Lochbaum)	Members of large organizations (8k in this case)	Specially selected documents per organization, like technical memoranda abstracts and project descriptions	Semantic structure analysis: - uses SVD to reduce dimensionality (tested at 30, 50, and 100 dimensions) - find best N matches using cosine similarity between the query vector and document vector
1997 *Yenta* (Foner)	Internet users; theoretically unbound	Text from emails, files, newsgroup articles	- similarity in grains, where *grain* is a document produced by a person - dot product of keyword vectors between grains - autonomous agents find each other based on referrals from other agents - hill climbing algorithm to cluster into group of like-minded agents
2000 *Expertise Recommender* (McDonald & Ackerman)	Members of medium-sized organizations (tech support in software company in this case)	- software change history - customer support database	Multiple heuristics possible; implemented two organizationally specific heuristics: - change history - tech support
2004–5 *ExpertFinding Framework* (Becks, Reichling, Wulf, 2004) (Reichling, Schubert, Wulf, 2005)	Any organization wanting to foster "social capital" (theoretically), but users of an online learning platform (e-Qualification framework) in this case	- personal profiles based on unstructured text documents and self-reported education and experience - individuals' learning histories (what learning modules have been taken)	- profile matching function (similarity in profiles) - completeness function (existence of relevant data in profiles) - history matching function (similarity in e-learning activity)
2007–12 *SmallBlue* (Ehrlich, Lin, Griffiths-Fisher, 2007) (Yarosh, Matthews, Zhou, 2012)	Members of very large organizations (150k at IBM in this case)	- email, chat, blogs, wikis, company directory, internal SNS status messages, geographic location - user profile (self-assessment & time in company) - LinkedIn connections (total connections, shared connections w/query user, degrees separated) - shared documents from 22 internal sources (# of links to each doc)	- relevance weighting between search terms and keywords in users' profiles - indexes map keywords to people

Method (Year, Authors)	Applicable to	Data used	Metric
2007 Z-Score Metric (Zhang, Ackerman, Adamic)	any Q&A system (theoretically), but dataset analysis using Java Forum	link network from question–answer relationships	Z-scores (called Z_number and Z_degree), where: Z_num = proportion of user's questions to answers Z-deg = proportion of user's indegree to outdegree
2010 ExpertScore Metric (Kao, Liu, Wang)	any Q&A system (theoretically), but dataset analysis using Yahoo! Answer in Taiwan	- user–question–answer tuples; - link network from question–answer relationships; - reputation (ratio of Best Answers to total answers provided by user)	ExpertScore = knowledgeScore + authorityScore, where: - k_score is knowledge profile and user reputation; - a_score is link analysis using HITS & PageRank
2014 Unsupervised Expert Identification (Munger & Zhao)	any Q&A system (theoretically), but empirically tested on Cisco Support Community users and managers	- post's *helpfulness* (answer ratings, speed of response, amount of content); - post's *sentiment* (sentiment analysis on post content)	user score = sum of their post scores weighted by recency (more recent is more favorable), where: post score = sum of a post's content, responsiveness, quality, and sentiment scores
2013 Selecting Experts from Social Networks (Bozzon et al.,)	anyone using social networks (theoretically), but Twitter, Facebook, & LinkedIn users in this case	content from SNS, including posts, likes, users following, comments, links to external sites, user profile	expertise score = # of resources related to the query - resources weighted differently depending on who created it (*directly* by the candidate or *indirectly* by someone else)
2010 Aardvark Social Search Engine (Horowitz & Kamvar)	anyone using social networks (theoretically), but Twitter & Facebook users in this case	- user's self-reports, friends' reporting, structured profiles, unstructured text (news feeds & messages), demographics, vocabulary, & politeness used; - frequency & length of messages and speed of responses; - link distance between users and common social connections	expertise score calculated at query-time using relevance metric, quality metric, and users' availabilities, where: - relevance addresses a user's topical expertise; - quality measures social connectedness; - availability is based on user preferences

organization members contributed questions to a company's "trivial pursuit" game, based on the knowledge required at the company. Those questions then enabled company members to estimate how others would do on the game, providing an expertise estimation of expertise under a realistic work context. Direct interactional indicators may be found in a publicized list of relational connections, such as those found in co-authored scholarly publications or networking sites like LinkedIn. Alternatively, Farrell et al. (2007) used social tagging (e.g. categorizing people based on their projects) and found it effective for characterizing people's expertise.

Indirect measures attempt to characterize the same information represented by direct observation, except this information typically must be construed from a person's activity. In the EF literature, a person's activity has generally been measured through two behaviors: what people create (artifactual) and with whom people communicate (interactional). Algorithms are used to turn documents or other artifacts (e.g. code, forum posts, or email content) into a mapping of people to keywords and topics. These artifactual indirect metrics measure what someone knows. Algorithms can also characterize a person's social network based on communications with others (e.g. email or question–answer forums); these become indirect interactional metrics when they are used to determine an entire network of relations (question-answering, communication, work projects, and so on).

Table 6.1 shows the many sources of data in the EF systems discussed. Others have been proposed and studied (such as Ackerman et al., 2003 and Farrell et al., 2007), but these are representative. Table 6.1 can be summarized as:

- Direct artifactual data have included user profiles from a company directory or from social networking sites, self-reported expertise(s), job duties (self-reported or assigned), time working at company, and current job title. It can also include periodic assessments by managers.
- Indirect artifactual data include technical memoranda abstracts, internal documentation, project descriptions (including research projects), local user files, email content, newsgroup articles, chat content, blogs, wikis, CoP, help-seeking forums or Q&A websites (content), number of positive votes in Q&A websites (including Best Answers and other ratings), message content on social networking sites, and even shared bookmarks. It can also include publicly shared documents such as papers and patents.
- Direct interactional data have included SNS followers (public or internal, as well as Facebook and LinkedIn, if permission is given).
- Indirect interactional data have included software change history (who was the last person to modify this code?), customer support history (who was the last person to work with this customer?), intra-organization social network site (status messages), geographic location, SNS or website profiles,

and number of links to publicly shared documents. Indirect interactional data from Q&A communities or CoP can also include question–answer social networks, timeliness of responses, and sentiment analysis. SNS such as LinkedIn or other systems incorporating social network data have provided such metrics as total number of connections, number of connections in common with querying user, and degrees of separation from the querying user.

It is important to note that the artifactual "what someone knows" and the interactional "whom someone knows" are analytical distinctions, since the two are often conjoint. In addition, some systems use mixed metrics for indicators of expertise. For example, Munger and Zhao (2014) applied sentiment analysis to Q&A posts to characterize whether an answer had a positive or negative sentiment (positive sentiment favorably influenced the answerer's expertise score). Sentiment analysis is arguably an effort toward adding social context to an expertise metric, but it does not so much measure expertise per se as how likely a candidate expert would be to helpfully fulfill an information need. Availability in SmallBlue (Yarosh et al., 2012) and responsiveness (Kao et al., 2010; Munger and Zhao, 2014) of candidate experts are more examples of features used to measure helpfulness. Indeed, in Kao et al. (2010), a person's "reputation" metric includes availability, responsiveness, and sentiment-based features.

Some initial EF systems used direct artifactual indicators. However, people's self-reports are unreliable. There are strong organizational, as well as personal, reasons to either hide or overpromote expertise. There are relatively few observational measures in organizations except for managers' periodic assessments, and these, too, can be unreliable and do not usually include the identification of topics of expertise.

Indirect artifactual indicators solved some problems associated with determining the expertise of individuals; indirect artifactual indicators could construct expertise profiles without intervention. Expertise profiles could be constructed from project reports or later, intranet documents. The list of potential sources became larger and larger over time, as can be seen in Table 6.1 and its summary.

Indirect measures solve two additional data problems. The first is the standard problem with explicit data collection: users lacking sufficient motivation to enter their data (Hinds and Pfeffer, 2003). The second is related: it is the problem of maintaining data over time, which requires the continued motivation to enter one's data accurately (Ehrlich, 2003). This can lead to non-consistent entry of data, incomplete entry of data, and out-of-date data. While incomplete entry and perhaps non-consistent entry can still result in useful EF systems, out-of-date data quickly lead to disuse. If an EF cannot be used for current needs or points to the wrong people, it is less than helpful.

Indirect measures, while they solve those problems, present other challenges. While standard information retrieval relies on incomplete or ambiguous representations of information sources, EF metrics use even more incomplete or ambiguous representations. While indirect measures solve self-report errors, they introduce many other sources of error. The issue of inferring topics from keyword vectors or even more suitable representations (e.g. topic models or LDA) has been mentioned, and there are difficulties of distinguishing mere interest in a topic versus expertise in that topic and of determining relative expertise. These issues can introduce error into an EF, and systems generally attempt to ameliorate this concern by producing a candidate set which can then be manually examined (but see Aardvark for a counter-example). Indirect measures also suffer from the problem of new employees and their cold start. New employees obviously will not have built a repertoire of suitable content. This issue introduces a form of incompleteness into the EF system by reducing the potential candidate set. It is not easily corrected, although in an organization of a sufficient size, this issue is likely to have negligible effect.

More importantly, indirect measures still rely on incomplete data. Not everyone has published material in the public domain or on organizational intranets. Not everyone even produces documents, even though they may have a great deal of organizational expertise (e.g. admins). Invisible work (Star and Strauss, 1999) is, indeed, often invisible and not captured by EF systems.

In the future, one can expect the kinds of data available to grow. Sensor data and other forms of big data will provide additional capabilities for knowing what people in an organization have done in their everyday practices. Best practices can be shared, and more importantly for EFs, the people who have developed and use these best practices could be found. Similarly, new forms of human computation and crowdsourcing (Bernstein et al., 2011) could create forms of knowledge on demand. Mixed-expertise models in crowdsourcing are only now being developed, and EF metrics and systems could create new forms of human computation and knowledge production. The history of EF shows that, every five or six years, new data and computational mechanisms become available and become incorporated. One might fully expect this to continue.

Advancing the Study of Expertise

CONTRIBUTION

EFs provide new capabilities to organizations and other collectivities by creating systems to identify, locate, and help utilize expertise among members. Organizations, for example, can achieve new efficiencies by more easily tying those with difficult questions to those who have specific technical expertise. Similarly, with an EF, one can find others who have experiences with specific clients. As organizations scale in size, EF systems can be particularly useful in helping sift through the mass of information communicated by workers and determine useful connections between expertise and those with expertise.

This chapter's contribution to an understanding of expertise is its socio-technical view. The chapter has argued that it is helpful to consider expertise finding, when augmented with technical EFs, as a socio-technical problem. The organizational and social requirements and possibilities for EFs have co-evolved with the technical capabilities and available data. Possibilities, limitations, and issues cannot be easily separated into social and technical components, and they change over time in a situated manner.

Most importantly, a socio-technical view of expertise shows that EFs consider expertise very differently than do humans. While many contextual and perceptual factors play into assessing expertise in social interaction (Yoon, Gupta, and Hollingshead, this volume; Liao, MacDonald, and Yuan, this volume; Fulk, this volume), EFs are substantially more limited. We must recognize that, even with advances in EFs, assessing expertise technically within an organizational setting is still difficult and limited. As is often the case, one is limited to assessing the most measurable characteristics of true expertise (Treem, 2012). We have discussed how EFs' ability to measure expertise in specific topics is constrained, and therefore the profiles, or representations, of users are also limited. As a result, an EF can use only a representation of "expertise" that is necessarily an approximation.

Nonetheless, even with their limitations, EF systems can provide organizations and other collectivities with a new ability to determine a candidate pool of people likely to have the requisite expertise to handle information needs *at scale*. In addition, EFs also allow expertise discovery and exploration, as well as the routing of questions and information queries, at scale. When people in organizations cannot find suitable expertise on their own, EFs can help. Even with limitations, EFs still substantially improve information flows and knowledge sharing within organizations. As a practical contribution, this chapter has argued that, despite EFs' limitations and constraints, EFs also can substantially improve the organization or other sociality.

FUTURE RESEARCH

There are many technical problems to be tackled. First, the routing of questions or information queries within social networking systems is still in its infancy. We also have not yet seen how to better route questions and information queries within large-scale online communities, nor have we seen how to have these communities reach out to non-members who have important expertise. Indeed, there recently has been work in using patients' expertise in the lived experience of medical conditions (Civan-Hartzler et al., 2010; Huh and Ackerman, 2012).

We believe, however, that most of the future technical research will be driven by new kinds of measurement and data. Better means of measuring expertise would necessarily lead to new technical forms of assessment and matching. We are currently exploring discount metrics for expertise measurement (Hung and Ackerman, 2015)—easy, cheap ways to determine a user's relative expertise by using readily available data and usage logs. With the rise of mobile device-based messaging (e.g. SMS texting) that influence everyday social and professional activities, new types of expertise metrics from artifactual data and social interactions are sure to be discovered. The chapter has also alluded to new types of data that are rapidly becoming available. Digital traces, or activity traces at the sensor level, will allow for different types of discovery—perhaps where people are more efficient or effective at their practices. These data types may also allow the detailed analysis of expertise flows within organizations. We strongly believe that new socio-technical possibilities will incorporate EFs. New forms of human computation and crowdsourcing (Bernstein et al., 2011) could create forms of knowledge on demand. Mixed-expertise models in crowdsourcing are only now being developed (Merritt et al., 2015), and incorporating elements of EFs could create new forms of human computation and knowledge production.

Finally, the major premise of this chapter has been that expertise finding is a socio-technical problem. The technology is nothing without the social and organizational requirements. There is a considerable interest currently in several research areas, including Computer-Supported Cooperative Work and Social Computing, in understanding the dynamics of socio-technical change. We know surprisingly little about the socio-technical change caused by EFs. How is organizational life affected by EFs? Do the patterns of communication change for the better or the worse? Future research could also examine the collective allocation of expertise in organizations, by allowing management to track what expertise is required for tactical and strategic goals (heeding the call of Fulk, this volume).

▓ REFERENCES

Ackerman, M. S. (2000). The Intellectual Challenge of CSCW: The Gap between Social Requirements and Technical Feasibility. *Human–Computer Interaction*, 15(2–3), 179–203. doi: 10.1207/S15327051HCI1523_5

Ackerman, M. S., and Halverson, C. (2004). Sharing Expertise: The Next Step for Knowledge Management. In M. Huysman and V. Wulf (eds), *Social Capital and Information Technology* (pp. 273–300). Cambridge, MA: MIT Press.

Ackerman, M. S., Boster, J. S., Lutters, W. G., and McDonald, D. (2003). Who's There? The Knowledge-Mapping Approximation Project. In M. Ackerman, V. Pipek, and V. Wulf (eds), *Beyond Knowledge Management: Sharing Expertise* (pp. 159–78). Cambridge, MA: MIT Press.

Ackerman, M. S., Dachtera, J., Pipek, V., and Wulf, V. (2013). Sharing Knowledge and Expertise: The CSCW View of Knowledge Management. *Computer Supported Cooperative Work (CSCW)*, 22, 531–73. doi: 10.1007/s10606-013-9192-8

Allen, T. (1977). *Managing the Flow of Technology*. Cambridge, MA: MIT Press.

Becks, A., Reichling, T., and Wulf, V. (2004). Expert Finding: Approaches to Foster Social Capital. In M. Huysman and V. Wulf (eds), *Social Capital and Information Technology* (pp. 333–54). Cambridge, MA: MIT Press.

Bernard, H. R. (2012). *Social Research Methods: Qualitative and Quantitative Approaches* (2nd edn). Thousand Oaks, CA: Sage.

Bernstein, M., Chi, E. H., Chilton, L., Hartmann, B., Kittur, A., and Miller, R. C. (2011). Crowdsourcing and Human Computation: Systems, Studies and Platforms. In *Proceedings of the 2011 Annual Conference: Extended Abstracts on Human Factors in Computing Systems* (pp. 53–6). New York: ACM. doi: 10.1145/1979742.1979593

Bozzon, A, Brambilla, M., Ceri, S., Silvestri, M., and Vesci, G. (2013). Choosing the Right Crowd: Expert Finding in Social Networks. In *Proceedings of the 16th International Conference on Extending Database Technology (EDBT '13)* (pp. 637–48). New York: ACM.

Civan-Hartzler, A., McDonald, D. W., Powell, C., Skeels, M. M., Mukai, M., and Pratt, W. (2010). Bringing the Field into Focus: User-Centered Design of a Patient Expertise Locator. In *Proceedings of the SIGCHI Conference on Human Factors in Computing Systems* (pp. 1675–84). New York: ACM. doi: 0.1145/1753326.1753577

Cohen, D., and Prusak, L. (2001). *In Good Company: How Social Capital Makes Organizations Work*. Boston: Harvard Business School Press.

Cohen, M. D., and Sproull, L. S. (1996). *Organizational Learning*. Thousand Oaks, CA: Sage.

Davenport, T. H., and Probst, G. J. (2002). *Knowledge Management Case Book: Siemens Best Practices*. Berlin: John Wiley & Sons, Inc.

Davenport, T. H., and Prusak, L. (1998). *Working Knowledge: How Organizations Manage What they Know*. Boston: Harvard Business School Press.

Ehrlich, K. (2003). Locating Expertise: Design Issues for an Expertise Locator System. In M. Ackerman, V. Pipek, and V. Wulf (eds), *Beyond Knowledge Management: Sharing Expertise* (pp. 137–58). Cambridge, MA: MIT Press.

Farrell, S., Lau, T., Nusser, S., Wilcox, E., and Muller, M. (2007). Socially Augmenting Employee Profiles with People-Tagging. In *Proceedings of the 20th Annual ACM Symposium on User Interface Software and Technology* (pp. 91–100). New York: ACM. doi: 10.1145/1294211.1294228

Fitzpatrick, G. (2003). Emergent Expertise Sharing in a New Community. In M. Ackerman, V. Pipek, and V. Wulf (eds), *Beyond Knowledge Management: Sharing Expertise* (pp. 81–110), Cambridge MA: MIT Press.

Foner, L. N. (1997). Yenta: A Multi-Agent, Referral-Based Matchmaking System. In *Proceedings of the First International Conference on Autonomous Agents (AGENTS '97)* (pp. 301–7). New York: ACM. doi: 10.1145/267658.267732

Foner, L., and Crabtree, I. B. (1997). Multi-Agent Matchmaking. In H. Nwana and N. Azarmi (eds), *Software Agents and Soft Computing towards Enhancing Machine Intelligence* (pp. 100–15). Berlin and Heidelberg: Springer.

Haas, R., Aulbur, W., and Thakar, S. (2003). Enabling Communities of Practice at EADS Airbus. In M. Ackerman, V. Pipek, and V. Wulf (eds), *Beyond Knowledge Management: Sharing Expertise* (pp. 179–98). Cambridge, MA: MIT Press.

Hinds, P. J., and Pfeffer, J. (2003). Why Organizations Don't "Know What They Know": Cognitive and Motivational Factors Affecting the Transfer of Expertise. In M. Ackerman, V. Pipek, and V. Wulf (eds), *Beyond Knowledge Management: Sharing Expertise* (pp. 3–26). Cambridge, MA: MIT Press.

Horowitz, D., and Kamvar, S. D. (2010). The Anatomy of a Large-Scale Social Search Engine. In *Proceedings of the 19th International Conference on World Wide Web* (pp. 431–40). New York: ACM. doi: 10.1145/1772690.1772735

Huh, J., and Ackerman, M. (2012). Collaborative Help in Chronic Disease Management: Supporting Individualized Problems. In *Proceedings of the ACM 2012 Conference on Computer Supported Cooperative Work* (pp. 853–62). New York: ACM. doi: 10.1145/2145204.2145331

Hung, P., and Ackerman, M. (2015). Discount Expertise Metrics for Augmenting Community Interaction. Work-in-progress paper, Communities and Technologies Conference.

Jannach, D., Zanker, M., Felfernig, A., and Friedrich, G. (2010). *Recommender Systems: An Introduction*. Cambridge: Cambridge University Press.

Kao, W., Liu, D., and Wang, S. (2010). Expert Finding in Question-Answering Websites: A Novel Hybrid Approach. In *Proceedings of the 2010 ACM Symposium on Applied Computing (SAC '10)* (pp. 867–71). New York: ACM. doi: 10.1145/1774088.1774266

Konstan, J., and Riedl, J. (2012). Recommender Systems: From Algorithms to User Experience. *User Modeling and User-Adapted Interaction*, 22, 101–23. doi: 10.1007/s11257-011-9112-x

Lave, J., and Wenger, E. (1991). *Situated Learning: Legitimate Peripheral Participation*. Cambridge: Cambridge University Press.

Lin, C.-Y., Ehrlich, K., Griffiths-Fisher, V., and Desforges, C. (2008). SmallBlue: People Mining for Expertise Search. *MultiMedia, IEEE*, 15(1), 78–84. doi: 10.1109/MMUL.2008.17

McDonald, D. W. (2001). Evaluating Expertise Recommendation. In *Proceedings of the 2001 International ACM Conference on Supporting Group Work* (pp. 214–23). New York: ACM.

McDonald, D. W., and Ackerman, M. S. (1998). Just Talk to Me: A Field Study of Expertise Location. In *Proceedings of the 1998 ACM Conference on Computer Supported Cooperative Work* (pp. 315–24). New York: ACM. doi: 10.1145/289444.289506

McDonald, D. W., and Ackerman, M. S. (2000). Expertise Recommender: A Flexible Recommendation System and Architecture. In *Proceedings of the 2000 ACM Conference on Computer Supported Cooperative Work* (pp. 231–40). New York: ACM. doi: 10.1145/358916.358994

Merritt, D., Ackerman, M. S., Newman, M. W., Hung, P., Mandel, J., Ackerman, E. (2015). Using Expertise for Crowd-Sourcing. Work-in-progress paper, 3rd AAAI Conference on Human Computation and Crowdsourcing (HCOMP-2015).

Munger, T., and Zhao, J. (2014). Automatically Identifying Experts in On-Line Support Forums Using Social Interactions and Post Content. In *2014 IEEE/ACM International Conference on Advances in Social Networks Analysis and Mining (ASONAM)* (pp. 930–5). Los Alamitos, CA: IEEE. doi: 10.1109/ASONAM. 2014.6921697

Orlikowski, W. J. (1992). Learning from Notes: Organizational Issues in Groupware Implementation. In *Proceedings of the 1992 Conference on Computer Supported Cooperative Work* (pp. 362–9). New York: ACM. doi: 10.1145/143457.143549

Petroski, H. (1994). *Design Paradigms: Case Histories of Error and Judgment in Engineering.* Cambridge: Cambridge University Press.

Pipek, V., Hinrichs, J., and Wulf, V. (2003). Sharing Expertise: Challenges for Technical Support. In M. Ackerman, V. Pipek, and V. Wulf (eds), *Beyond Knowledge Management: Sharing Expertise* (pp. 111–36). Cambridge, MA: MIT Press.

Reichling, T., Schubert, K., and Wulf, V. (2005). Matching Human Actors Based on their Texts: Design and Evaluation of an Instance of the ExpertFinding Framework. In *Proceedings of the International Conference on Supporting Group Work (Group 05)* (pp. 61–70). New York: ACM. doi: 10.1145/1099203.1099213

Reichling, T., Veith, M., and Wulf, V. (2007). Expert Recommender: Designing for a Network Organization. *Computer Supported Cooperative Work (CSCW)*, 16, 431–65. doi: 10.1007/s10606-007-9055-2

Senge, P. M. (2006). *The Fifth Discipline: The Art and Practice of the Learning Organization (Revised Edition).* New York: Doubleday.

Star, S. L., and Strauss, A. (1999). Layers of Silence, Arenas of Voice: The Ecology of Visible and Invisible Work. *Computer Supported Cooperative Work (CSCW)*, 8, 9–30.

Stewart, Thomas A. (1991). BrainPower: How Intellectual Capital is Becoming America's Most Valuable Asset. *Fortune* (June 3), 44–60.

Streeter, L. A., and Lochbaum, K. E. (1988). Who Knows: A System Based on Automatic Representation of Semantic Structure. In *RIAO 88 (Recherche d'Information Assistée par Ordinateur) Conference* (pp. 380–8). Cambridge, MA: MIT.

Treem, J. W. (2012). Communicating Expertise: Knowledge Performances in Professional-Service Firms. *Communication Monographs*, 79, 23–47.

Wenger, E. (1999). *Communities of Practice: Learning, Meaning, and Identity.* Cambridge: Cambridge University Press.

Yarosh, S., Matthews, T., and Zhou, M. (2012). Asking the Right Person: Supporting Expertise Selection in the Enterprise. In *Proceedings of the SIGCHI Conference on Human Factors in Computing Systems (CHI '12)* (pp. 2247–56). New York: ACM. doi: 10.1145/2207676.2208382

Zhang, J., and Ackerman, M. S. (2005). Searching for Expertise in Social Networks: A Simulation of Potential Strategies. In *Proceedings of the 2005 International ACM SIGGROUP Conference on Supporting Group Work* (pp. 71–80). New York: ACM. doi: 10.1145/1099203.1099214

Zhang, J., Ackerman, M. S., and Adamic, L. (2007). Expertise Networks in Online Communities: Structure and Algorithms. In *Proceedings of the 16th International Conference on World Wide Web* (pp. 221–30). New York: ACM. doi: 10.1145/ 1242572.1242603

Zhang, J., Ackerman, M. S., Adamic, L., and Nam, K. K. (2007). QuME: A Mechanism to Support Expertise Finding in Online Help-Seeking Communities. In *Proceedings of the 20th Annual ACM Symposium on User Interface Software and Technology* (pp. 111–14). New York: ACM. doi: 10.1145/1294211.1294230

Judging the Competence (and Incompetence) of Co-Workers

KAY YOON, NAINA GUPTA, AND ANDREA
B. HOLLINGSHEAD

Expertise has often been described as deep knowledge related to specific domain (e.g. Canary and McPhee, 2010). For instance, a software engineer who demonstrates computer programming skills and an oncologist who specializes in breast cancer are considered to have expertise in their respective domain areas. Competence, on the other hand, has been described as a perception of abilities in another person or in one's self (Sandberg, 2000; Sternberg, 1990). The abilities may include intelligence, specific knowledge and skill sets to perform a task, problem-solving skills, creativity, interpersonal relationship-building and collaborative abilities, to name a few. Although competence is often used interchangeably with expertise (Liao, MacDonald, and Yuan, this volume) and has also been conceptualized as a precursor to expertise (Dreyfus and Dreyfus, 2005), we conceptualize competence as the larger, more comprehensive category that includes expertise.

Judgments about the competence of co-workers influence many aspects of organizational life. Employees perceived to be competent are often assigned meaningful tasks, sought out for advice and input in key decisions, and are likely to feel respected and valued by their co-workers and employers. In contrast, employees deemed to be incompetent may face social and work-related isolation, negative performance appraisals, and decreased job satisfaction and organizational commitment (Wittenbaum et al., 2010). In addition, inaccurate judgments of competence and incompetence may lead to overconfidence in employees' knowledge, skills, and abilities or the under-utilization of their abilities respectively. Therefore, whether an employee is judged to be competent or incompetent is consequential for future career opportunities, job satisfaction, and performance at the individual, group, and organizational levels.

In this chapter, we examine how competence and incompetence in the workplace are conceptualized and judged. In doing so, we address (1) what types of information are used as a cue to the judgment of competence and incompetence, (2) how judgments of competence and incompetence are related to the affective dimension (e.g. liking), and (3) how information about co-workers' competence and incompetence is gathered. When addressing each of these areas, we draw on several areas of relevant research including social judgment and impression formation in psychology, education, and human resource management, and information-seeking behavior in uncertainty management theory. Then, we present empirical data from a large survey study that sheds light on the conceptualizations of competence and incompetence and formation of its perceptions as well as the connections between competence and expertise. We conclude the chapter by discussing theoretical and practical implications of studying competence and incompetence, and ways in which this work can aid our understanding of expertise in organizations.

Information Types in Judgments of (In)Competence

Previous research on social judgment offers some insights on the cognitive processes through which competence impressions are formed (Fiske and Neuberg, 1990; Reeder and Brewer, 1979). This research focuses on how people process category-based versus individuating information about others to form a judgment. Category-based information includes stereotypes based on categories such as gender and race, whereas individuating information includes attributes unique to the individuals beyond surface characteristics such as personalities and abilities (Fiske and Neuberg, 1990). For example, an employee judging their Asian co-worker to be competent at statistical analysis can be basing their perception on category information such as the co-worker's race as well as on individuating information collected during their shared experience in working on an earlier project. The focus in this line of research has been on how these two types of information contribute to stereotyping (Operario and Fiske, 2004) and impression formation accuracy (see Fiske et al., 1999, for review) and on the factors that influence people's use of one type of information over the other in their social judgments (Fiske et al., 1987; Ruscher et al., 2000).

Previous research on competence examined judgments based on both category and individuating information cues. With regard to category-based judgments, social stereotypes associated with gender, race, and status can lead to inaccurate judgments of competence (Heilman and Welle, 2006; Hollingshead and Fraidin, 2003; Ridgeway, 1981). For instance, Asians are perceived to be more competent in stereotypically Asian domain areas (e.g. math) than stereotypically white American domain areas (e.g. English language; Yoon and Hollingshead, 2010); high-status individuals are expected to deliver a high performance while the same is not expected from low-status individuals (Berger et al., 1972).

Research has also identified individuating behaviors that signal one's competence to others. These include demonstration of intellectual abilities, goal accomplishment, communication behaviors, and social skills. Studies indicate that intellectual abilities including problem-solving skills, learning abilities, and logical reasoning skills affect competence judgments (DePaulo et al., 1987; O'Neil et al., 1992; Ramsay et al., 1997). Accomplishment of goals and display of relevant knowledge (Heilman and Welle, 2006; Sheldon et al., 2006) can also influence competence judgments. Some researchers suggest that social skills such as team work and interpersonal skills can also be viewed as signs of competence (O'Neil et al., 1992; Vonk, 1998). Communication behaviors such as talkativeness, displays of dominance and of confidence, listening skills, and argumentation have been positively linked to competence judgments (Littlepage and Mueller, 1997; Ramsay et al., 1997). Liao, MacDonald, and Yuan (this volume) provide an extensive review on the role of communication in expertise recognition from an expectation states theory perspective and argue that communication opportunities, styles, and accommodations derived from status cues are significant indicators of competence.

In contrast, researchers have paid less attention to impression formation processes for incompetence and how those impressions are communicated in the workplace. It is possible that the lack of attention stems from the assumption that the *absence* of any of the competence-signaling abilities in a person signals that he/she is incompetent. Hence, the lack of intellectual abilities, communication behaviors, social skills, and/or goal accomplishment might indicate that the target is incompetent. However, people treat positive and negative information about targets differently (Reeder and Brewer, 1979). For instance, according to Reeder and Brewer (1979), positive information about a target's ability is likely to lead to an impression of the target's competence. But, negative information about a target's ability does not always lead to an impression of the target's incompetence. In addition, certain types of skills and abilities are considered minimum workplace skills required by employees (O'Neil et al., 1992; Treem, 2013). The use of the term 'minimum' suggests that the display of such skills is not considered commendable but a lack of their display would be noticed. For example, the ability to use mundane communication technologies such as email is not considered as an indicator of high level of proficiency because everyone is expected to be adept at it, but errors made using mundane technology can be a significant cue to incompetence (Treem, 2013). Therefore, if positive information is more diagnostic than negative information and if the presence of certain skills and abilities does not lead to a judgment of competence but of 'not incompetent', then it is possible that there are potential differences between competence and incompetence judgments that warrant separate investigation.

Affect and Judgments of (In)Competence

Judgments of someone's competence and incompetence may influence socio-emotional reactions or attitudes toward the target. Do co-workers form positive socio-emotional attitudes (e.g. liking, trust, closeness) toward those they judge as competent, and similarly, do they form negative socio-emotional attitudes (e.g. disliking, mistrust, distance) toward those judged as incompetent? The two-dimensional model of social judgment is informative in addressing this question.

Social judgment research has identified two predominant dimensions in person judgment: the intellectual dimension (e.g. intelligent, competent, efficient) and the social dimension (e.g. warm, friendly, nice; Fiske et al., 2007; Judd et al., 2005; Rosenberg et al., 1968). This research argues that the domains of person perceptions, including traits, personalities, and abilities, can be reduced to these two dimensions in which people form impressions of others.

While there is much consensus on the validity of both intellectual and social dimensions in the literature (Cuddy et al., 2011; Fiske et al., 2007; Wojciszke, 1994), the relations between the two dimensions are less clear. The judgment of one dimension could be positively or negatively correlated with that of the other dimension. On one hand, some research findings suggest that the judgment of one dimension parallels with the other, known as a halo effect (Judd et al., 2005; Rosenberg et al., 1968). It means that when someone is judged to be competent (intellectual dimension), the person will likely be judged to be warm (social dimension) as well, and vice versa. For example, Rosenberg et al. (1968) used multidimensional analysis to report positive correlation between the two dimensions across sixty-four traits. Individuals who were perceived to have a high level of intellectual abilities were also perceived to have positive social abilities.

On the other hand, the judgments of the two dimensions can be negatively related so that positive or negative direction of the judgment in one dimension does not mirror the other dimension. This is known as a compensation effect (Carlsson et al., 2012; Judd et al., 2005; Kervyn et al., 2009). According to the research on the compensation effect, positive judgment in one dimension leads to negative judgment in the other dimension. For instance, many people are perceived to be competent but cold (e.g. he is smart but arrogant) or to be incompetent but warm (e.g. he is inefficient in getting the work done but friendly). Experiments on this compensation effect show that people infer strength in one dimension to imply deficiency or weakness in the other dimension (Judd et al., 2005; Kervyn et al., 2009). Particularly, this compensation effect is pronounced when it comes to the judgment of groups. For instance, successful women and model minorities (e.g. Asians) are judged to be competent but cold, whereas the elderly, disabled, and housewives are judged to be warm but incompetent (Cuddy et al., 2008; Fiske et al., 2002). It is not clear whether the relations between the judgments of (in)competent co-workers and the affective attitude toward them exhibits halo or compensation effects, or if different effects occur for the judgments of competence and incompetence.

Information Gathering for Judgments of (In)Competence

It is important to understand the types of information that people use to form judgments of their co-workers' (in)competence, but it is also essential to learn about the ways in which people infer competence and incompetence. Uncertainty reduction theory (URT) argues that in early stages of social relationships, reducing uncertainty about relational partners is one of the primary concerns to explain or predict one's own and their partner's behavior (Berger, 1979; Berger and Calabrese, 1975). Communication is the major medium through which information becomes available for social judgment and, hence, uncertainty is reduced (Berger, 1979; Kellermann, 1987).

Previous research on social information acquisition in interpersonal communication offers a useful typology for how people learn about others (Berger 1979; Berger and Kellermann, 1983, 1994). Berger (1979) argues that information-seeking strategies can be passive, active, or interactive. Passive strategies involve unobtrusive observation without direct interaction or verbal/nonverbal exchange of information between the observer and the target. Active strategies, however, require the observer to take explicit actions to gain information about the target by either asking others about the target or creating an environment in which the target's behavior is induced or observed. Interactive strategies not only involve the observer's proactive actions for information acquisition but also require direct communicative exchanges with the target such as verbal interrogation and self-disclosure (in the hopes that the target would do the same). These information-seeking strategies have been applied to a variety of contexts including close relationships (Knobloch and Solomon, 2002), health care (Brashers et al., 2002), intercultural interactions (Baldwin and Hunt, 2002; Gudykunst et al., 1985), and organizations (Comer, 1991; Gallagher and Sias, 2009;

Kramer, 2004; Kramer et al., 2013; Miller and Jablin, 1991; Morrison, 1993, 1995; Teboul, 1994).

The passive, active, and interactive strategies that Berger (1979) proposed provide us with a useful starting point to conceptualize specific processes through which information about someone's competence and incompetence is gathered. We identify two distinctive communicative dimensions from Berger's (1979) three types of strategies (passive, active, and interactive) that are relevant for inference methods for competence and incompetence: conversational involvement and source of information. *Conversational involvement* refers to the extent to which the judge interacts with the target to learn about the target's level of competence. Working with the target on projects or asking questions of the target are high on conversational involvement, whereas observation and surveillance of the target are low on conversational involvement.

The other dimension is *the source of information*: whether information about competence is inferred directly from the target's performance or indirectly through a third party. Direct sources of information would include first-hand work experience with the target and observation of the target's performance; indirect sources of information would include another co-worker's previous experience with the target and overall reputation of the target's competence.

Given the two dimensions, conversational involvement (high and low) and information source (direct or indirect), judgment formation processes can be organized into four different types: interaction, description, observation, and reputation (see Figure 7.1).

Interaction is the method of direct source and high conversational involvement whereby co-workers fully participate in activities together through verbal and nonverbal exchanges. This inference method may involve overt

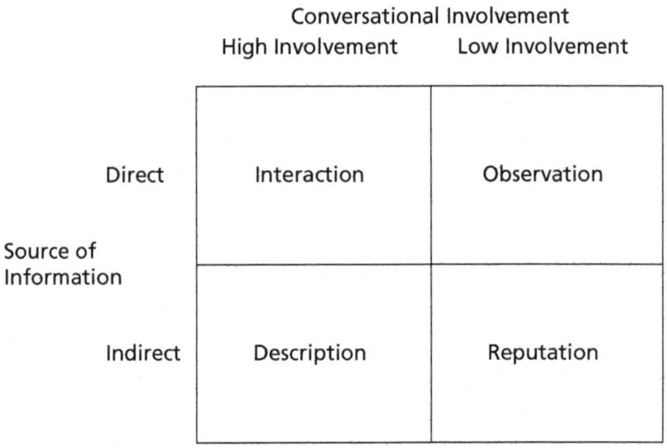

| | Conversational Involvement | |
	High Involvement	Low Involvement
Direct	Interaction	Observation
Indirect	Description	Reputation

Source of Information

Figure 7.1 Information-Seeking Methods for Judging Competence and Incompetence

questioning (Gallagher and Sias, 2009; Miller and Jablin, 1991). Interactions allow for reciprocal information exchange and verbal interrogation whereby rich evidence is potentially available for making inferences about co-workers' competence and incompetence.

Description is conceptualized as the inference method of indirect source and high conversational involvement. This method is similar to Miller and Jablin's (1991) self-disclosure in which the target voluntarily reveals his or her own knowledge, skills, or abilities. Unlike the interaction method, description does not require a direct working relationship with the target co-worker. For example, a marketing manager may describe her previous success in a product launch when talking to a new co-worker.

Observation is the method of direct source and low conversational involvement. Instead of participating in activities together, one obtains the information about the person with a perspective of a distant observer (Gallagher and Sias, 2009; Stafford et al., 1989). When a sales person watches her co-worker handle a complaint from a customer, she gathers information about the co-worker's competence through observation without engaging in any conversation or being involved in the situation.

Lastly, *reputation* is the method of indirect source and low conversational involvement. In this method, information about a co-worker's competence comes from a third party's description (Gallagher and Sias, 2009). For example, an accounting manager may gather information about a particular marketing manager's competence by listening to the marketing department staff.

Empirical Investigation of Judgments of (In)Competence

As noted earlier, little empirical work has explored the processes by which individuals working in organizations evaluate the competence or incompetence of their co-workers. To begin, we asked a sample of 533 college students (287 males and 246 females) with work experience to (1) define competence and incompetence, and then, (2) to describe an incident involving a competent and an incompetent co-worker and to report their information-gathering methods and liking toward those co-workers. We coded the definitions that participants provided of competence and incompetence, and then we used the thematic categories that emerged from the definitions to code the incidents.

For the definition coding process, we used Becker and Martin's (1995) three-stage analysis. First, we unitized the definitions by identifying different attributes within a definition. For example, one participant defined competence by stating that "[competent individuals] are hard-working and if they are given a job to do, it can be expected that it will be done on time and will be of quality work." This response was unitized into three separate attributes: (a) hard-working, (b) punctual, and (c) quality work. Second, we developed the categories by identifying discrete themes. The coder sorted the units into themes containing similar attributes. For example, "intelligent" and "smart" were grouped together in the definition of competence, and all responses indicating either of the two were included in that group. Likewise, "stupid" and "slow learner" were grouped together in the definition of incompetence. While many categories were similar for competence and incompetence defin- itions, some belonged to only one or the other. To further narrow down the themes, the three authors inductively generated three information types: (1) Person-trait characteristics, (2) Task-specific knowledge, and (3) Perform- ance outcomes. Third, we coded the definitions by assigning each unit into one of the three information types. The inter-coder reliability between the independent coder and the first author was acceptable at $\kappa = .71$ and $\kappa = .83$ for competence and incompetence, respectively.

For the incident coding process, each incident was assigned into one of three information types identified from the definitions. The first and second authors each coded 100 incompetence incidents. The reliability between coders was .89, measured as the ratio of total agreements to total agreements plus disagreements (Miles and Huberman, 1994). The few disagreements were resolved through discussion. The first author then coded the rest of the incompetence incidents, and the second author coded the rest of the competence incidents.

Results

Mirroring the three main areas with regard to judgment of competence and incompetence that we discussed earlier, we present the results of the data analysis in those three areas: (1) Information types, (2) Affect, and (3) Information-gathering methods.

INFORMATION TYPES UNDERLYING (IN)COMPETENCE JUDGMENTS

Our analysis of the qualitative responses for the definitions of competence and incompetence revealed three information types that are used for the judgment of both competence and incompetence: (1) Person-trait characteristics, (2) Task-specific knowledge, and (3) Performance outcomes. These three types were also used to code the descriptions of the incidents where our participants judged their co-worker's competence and incompetence.

Person-trait characteristics

This information type refers to abilities and attributes that generalize the person's character. In this type, competence and incompetence are defined without any reference to specific tasks and are applicable across contexts. Many definitions of competence included general traits like "smart," "trustworthy," "independent," "hard-working," and "enthusiastic," and similarly many definitions of incompetence mentioned "stupid," "unintelligent," "slow learner," "always late," and "careless." Incidents of this type focused on general traits rather than task-specific skills. Person-trait characteristics describing competence tended to be positively framed; those describing incompetence were negatively framed. The following description about a manager's competence highlights her organizing skills.

Every once in a while, important Banana Republic people come around to the stores to make sure the store looks good and everything is folded and the sizes are arranged appropriately. Allyson, my competent manager, is very good at getting employees to be efficient and quickly get the store in order. She is very organized and gets things done well on time.

This account was centered on the competent individual's broad skills in organization and efficiency instead of matching an assigned task with her abilities to perform that task.

Motivation (or lack thereof) emerged in the following responses as general traits. The first is for competence; the second is for incompetence.

I thought he was competent during his first week at Domino's pizza because he did not get frustrated with the learning curve during the "rush" part of the workday, he showed eagerness to learn the system, and he used his mind before asking about locations of deliveries.

When overloaded with customers at the front desk, my co-worker just lost all will, and then just vanished from the job.

Interpersonal abilities were mentioned frequently. Such abilities were framed as "getting along," "team player," or "helping" for competence; and the lack thereof for incompetence. For example:

She stepped up to help the other workers when we couldn't figure out a problem. She was able to help us while also completing her responsibilities to keep her customer happy.

Getting along with your co-workers is important, and once she started a fight with another co-worker. In order to be competent you have to be able to work well with others, she could not.

Task-specific knowledge

This information type refers to the possession of knowledge specifically required to perform certain tasks or lack thereof, for example, foreign-language proficiency for translators, and programming skills for computer engineers. Competence and incompetence definitions fitting this type were specifically linked to tasks at hand. The importance of task-specific knowledge in competence judgments is illustrated in the following two incidents.

He is the production manager for an armored car factory. When there was a problem with the pieces not fitting right he found the root of the problem. It was in the CAD drawing that the laser uses to cut out the pieces. He knew where to look first and what to look for right away.

This individual was working on budget preparation, a process which the managers did not fully understand. She was able to explain to them the variances in their budgets, the challenges they would face, and put potential solutions in front of them so they could make a decision. She displayed background knowledge of what was going on behind the numbers and an understanding of what future events will impact the results.

The following examples of incompetence similarly focus on how the co-worker did not have knowledge and skills required to perform a specific task in a variety of work settings: car factory, library, and office.

He was a mechanical engineer at the armored car factory with many years of experience. I asked how to fix a drawing and he had no idea of what to do even though he worked with the program every day and it was something that I later found out was a simple thing to change.

A student needed help in searching for materials for a research paper. My supervisor didn't know how or what subject headings to look under as a topic to find the materials.

He did not know anything about the daily duties he should know how to do.

These descriptions of both competent and incompetent co-workers focused on the co-worker's knowledge. Specifically, the responses in this type connected specific tasks assigned to the target person to his/her knowledge about those tasks. This information type seems to fit how expertise is often defined, deep knowledge in specific domains (e.g. Canary and McPhee, 2010).

Performance outcomes

The last information type refers to the success or failure of the end result. For example, one participant defined a competent person as someone who "is able to complete a task in a quality and timely fashion." The definitions in this type all had the notion of "getting the job done." The same theme was present in the definitions of incompetence as well. Incompetence was defined as "never completing the job," "not being able to perform the job well," and "screwing up required duties."

Participants' descriptions of specific incidents involving competent and incompetent co-workers mirrored the outcome-oriented evaluation. One participant described:

When I was working for an accounting company, that company just took on a new client. However, there were troubles with the importing of information from the previous company that was handling the account. I saw my boss's competence when she was able to fix any mix ups that constantly came up as the job went on.

In this account, competence was evaluated with a strong focus on the outcome: whether the person got the job done successfully or not. Similarly, the following response was also purely outcome-driven. In this incident, the criterion for competence was the amount of work completed during a given period of time.

As a telecommunications operator we were assessed by the number of completed calls per hour. While the average was 14, I was at 21 and he was at 23.

The following incompetence incidents demonstrated poor performance outcomes:

I worked in retail with her and when we were closing the store, she did nothing to help. Therefore another co-worker and I had to do her part before we could leave for the day.

When I worked at a produce store, one of my co-workers never completed the jobs he was supposed to.

Additionally, we compared the data between competence and incompetence to examine if there was any difference between the two in terms of the types of information used to form judgments. We counted the number of occurrences for each information type for both definitions and incidents and compared the frequencies. The results indicated that more participants defined competence in terms of task-specific knowledge and performance outcomes than incompetence. On the other hand, participants described incompetence in terms of person-trait characteristics more often than competence. The same pattern emerged in the incident analysis. Task-specific knowledge and performance outcomes appeared more often in the incidents of competent than incompetent co-workers, while person-trait characteristics appeared more often in incidents depicting incompetent than competent co-workers.

AFFECT AND (IN)COMPETENCE JUDGMENTS

We conducted a chi-square analysis comparing the frequencies of liking and disliking for competence and incompetence separately. Significantly more participants reported liking than disliking their competent co-worker. However, there was no statistically significant difference between the number of participants who liked and the number who disliked their incompetent co-worker. These results suggest that although people generally like competent co-workers, they do not necessarily dislike incompetent co-workers.

The asymmetries between competence and incompetence revealed in the data suggest that each concept generates different affective consequences and that incompetence is not simply a lack of competence.

INFORMATION-GATHERING METHODS FOR MAKING IN(COMPETENCE) JUDGMENTS

Our third set of analysis pertained to the information-gathering methods used in making competence and incompetence judgments. We conducted chi-square McNemar tests to compare the information-gathering methods participants used for learning about competence and incompetence of co-workers.

For competence judgments, Reputation was the most often used method, followed by Observation, Description, and Interaction. The same pattern was discovered for incompetence, Reputation, Observation, Description, and Interaction.

We tested for differences in terms of conversational involvement and source of information. To compare frequencies for these dimensions, we combined the frequencies of interaction and self-description to calculate a total frequency for high conversational involvement. Similarly, we combined the frequencies of observation and reputation to calculate a total frequency for low conversational involvement. We used the same calculation method for direct and indirect information sources.

Our chi-square Wilcoxon signed-rank test revealed that, for competence judgments, participants used low involvement methods more often than high involvement methods, and used methods with indirect sources more often than direct sources. Similar results were discovered for incompetence. Participants reported using low involvement methods more often than high involvement methods for incompetent co-workers, and used methods with indirect sources more often than direct sources.

Discussion

This chapter examined how competence and incompetence are judged in the workplace. We reviewed previous research on social judgment and impression formation from a variety of disciplinary perspectives that inform the judgment of competence and incompetence and presented the results of an empirical investigation that directly addresses information types as a basis of judgment, the relationship between the judgment and affect, and information-gathering methods.

Advancing the Study of Expertise

CONTRIBUTIONS

One of the key insights from our empirical data is that competence and incompetence may be two separate constructs rather than two end-points of the same continuum. The comparative analysis between competence and incompetence in terms of information types and affect provides useful insights for the conceptualization of competence and incompetence. Although it is evident that the formation of the judgments for both competence and incompetence is based on two primary dimensions, person-trait characteristics and task-specific abilities, it is notable that these two dimensions carry differing weights for competence and incompetence. Also, the relation between competence and liking does not mirror the relation between incompetence and disliking. The asymmetries between competence and incompetence revealed in the data suggest that each concept generates different affective consequences and that incompetence is not simply a lack of competence. Instead, each concept may require a separate set of criteria when it comes to its judgment.

In addition, the two dimensions associated with competence judgment suggest that competence and expertise may not be conceptually interchangeable. While expertise is often connected to specific domain areas of task (see Merritt, Ackerman, and Hung, this volume), the conceptualizations of competence from our empirical data include not only task-specific domains but also person-traits that transcend task types. This clarifies our assertion at the beginning of the chapter that the concept of expertise could be subsumed in the larger concept of competence.

Treating competence and incompetence as separate constructs and considering two distinctively different dimensions associated with the constructs present a significant implication for the recognition and utilization of expertise in organizations. There seems to be a hierarchical order of priority in terms of the types of abilities that are considered for judgment. The two dimensions, generic and task-specific, are both important cues when judging someone's abilities. However, the fact that the generic dimension plays a larger role in identifying someone's incompetence and that the judgment of incompetence is assumed to preclude recognition and utilization of the person's expertise suggests that generic abilities are lower in the hierarchy than task-specific abilities and that those generic abilities are necessary but not sufficient determinants for the recognition of one's expertise. In other words, demonstration of positive generic abilities (e.g. intelligent, diligent, organized) is only helpful not to be judged as incompetent or not to be excluded from the possibility for being considered as an expert. For someone's expertise to be recognized and ultimately used, the higher order abilities in the task-specific dimension (e.g. Java language for computer programmers, proficiency in SPSS for statisticians) would need to be displayed in addition to the generic abilities.

Our results demonstrated that participants relied more on information-gathering methods with low conversational involvement and indirect sources than those with high conversational involvement and direct sources when inferring their co-workers' competence and incompetence. Reputation, which is the least engaged method in terms of communication and directness, was in fact the most often adopted method, even if information from one's own experiences with the target person is likely to provide more accurate information about the target's competence and incompetence (Stafford et al., 1989).

The reliance on reputation indicates the power of social influence on the recognition of expertise in the workplace. This suggests that one's competence is demonstrated to and communicated by people inside as well as outside current working relationships and sometimes without their knowledge. Given that learning involves both individual and collective processes (Canary, 2010; Choo, 2006; Kuhn and Jackson, 2008), a co-worker's perceived level of competence can be heavily influenced by other co-workers' evaluations. Such influence may enhance the accuracy of judgments, suppress the revelation of true abilities, or reinforce already existing biases. It would be useful to use the perspective that focuses on how communicative activities shape how expertise is identified (e.g. Iverson and McPhee, 2002; Kuhn and Jackson, 2008) to investigate deeper into the impact of social influence on expertise recognition.

These considerations of social influence in understanding how expertise is identified and recognized challenge the view that considers expertise (or competence) as a fixed property located in individuals and as a set of qualities that are to be objectively evaluated and universally applied. As Kuhn and Rennstam argue in this volume, expertise may be accomplished and established based on a variety of situational features (e.g. shifts of authority and values) and through continuously emerging processes of interaction among organizational members. Then, the evaluation of who is most competent or has the most expertise and whose knowledge is given most influential power may shift from one situation to another or throughout the course of one situation. This perspective provides an alternative analytical framework that pushes our study of expertise recognition beyond individual-level psychological processes.

Our empirical investigation offers a practical implication as well with regard to impression management. The prevalent view of impression management is that employees seek to be judged favorably to positively influence the appraisals of their performance, to improve their chances of promotion, or to enhance their competitiveness in being selected to key teams (Hinds et al., 2000; Wayne and Liden, 1995). Our data offer a few practical suggestions for how to be judged as competent. The differential weights placed on task-specific and person-trait dimensions for competence and incompetence indicate that employees need to use different strategies to appear competent. Because people focus more on the task-specific dimension when judging co-worker's competence, showcasing task-specific skills will be more effective in engendering judgments of competence than person-trait characteristics. Simply demonstrating positive person-trait characteristics will not be convincing enough for others to believe one's competence. Similarly, in order to avoid appearing incompetent, displaying positive person-traits across different tasks such as organizing skills, punctuality, and effort may be more helpful.

The finding that incompetence judgments are more focused on person-trait characteristics than task-specific knowledge implies that it may be difficult to change impressions of incompetence. Person-trait characteristics (e.g. organizing skills, helpfulness, interpersonal skills) tend to be applicable to many types of tasks, whereas task-specific knowledge is isolated to a specific task (e.g. computer programming skills for database construction). Because person-trait characteristics are more likely to transcend task types, one observation of a negative person-trait in a task situation could be considered diagnostic of an employee's performance in other task situations. For example, when a cashier constantly comes to work late, the cashier is more likely to be expected to show tardiness even when his/her position moves to inventory. This transferability of negative person-trait characteristics across tasks makes the impression of incompetence more 'sticky' than that of competence.

FUTURE RESEARCH

The insights gained from our data provide a starting point for understanding how young adults form judgments about the competence of co-workers. Future research should test whether the study's results hold among more experienced workers, particularly workers in the knowledge industry where judgments of competence and incompetence might be more consequential in determining rewards, assigning responsibilities, and accomplishing organizational goals. It would also be useful to examine how perceptions of competence and information-gathering methods might evolve as employees gain more experience and responsibilities. The likelihood of using more accurate and direct information-seeking methods may increase over time as employees accumulate experience, knowledge, and confidence.

Work experiences of young adults at the entry level may not be significantly affected by the performance of incompetent co-workers, hence the ambivalence displayed in affective judgments of incompetent targets. Future research should investigate whether the liking asymmetry generalizes to managers and more experienced full-time employees who are held accountable for their co-workers' incompetent performance.

Lastly, the usage of technology to communicate and interact is ubiquitous today. Future research should investigate the display of task-specific and generic traits by individuals working virtually. Merritt, Ackerman, and Hung in this volume articulate how technological tools (e.g. expertise finding systems) could locate experts and expertise in a variety of virtual spaces (e.g. database systems, online communities, open source communities). While such technological tools are successful in capturing data about specific knowledge shared in online spaces, which would lead to identification of experts based on the factual data, they are limited in capturing the impressions and perceptions formed behind the factual data. Particularly, the impressions of generic traits that don't pertain to domain-specific knowledge and information would be extremely difficult to form through those tools. Given that virtual teams prefer task-related communication to social communication (Walther, 2013), task-specific knowledge might be displayed more often in the technology-mediated environment, facilitating competence judgments. However, judging generic traits might be more of a challenge and could veer more toward negative judgments because of attribution errors. For instance, when a person doesn't respond quickly to email information requests and synchronous communication technology cannot be used due to time zone differences, would their peers use that information to judge them as being lazy—a generic trait? Virtual work arrangements might also affect the information-gathering methods as individuals may rely on indirect methods even more because of technological constraints. Hence, we might expect the reliance on indirect methods like reputation to continue or become even stronger when employees work virtually.

▨ REFERENCES

Baldwin, J. R., and Hunt, S. K. (2002). Information Seeking Behavior in Intercultural and Intergroup Communication. *Human Communication Research*, 28, 272–86.

Becker, T. E., and Martin, S. L. (1995). Trying to Look Bad at Work: Methods and Motive for Managing. *Academy of Management Journal*, 38, 174–200.

Berger, C. R. (1979). Beyond Initial Understanding: Uncertainty, Understanding, and Development of Interpersonal Relationships. In H. Giles and R. N. St. Clair (eds), *Language and Social Psychology* (pp. 122–44). Oxford. Basil Blackwell.

Berger, C. R., and Calabrese, R. (1975). Some Explorations in Initial Interaction and Beyond: Toward a Development Theory of Interpersonal Communication. *Human Communication Research*, 1, 99–112.

Berger, C. R., and Kellermann, K. A. (1983). To Ask or Not to Ask: Is that a Question? In R. N. Bostrom (ed.), *Communication Yearbook*, 7 (pp. 342–68). Beverly Hills, CA: Sage.

Berger, C. R., and Kellermann, K. A. (1994). Acquiring Social Information. In J. A. Daly and J. M. Wiemann (eds), *Strategic Interpersonal Communication* (pp. 1–31). Hillsdale, NJ: Lawrence Erlbaum.

Berger, J., Cohen, B. P., and Zelditch Jr., M. (1972). Status Characteristics and Social Interaction. *American Sociological Review*, 37, 241–55.

Brashers, D. E., Goldsmith, D. J., and Hsieh, E. (2002). Information Seeking and Avoiding in Health Context. *Human Communication Research*, 28, 258–71.

Canary, H. (2010). Constructing Policy Knowledge: Contradictions, Communication, and Knowledge Frames. *Communication Monographs*, 77, 181–206.

Canary, H. E., and McPhee, R. D. (2010). Introduction: Toward a Communicative Perspective on Organizational Knowledge. In H. E. Canary and R. D. McPhee (eds), *Communication and Organizational Knowledge: Contemporary Issues for Theory and Practice* (pp. 1–14). New York: Routledge.

Carlsson, R., Bjorklund, F., and Backstrom, M. (2012). Mixed Discriminatory Judgments of Individuals' Warmth and Competence-Related Abilities. *Social Psychology*, 43, 160–7.

Choo, C. W. (2006). *The Knowing Organization: How Organizations Use Information to Construct Meaning, Create Knowledge, and Make Decisions*. New York: Oxford University Press.

Comer, D. R. (1991). Organizational Newcomers' Acquisition of Information from Peers. *Management Communication Quarterly*, 5, 64–89.

Cuddy, A. J. C., Fiske, S. T., and Glick, P. (2008). Warmth and Competence as Universal Dimensions of Social Perception: The Stereotype Content Model and the BIAS Map. In M. P. Zanna (ed.), *Advances in Experimental Social Psychology*, 40 (pp. 61–149). New York: Academic Press.

Cuddy, A. J. C., Glick, P., and Beninger, A. (2011). The Dynamics of Warmth and Competence Judgments, and their Outcomes in Organizations. *Research in Organizational Behavior*, 31, 73–98.

DePaulo, B. M., Kenny, D. A., Hoover, C. W., Webb, W., and Oliver, P. V. (1987). Accuracy of Person Perception: Do People Know What Kinds of Impressions they Convey? *Journal of Personality and Social Psychology*, 52, 303–15.

Dreyfus, H., and Dreyfus, S. (2005). Peripheral Vision: Expertise in Real World Contexts. *Organization Studies*, 26, 779–92. doi: 10.1177/0170840605053102

Fiske, S. T., and Neuberg, S. L. (1990). A Continuum of Impression Formation from Category-Based to Individuating Processes: Influences of Information and Motivation on Attention and Interpretation. In M. P. Zanna (ed.), *Advances in Experimental Social Psychology* (pp. 1–74). San Diego, CA: Academic Press.

Fiske, S. T., Cuddy, A. J. C., and Glick, P. (2007). Universal Dimensions of Social Cognition: Warmth and Competence. *Trends in Cognitive Sciences*, 11, 77–83.

Fiske, S. T., Glick, P., and Xu, J. (2002). A Model of (Often Mixed) Stereotype Content: Competence and Warmth Respectively Follow from Status and Competition. *Journal of Personality and Social Psychology*, 82, 878–902.

Fiske, S. T., Lin, M., and Neuberg, S. L. (1999). The Continuum Model: Ten Years Later. In S. Chaiken and Y. Trope (eds), *Dual-Process Theories in Social Psychology* (pp. 231–54). New York: Guilford Press.

Fiske, S. T., Neuberg, S. L., Beattie, A. E., and Milberg, S. J. (1987). Category-Based and Attribute-Based Reactions to Others: Some Informational Conditions of Stereotyping and Individuating Processes. *Journal of Experimental Social Psychology*, 23, 399–427.

Gallagher, E. B., and Sias, P. M. (2009). The New Employee as a Source of Uncertainty: Veteran Employee Information Seeking about New Hires. *Western Journal of Communication*, 73, 23–46.

Gudykunst, W. B., Yang, S. M., and Nishida, T. (1985). A Cross-Cultural Test of Uncertainty Reduction Theory: Comparisons of Acquaintances, Friends, and Dating Relationships in Japan, Korea, and the United States. *Human Communication Research*, 11, 407–54.

Heilman, M. E., and Welle, B. (2006). Disadvantaged by Diversity? The Effects of Diversity Goals on Competence Perceptions. *Journal of Applied Social Psychology*, 36, 1291–1319.

Hinds, P. J., Carley, K. M., Krackhardt, D., and Wholey, D. (2000). Choosing Work Group Members: Balancing Similarity, Competence and Familiarity. *Organization Behavior and Human Decision Processes*, 81, 226–51.

Hollingshead, A. B., and Fraidin, S. N. (2003). Gender Stereotypes and Assumptions about Expertise in Transactive Memory. *Journal of Experimental Social Psychology*, 39, 355–63.

Iverson, J. O., and McPhee, R. D. (2002). Knowledge Management in Communities of Practice: Being True to Communicative Character of Knowledge. *Management Communication Quarterly*, 16, 259–66.

Judd, C. M., James-Hawkins, L., Yzerbyt, V., and Kashima Y. (2005). Fundamental Dimensions of Social Judgment: Understanding the Relations between Judgments of Competence and Warmth. *Journal of Personality and Social Psychology*, 89, 899–913.

Kellermann, K. (1987). Information Exchange in Social Interaction. In M. E. Roloff and G. R. Miller (eds), *Interpersonal Processes: New Directions in Communication Research* (pp. 188–219). Newbury Park, CA: Sage.

Kervyn, N., Yzerbyt, V. Y., Judd, C. M., and Nunes, A. (2009). A Question of Compensation: The Social Life of the Fundamental Dimensions of Social Perception. *Journal of Personality and Social Psychology*, 96, 828–42.

Knobloch, L. K., and Solomon, D. H. (2002). Information Seeking beyond Initial Interaction: Negotiating Relationship Uncertainty within Close Relationships. *Human Communication Research*, 28, 272–86.

Kramer, M. W. (2004). *Managing Uncertainty in Organizational Communication*. Mahwah, NJ: Lawrence Erlbaum.

Kramer, M. W., Meisenbach, R. J., and Hansen, G. J. (2013). Communication, Uncertainly, and Volunteer Membership. *Journal of Applied Communication Research*, 41, 18–39.

Kuhn, T., and Jackson, M. H. (2008). Accomplishing Knowledge: A Framework for Investigating Knowing in Organizations. *Management Communication Quarterly*, 21, 454–85.

Littlepage, G. E., and Mueller, A. L. (1997). Recognition and Utilization of Expertise in Problem-Solving Groups: Expert Characteristics and Behavior. *Group Dynamics: Theory, Research, and Practice*, 1, 324–28.

Miles, M. B., and Huberman, A. M. (1994). *Qualitative Data Analysis: An Expended Sourcebook*. Thousand Oaks, CA: Sage.

Miller, V. D., and Jablin, F. M. (1991). Information Seeking during Organizational Entry: Influences, Tactics, and a Model of the Process. *Academy of Management Review*, 16, 92–120.

Morrison, E. W. (1993). Newcomer Information Seeking: Exploring Types, Modes, Sources, and Outcomes. *Academy of Management Journal*, 36, 557–89.

Morrison, E. W. (1995). Information Usefulness and Acquisition during Organizational Encounter. *Management Communication Quarterly*, 9, 131–55.

O'Neil, H. F., Allred, K., and Baker, E. L. (1992). *Measurement of Workforce Readiness: Review of Theoretical Frameworks*. Los Angeles: University of California.

Operario, D., and Fiske, S. T. (2004). Stereotypes: Contents, Structures, Processes, and Contexts. In M. B. Brewer and M. Hewstone (eds), *Social Cognition* (pp. 210–41). Malden, MA: Blackwell Publishing.

Ramsay, S., Gallois, C., and Callan, V. J. (1997). Social Rules and Attributions in the Personnel Selection Interview. *Journal of Occupational and Organizational Psychology*, 70, 189–203.

Reeder, G. D., and Brewer, M. B. (1979). A Schematic Model of Dispositional Attribution in Interpersonal Perception. *Psychological Review*, 86, 61–79.

Ridgeway, C. L. (1981). Nonconformity, Competence, and Influence within Groups: A Test of Two Theories. *American Sociological Review*, 46, 333–47.

Rosenberg, S., Nelson, C., and Vivekananthan, P. S. (1968). A Multidimensional Approach to the Structure of Personality Impressions. *Journal of Personality and Social Psychology*, 9, 283–94.

Ruscher, J. B., Fiske, S. T., and Schnake, S. B. (2000). The Motivated Tactician's Juggling Act: Compatible vs. Incompatible Impression Goals. *British Journal of Social Psychology*, 39, 241–56.

Sandberg, J. (2000). Understanding Human Competence at Work: An Interpretative Approach. *Academy of Management Journal*, 43, 9–25.

Sheldon, O. J., Thomas-Hunt, M. C., and Proell, C. A. (2006). When Timeliness Matters: The Effects of Status on Reactions to Time Delay within Distributed Collaborations. *Journal of Applied Psychology*, 91, 1385–95.

Stafford, L., Waldron, V. R., and Infield, L. L. (1989). Actor–Observer Differences in Conversational Memory. *Human Communication Research*, 15, 590–611.

Sternberg, R. J. (1990). Prototypes of Competence and Incompetence. In R. J. S. J. Kollingian (ed.), *Competence Considered* (pp. 117–45). New Haven: Yale University Press.

Teboul, J. C. (1994). Facing and Coping with Uncertainty during Organizational Encounter. *Management Communication Quarterly*, 8, 190–224.

Treem, J. W. (2013). Technology Use as a Status Cue: The Influences of Mundane and Novel Technologies on Knowledge Assessments in Organizations. *Journal of Communication*, 63, 1032–53.

Vonk, R. (1998). Effects of Cooperative and Competitive Outcome Dependency on Attention and Impression Preferences. *Journal of Experimental Social Psychology*, 34, 265–88.

Walther, J. B. (2013). Groups and Computer-Mediated Communication. In Y. Amichai-Hamburger (ed.), *The Social Net: Understanding our Online Behavior* (pp. 165–79). New York: Oxford University Press.

Wayne, S. J., and Liden, R. C. (1995). Effects of Impression Management on Performance Ratings: A Longitudinal Study. *Academy of Management Journal*, 38, 232–60.

Wittenbaum, G. M., Schulman, H. C., and Braz, M. E. (2010). Social Ostracism in Task Groups: The Effects of Group Composition. *Small Group Research*, 41, 330–53.

Wojciszke, B. (1994). Multiple Meanings of Behavior: Construing Actions in Terms of Competence or Morality. *Journal of Personality and Social Psychology*, 67, 222–32.

Yoon, K., and Hollingshead, A. B. (2010). Cultural Stereotyping, Convergent Expectations, and Performance in Cross-Cultural Collaborations. *Social Psychological and Personality Science*, 1, 160–7.

Part III

Expertise as Communicated within Professional Contexts

8 Expertise in Context

Interaction in the Doctors' Room of an Emergency Department

JOHN C. LAMMERS, NATALIE J. LAMBERT, BRYAN
ABENDSCHEIN, TOBIAS REYNOLDS-TYLUS,
AND KIRA A. VARAVA

The medical profession is widely recognized as a site of highly developed expertise. Indeed, Starr (1982, 5) referred to medicine as the "sovereign profession" for its sustained technical, political, and economic dominance over other healing systems as well as over a vast health care establishment. The profoundly developed social context of medicine stands in sharp contrast to its technical aspects, however, which remain housed in individual practitioners in local settings. Sternberg (1997, 150) reviewed at least seven different views of expertise that all varied around individuals using stores of special knowledge to solve complex problems rapidly. Patel and Ramoni summarized medical expertise with respect to diagnosis in a particular way:

All hypotheses needed to explain the current case had to be available when the diagnostic process starts, and the generation of hypotheses is a process of selection rather than a process of creation. This factor makes diagnostic reasoning different from the process of scientific discovery or creative thinking, in which all knowledge cannot be assumed always to be available. (1997, 71)

Thus medical expertise is seen to rely on a store of knowledge held by individuals and applied on a case-by-case basis. However, medical organizations are also powerfully structured places of roles, rules, and routines governed by conventions, policies, and laws (Apker, 2011; Apker et al., 2007, 2010; Lammers and Proulx, 2016; Lammers et al., 2003). They therefore offer an opportunity to study expertise simultaneously as a property of individuals and as socially situated phenomena (Treem, 2012).

The multifaceted, dynamic nature of expertise is highlighted in the emergency departments (EDs) of local hospitals, where individual physicians apply their diagnostic, prognostic, and prescriptive expertise to a steady stream of patients who come to them with a broad range of health conditions. The organization of emergency medicine is a product of the habits and preferences of practitioners as well as of the social, economic, and technological constraints and affordances of the delivery of emergency medical care (see Agnew et al., 1997; Stein, 1997).

Since medicine made its big moves to dominance early in the first half of the twentieth century (Starr, 1982), as a profession it has been increasingly constrained by at least three forces. First, the growth of medical organizations, including hospitals and group medical practices, has placed restrictive administrative arrangements on the once-autonomous solo practice of medicine (Leicht and Fennell, 2001). Second, especially since the advent of Medicare and Medicaid in 1965, the provision of health care, at least in the US, has experienced an increasing regulatory burden from both governmental and proprietary payers. Managed care, a set of principles followed by both public and private funders (Lammers et al., 2003), has restricted *who* can be compensated for doing *what* for *whom* in American medical care. Finally, a host of medical and information technologies, some clinical and some administrative, has arisen to replace or augment the traditional diagnostic, clinical, and administrative routines of physicians. Together these forces have changed, and we argue constrained, the environment in which medical expertise is applied.

The built-up, institutionalized environment in which medical expertise is applied suggests that a single approach to expertise in this case may not be warranted. Treem (2012) identified three broad approaches which might be employed to study expertise. The cognitive approach emphasizes the knowledge and skills of practitioners, the sociological approach the status of professionals, and a communicative approach the social relationships and interactions among practitioners. The setting of emergency medicine is certainly characterized by frequent cognitive behaviors associated with diagnosis, prognosis, and prescription, but it is also characterized by professional status differentials and coordinative interaction among personnel. However, it has not been tapped as a setting in which expertise might be studied. In fact, aside from our general knowledge of the institutional context of medical work, we know very little about what expert knowledge is communicated, to whom, with what frequency, and in the context of what particular constraints. Thus to get at expertise in the emergency medical setting we need an empirical strategy that is ecumenical with respect to its approach, and explores the cognitive, sociological, as well as the communicative features of the manifestation of expertise.

In his analysis of professional-service firms Treem (2012, 27) asked, "How do people make determinations about who is an expert in environments where the conduct of work is largely invisible and the outputs of that work are highly ambiguous?" This is an important question in the context of an emerging arena of expertise such as professional-service firms, particularly in the context of new media. In the ED, however, there is little ambiguity about *who* is the expert. And the conduct of ED work, while partially concealed in examination rooms and by privacy protocols, is hardly concealed from other workers, notwithstanding its individualized conduct. Moreover, ambiguity in medical diagnosis and treatment is precisely what medical science and the edifice of administrative rules and regulations have sought for the last four decades to reduce. Thus in the case of emergency physicians, the question is, "How is the expertise of ED physicians expressed, constrained, and applied in the conduct of their work?"

Our thesis is that expertise in the ED is an emergent property both of licensed, certified, and previously recognized individuals *and* of the communicative interactions between and among them. Key questions include communication and interaction *with* whom (or what) and *about* what? The "whom" involves actors both human and nonhuman and present and not present. And the topics, too, is an empirical question, because expertise is always about something. Beyond the content and interaction that constitute expertise are the professional identities and awareness of the actors. Therefore, our operational question is, "How do people communicate, constitute, and enact expertise in a built-up environment where the conduct of work is individualized and the outputs of that work are not highly ambiguous?"

The project we report in this chapter investigates expertise through observations of the consultations of ED physicians, nurse practitioners (NPs), and physician's assistants (PAs) with other clinicians, which we view as interactions about expertise. The current literature on expertise interactions in the ED setting is quite limited. A study of hand-offs, communication related to consultations in an ED (Maughan et al., 2011) identified communication problems related to failure to repeat requests or orders, physical examinations, and laboratory reports: "Physical examination handoff errors and omissions were observed in 130 (13.1%) and 447 (45.1%) handoffs, respectively. Laboratory errors and omissions were noted in 37 (3.7%) and 290 (29.2%) handoffs, respectively" (p. 506). As Kessler et al. (2011) noted, the consultation process is something learned by doing in the medical profession; there is little to no actual training of this important skill and very little research has explored the subject. The literature that does exist has looked at developing a model of ED consulting (Kessler et al., 2011, 2012) and creating a taxonomy of the types of ED consulting (Kessler et al., 2013). Limited initial work focused on testing a model for training on how to consult (Nokes et al., 2011).

The current study expands this body of work by investigating ED consultations in a community hospital while previous literature described similar consultations at a Veterans Administration (VA) hospital and at academic medical centers (Eisenberg et al., 2006, 2005). This is an important distinction as the physicians in the two types of hospitals may be motivated in different ways which in turn may affect their consultation behaviors. VA physicians are employed by their hospitals whereas community hospital physicians are members of private medical practices contracted to work in local hospitals. As self-employed individuals their reimbursement incentives, liabilities, and practice patterns may vary. Thus while the initial impetus for our study was to observe a baseline of consultation behaviors in a community hospital setting, we also aim to make a broader theoretical contribution toward understanding how expertise is exercised in an environment with recognized individual experts and visible work.

Physical Setting and Work Routine

"Care Hospital" is a 325-bed nonprofit community hospital located in a small Midwestern city. About two-dozen full-time physicians staff the ED at Care Hospital. Because the ED at Care Hospital never closes, ten-hour shifts are staggered throughout the day. More staff members are present during busier periods, with the majority of patient visits occurring Fridays through Mondays. Similar to other EDs in the US (Côté et al., 2013), the majority of patients visit the ED at Care Hospital between the hours of 3 p.m. and 11 p.m.

Our observations took place in the "doctors' room" in the ED at Care Hospital. The doctors' room is reserved primarily for ED physicians, although there are about half-a-dozen non-physicians including PAs, NPs, and Advanced Practice Nurses (APNs) who work there as well during any given shift. In addition, residents in several training programs are sometimes present in the doctors' room. Finally, other Care Hospital staff such as nurses, janitorial staff, administrators, and consulting physicians enter the doctors' room regularly.

The doctors' room is located in a back hallway of the ED next to a nurse's station. Outside the doctors' room a sign designates the area as "Staff Only." The doctors' room is roughly 22 feet by 15 feet (see Figure 8.1) and the walls are lined with carrels or stations where dual monitors are set up to allow physicians access to patient medical records and images such as x-rays and scans. In addition to workstations, the doctors' room also has a refrigerator, microwave, sink, and a coffee maker.

The physical makeup of the room is cramped and perfunctory. The layout contains seven small work stations where the physicians and other personnel make phone calls for consultations, discuss admission with hospitalists, or dictate information into the electronic medical record system (the hospital uses EPIC). The room serves less formal purposes as well. Physicians and others consult with each other, discuss possible courses of action, and review previous treatment strategies on repeat patients or situations. There is a fair amount of small talk and talking-to-the-room as members think out loud or address the room in general. There is an element of intensity that grows out of the moment-to-moment urgency of the environment. In this tangible backstage space (Goffman, 1959), interactions are friendly but mostly

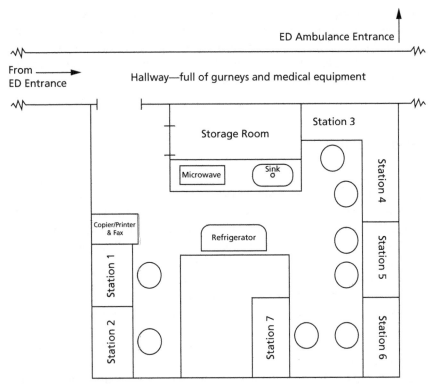

Figure 8.1 Schematic of the Doctors' Room

task-oriented; there is a sense of some detachment from the stress of the patient care areas, yet there is never an opportunity to fully relax.

At the beginning of their shifts—staggered to maintain a constant supply of personnel—a physician would enter the room, find an empty work station (these were not assigned but we typically saw the same physicians at the same work stations over multiple observations), and sign in to the electronic medical record system. The system employed voice recognition software that most physicians used. One of the windows at the work stations continually displays the patients in need of attention; physicians would typically take the case that had been waiting the longest or had the highest urgency. NPs and PAs would follow a similar routine.

Within the ongoing state of urgency there were also constant interruptions. Everything seemed to be given a level of importance that grew out of the ED culture, yet the participants attended to the steady flow of immediacy. Coupled with the intensity of treating sometimes life-and-death cases on a daily basis, there were also stories about someone's most recent home repair, weekend plans, jokes, and intimate family stories. Finally there was the mundane aspect of care in an urban ED, where a significant number of cases involved patients who were seeking drugs to satisfy an addiction, coming to the ED because they had no regular insured source of care, or might have just been looking for attention (Shem, 1978). Thus these are regular sources of commentary characterized by cynicism.

Study Design

Because expert consultations had not been systematically studied in community hospitals before, we approached this study as an opportunity to collect baseline information about how expertise was communicated in the ED setting. Our study was approved by both our university's and the hospital's Institutional Review Boards, and all the staff who participated were aware of our study and voluntarily consented in writing to participate. Privacy and logistic concerns meant that we were somewhat constrained to observations in the doctors' room. However, within that context we were privy to everything that was said, and to our knowledge there was minimal filtering while we were there. Thus without an a priori definition of consultation or expertise, we aimed to record to the extent possible every utterance we observed. We analyzed the data using an explanatory sequential mixed data analysis strategy (Creswell and Clark, 2007; Teddlie and Tashakkori, 2009), first using network analysis of the observational data, followed by interviews with ED physicians. Our network analyses aimed to identify what expertise was communicated with whom, while our interview data aimed to more carefully sort out the usefulness of the cognitive, sociological, and communicative approaches to expertise.

According to national studies (Côté et al., 2013), EDs most frequently see patients, and therefore have a higher likelihood of requiring consultations, on Fridays, weekends, and Mondays during the hours of 3 p.m. to 11 p.m. We originally had hoped to shadow physicians during those hours, but learned that nearly all consultations occur in the doctors' room rather than during examinations or treatments with patients. Thus, we arranged to post researchers in the doctors' room Friday through Monday for around-the-clock observations. With Care Hospital and the physician participants' consent, the investigators observed the way in which ED physicians communicated with other physicians, residents, NPs, and PAs during medical consultations over the telephone and in the office areas of the ED. The "secondary" physicians, that is, doctors who consulted on the telephone or are in discussion with ED physicians were not the focus of our study, and no personal identifying information about them nor their comments were collected during our observations.

In the initial phase of our study, our team observed the doctors' room in two- or three-hour shifts and covered nearly all the hours from Friday morning at 5 a.m. until Monday at 4 p.m. for a total of ninety hours of direct observation. For each of these observations, we recorded as many verbal interactions as possible and all our observations of the behavior of the physicians, NPs, PAs, and residents. A member of our team would take a chair at one of the empty work stations and record observations on a laptop. In this way we were able to capture much, if not all, that was said in the doctors' room (simultaneous conversations meant that some interactions were not recorded, thus our observations could not include everything that was said). Based on our first ninety hours of observations we accumulated 159 pages of field notes. The analysis of these data is described in this chapter.

In the second phase of our study, we interviewed ED physicians ($N = 7$) either before or immediately following a shift based on participants' availability (with a single exception of a physician who met us at an off-site location). Interviews lasted between ten and forty minutes, with most interviews lasting approximately twenty minutes. During these interviews, we presented participants with two anonymized, composite scenarios based on our observations in the doctors' room, and asked them to explain what was happening in the scenarios. We used composites to explore physicians' views of expertise, rather than directly asking them about expertise initially, to avoid bias and priming effects. The two composite scenarios we developed were as follows:

SCENARIO 1

Doctor approaches PA in the doctors' room of the ED.
Doctor: Are you available?
PA: I just put in orders on that lady. One of her sons is sick, she was feeling fine this morning, she was at the store with her son when she started to feel dizzy, she sat down and drank some water and felt better, aside from that she had a right side chest tingle that went away. Everything else is normal, her workup is normal ... so she's in bed five ... and I had one other one that you took. He had a drainage tube removed today, he said he has 9/10 pain, he was moaning, so I ordered a CBC scan and a milligram of Dilaudid.
Doctor: Why don't you call Dr [name] and see what he wants?

SCENARIO 2

An ED Doctor talks to a hospitalist on the phone.
Doctor: I have this 8-year-old boy that I'm on the fence about sending home. He was getting out of a car and his dad had left the car in neutral, and he got

drug partially under the car, he has a fracture in his left elbow, can't ambulate yet. The left elbow is from the injury, the right knee is from an accident a few weeks ago. No, no, it was total coincidence. Would you come look at him, and say what you think? I just feel bad about sending him home in a wheelchair. If you would just see him...I would feel better about sending him home.

The Doctor hangs up the phone.

After sharing the scenarios with our participants, we then asked direct questions about their communication processes and views on expertise including:

Do you recognize this kind of interaction?
Does this sound typical?
In this case, what's going on here?
What makes this an easier or more difficult interaction?
What makes this effective or ineffective?

Finally we asked more directly about expertise, respondents' definitions of it, and who possessed it. In the following sections we discuss the role network and sematic network analyses that identify the content of expertise and the interactions involved in expert consultations, and we then turn to the interview data to better understand the salience of the cognitive, sociological, and communicative aspects of expertise as manifested in the ED.

Network Analyses

THE NETWORK OF ROLES

Consultations were extracted from all communication episodes we recorded in a format that listed the speakers and the verbatim spoken content. For data analysis, we defined a consultation as communication between two medical personnel in the ED where at least one speaker was a physician and one speaker solicited a conversation regarding patient care with another. Data collection yielded 421 such verbatim medical consultations. NP and PA roles were collapsed into the same occupational group, as their work roles in practice were indistinguishable to our team. We generated a network map of the frequency of consultations between the different medical roles in the ED using the network graphing software NodeXL (see Figure 8.2). In this way we are able to identify precisely with whom expertise is shared. In this graph, each node represents a professional role in the ED and each edge represents an observed consultation between these role types. The weight (thickness) of the edges indicates the relative amount of consultations between each of the role types.

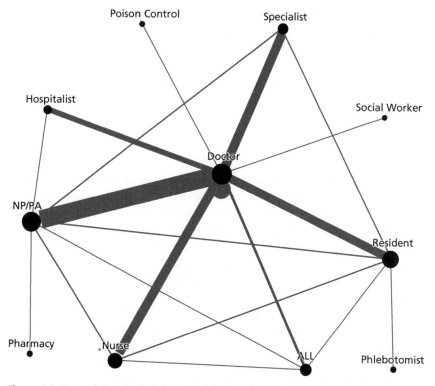

Figure 8.2 Network Graph of ED Roles and the Relative Number of Consultations between Each Role Type

Medical consultations are widely conceptualized as requests by one physician to another physician for expert advice about patient care. Our observations of medical professional interactions in the ED indicated, however, that physicians interact and share their expertise with many other role types (see Figure 8.2) in order to coordinate and accomplish patient care. In fact, perhaps the rarest form of interaction was the case of an ED physician specifically asking for knowledge she or he did not hold. The most frequent consult occurred between physicians and the NP/PA group, followed by the physicians and nurses, specialists, residents, and hospitalists. Consultations between physicians and the NPs, PAs, and nurses involved coordination of care for a patient. NPs and PAs were in much of their practice indistinguishable from physicians, except that the physicians were responsible for overseeing the care NPs and PAs provided, so there were frequent exchanges of information and advice given by physicians to NPs and PAs. Consultations between ED physicians and hospitalists are part of the routine by which patients are admitted to the hospital from the ED; we learned that for each kind of patient condition, hospitalists enforce standards consisting of symptoms, tests, and other indicators that must be satisfied before the hospitalist would authorize admission. While this kind of consult was not the most frequent we observed, it tended to follow a pattern of negotiation, depending on the ED physician, of either asserting that the patient required immediate admission, or inquiry and exchange to determine whether the patient would satisfy criteria for admission.

THE SEMANTIC NETWORKS

In an effort to sort out the differences between types of expert consultations, we conducted text analytics on two subgroups of our data (physician-to-physician consultations and physician-to-all-other medical roles) in order to compare the ways in which expertise was enacted in these two groups. Data preprocessing and semantic analysis took place in AutoMap text-to-network analysis software. Preprocessing removed noise words (i.e. articles and simple verbs), pronouns, symbols, and numbers. The next step extracted a semantic network co-reference list using a window size of 2 (i.e. a word occurred within two sentences of another word) with a sentence as the default window. We visualized the resulting semantic network list in NodeXL network graph exploration software. Cluster analysis is a useful exploratory data analysis tool for looking for underlying structure within a dataset. This method suited our data-driven exploration of looking for patterns of expert medical consultations in an observational dataset. We used the Clauset-Newman-Moore (2004) cluster algorithm to analyze the data for structural clusters, and then visually grouped the vertices of the semantic network according to the resulting clusters. We performed the same analytic method on the second subgroup of our data, physician consultations with all other medical roles. Figure 8.3 is the largest cluster within the physician-to-physician medical consultation semantic network, and Figures 8.4 and 8.5 are the largest clusters for the semantic network of physician consultations with all other ED medical professional roles.

Figure 8.3 shows that the largest cluster in the physician-to-physician communication network concerned patients' pain and how to handle it. This cluster and its salience in our data is a reminder that a key reason that patients come to the ED is that they suffer from pain that they cannot treat themselves or are unwilling to wait to have treated. The cluster suggests that a substantial portion of interaction with other physicians concerns describing the pain that patients exhibit, which contextually is often represented by terms associated with anatomical parts. Recognizing that articles have been removed from the analysis, the consults regarding pain can be reconstructed by connecting nodes on the graph in Figure 8.3 (e.g. "chest pain," "pain medication," "severe pain," "increased pain," "pain (on the) left side").

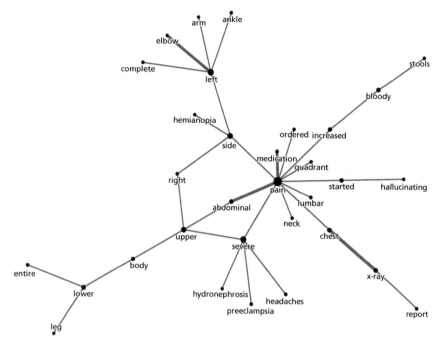

Figure 8.3 Physician-to-Physician Consultation Cluster 1: Communication Having to Do with Pain Treatment

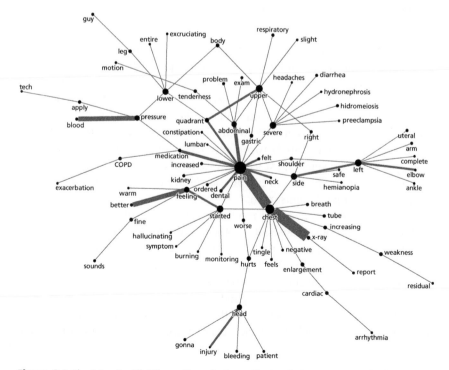

Figure 8.4 Physician-to-All-Others Consultations Cluster 1: Treatment and Diagnosis of Pain during Medical Consultation

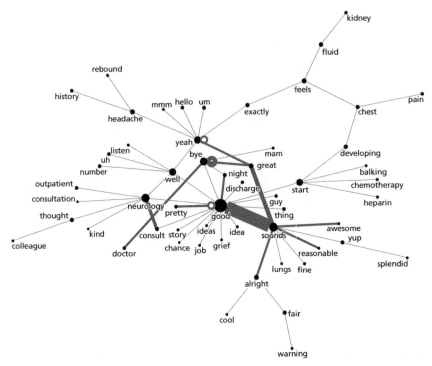

Figure 8.5 Physician-to-All-Others Consultations Cluster 2: Communication/Coordination, Feedback during Medical Consultation

Figure 8.4 shows that the largest physician-to-all-others cluster also represents pain as the most commonly discussed topic, with even more details, and reveals that "chest pain" was the most common word pair, followed by "chest x-ray," "abdominal pain," and "feeling better." While an examination of medical records or patients' complaints upon admission to the ED might suggest other issues of concern in the ED, it is revealing that in simply examining the interactions between physicians and others in the doctors' room, pain was the single most frequent topic of discussion when coordinating patients' care. Experienced ED physicians are therefore experts in identifying and managing patients' pain.

Figure 8.5 displays the second most common cluster of terms used in consultations between physicians and all others in the doctors' room. While more difficult to interpret than the pain-centered cluster, it does capture the coordinative action associated with consultations. The term "good" clearly plays a number of roles in association with other terms, such as the affirmatives "sounds good" and "good thing" as well as "good start" and "good chance." "Yeah" also played that affirmative role. Looking at these affirmative words in the context of the consultations in which they occur, it is clear that, during communication of expertise, affirmative feedback is important. Other terms with some centrality in the network included "nurse," "asks," and "neurology." The frequency of neurology is a reminder that pain brings a fair number of patients to the ED, and that therefore a central feature of expertise in the ED is coordinative communication in the management of pain.

DISCUSSION OF ROLE AND SEMANTIC NETWORK ANALYSIS

The network analyses suggest a communicative structure and content of expertise interaction in the ED. There are similarities between the two data subgroups (physician-physician vs. physician-all-others) in the first subgraphs, but examining only physician-to-physician medical consultations leaves us with an incomplete view of expertise as it is enacted in EDs. Physician-to-physician consultations account for only a small portion of the total body of observed expert consultations (about one-fifth; see Figure 8.2) and they are also only part of the larger patient care coordination process. NPs, PAs, residents, nurses, and other medical personnel regularly interact with physicians to gain expert guidance and to share patient information in order to collaboratively provide patient care.

Data-driven methods are very useful for research projects where little is known observationally about the object of study. Observational data collection in combination with data-driven methods like text analysis can reveal structure in datasets that can then be compared with existing frameworks or can be used to create new frameworks. Carefully made choices during text analysis, such as the use of a sentence as the unit of analysis, can help to preserve natural language patterns that otherwise might be lost during some types of quantitative analysis. In particular, text analyses of observational data like the foregoing allowed us to see how expertise on particular topics is enacted through communicative interactions with particular others, and to investigate how role types can affect expression of expertise during interaction. Indeed, the network analyses give a clear view of what expertise is expressed, known, judged, or acted upon.

However, semantic network analysis does not reveal participants' own self-awareness of expertise sharing. In order to develop a more nuanced understanding of expertise sharing, we interviewed ED physicians using the composite scenarios. We discuss the findings of those interviews in terms of cognitive, sociological, and communicative perspectives on expertise.

PHYSICIANS' VIEWS OF THEIR WORK

In our analysis of the interview data, we questioned our participants using composites of the interactions we observed, and we looked for evidence of different perspectives on expertise. Following Treem (2012), we assess here how ED physicians discussed expertise according to three different perspectives on what constitutes expertise (cognitive, sociological, and communicative). We acknowledge that these are not types of expertise, but ways of viewing expertise that allow for certain phenomena to be foregrounded depending on the perspective. While each of these perspectives concerns expert knowledge, they each also emphasize distinct and common features of the social setting of the ED—cognition, professionalism, and interaction. In the following section, we both expand on this multi-perspective on expertise, and we articulate what our data reveal from each of these perspectives.

THE COGNITIVE PERSPECTIVE ON EXPERTISE

In the cognitive perspective, expertise is seen as an attribute of the individual, with experts "having different mental approaches to tasks than other individuals" (Treem, 2012, 24). Thus, experts are said to be able to interpret information in abstract and meaningful ways, and are able to apply this information in different contexts appropriately. In this perspective, expertise is born of immersion in the field of study, as well as through rigorous training and practice. The theme of expertise as a cognitive attribute arose several times in our interviews. One of the most salient themes that reflected the cognitive perspective was the ability of ED physicians to deal with the large amount of information inherent in their jobs. In general, physicians saw themselves as broad specialists. When asked about what type of expertise that ED physicians have, one physician responded, "We are jack-of-all-trades, we know a little about a lot." Another physician noted,

As an ED doctor, my specialty is emergencies. We are "emergentologists." I consider my specialty to identify and treat emergencies: this includes things such as strokes, heart attacks, fractures, abdominal pain, chest pain, toxicology (such as accidental or intentional poisoning, or poisoning brought on by environmental exposure).

Thus the nature of ED work is medically technical, and yet very broad, but frequently interrupted. As one physician put it, "You have to be good at multitasking to do this job." Another physician noted that being an expert meant being able to "prioritize the sea of information, and focus on the one or two things you need to see." The physician continued, noting that:

When you are at your peak, you start to minimize the noise and [to] focus...When you start having all the noise, you have all this information, when you have a sick patient, you cut out the noise and focus on what needs to be done.

Another physician used the metaphor of a cognitive juggler to describe the work of an ED physician:

[Our work] looks like a juggler juggling balls, with each ball representing an individual patient. As the balls go around in the air, sometimes new balls are being thrown in. As the ball turns, as the patient comes back into my memory, I reassess everything I know about this patient and move them on. So all the while these balls are constantly circling in my mind. There may be 8 or 9 of them, so I am constantly recirculating back to them. Also, there are interruptions, things that may be thrown in that aren't balls, like a pen. With the interruptions, I throw them out as I get them done. The balls get thrown out as I admit the patient or as they leave the ED, and new balls, new patients, come in. All the while, nobody, no ball, really ever goes completely away. There may be many balls sitting in the back of my head. These may be things that I need to document at the end of my shift about a particular patient. So even the balls that leave never really go away, as these balls are shifted to the back of my head.

When asked how often ED physicians were interrupted, one physician answered succinctly: "constantly." Other physicians gave specific estimates of how often they were interrupted. For example, one physician estimated interruptions occurred "on average, probably 10 times in an interaction." Likewise, when asked what the biggest challenge of the job was, many ED physicians indicated issues related to balancing a cognitive load alongside constant interruptions. As one physician responded to the question on the biggest challenge, "Without a doubt it is how busy we are and trying to multitask." Another physician commented, "Here we are making life and death decisions, on top of being interrupted."

Several physicians noted that their work is a function of immersion and experience dealing with the unique challenges of working in the ED. When asked to describe what factors result in expertise, one physician responded, "Residency training and practicing, like anyone else. The more patients you see the more experienced and a better clinician you are. Not always, but often this is the case." In another interview, when asked how long it takes to acquire the cognitive ability to handle all this information, one physician suggested between three to five years, noting, "By the end of your residency, you are usually able to juggle this information effectively." The same physician also noted that, "When I first started I had to carry around a notebook just to keep up with all the information. As the years went on, it got less and less difficult to juggle that information."

In short, we found ample evidence to support a cognitive view of expertise as our participants described their work. Mentally retaining information, balancing many patients, tracking details, and handling interruptions to their thought processes are all cognitive aspects of ED work. The physicians we spoke to accepted this as part of what distinguished ED work from that of other specialties.

THE SOCIOLOGICAL PERSPECTIVE ON EXPERTISE

In the sociological perspective, expertise is seen as an attribute of the individual, with expertise being "born of and reified by immersion in professional groups"

(Treem, 2012, 25). Aspects associated with professionalism (e.g. titles, credentials, professional standards, and governing bodies) allow for a boundary to be established around who is considered an expert and who is not, allowing for clarity in who can claim expertise in different contexts. We saw some evidence of the sociological perspective in our interviews with ED physicians.

Several physicians mentioned that they relied on a variety of sources for information related to patient care, yet were careful in describing which of these sources were considered experts. When asked about who was a potential source of information for patient care, physicians responded with a wealth of sources, including nurses, NPs, PAs, medical students, specialists (e.g. hospitalists, radiologists, cardiologists), patients, patients' families, police officers, crisis workers, nursing home staff, emergency medical technicians (EMTs), and medical technicians. As one physician put it, "Everybody may be useful; you shouldn't exclude any of your possibilities [as a source of information]." However, when asked about who holds expertise, some physicians articulated expertise as a function of credentialing. For example, one physician said, "Residents, PAs, and NPs would not be considered as having expertise." When asked if physicians would ever consult with a NP or PA for advice, most physicians disagreed. One physician stated, "I think it is pretty rare." Another physician agreed, noting that "[PAs] assist us physicians. They do not operate without our oversight." However, one physician did mention, "It does happen every now and then. For example, we have one PA here who has a background in radiology, and her radiology skills are better than many of our docs." No physicians noted residents as a source of advice. As one physician put it, "Residents are students, so by definition they have no expertise." Another physician noted, "I can't say I would ever consult with a medical student, but that seems pretty self-evident." The credential as a mark of expertise seemed taken for granted, and rarely explicitly invoked. From our observations, the work routines of the NPs and PAs seemed almost indistinguishable from those of the physicians. NPs and PAs would take cases from the board, see patients, treat them, chart diagnoses, and write prescriptions, intermittently conferring with their supervising physicians, depending on the cases and the busyness of the department.

THE COMMUNICATION PERSPECTIVE ON EXPERTISE

In the communication perspective, expertise is viewed as "a product of social relationships as opposed to a property held by an individual through either cognitive skill or professional standing" (Treem, 2012, 25). Thus, in this perspective, expertise arises through the process of social interaction with others. We saw evidence of the communication perspective in our interviews with ED physicians.

Several ED physicians reported that expertise was the result of communicating with a variety of sources. Referring to communication with patients, one physician noted, "You have to effectively communicate with the patient in order to know what is wrong. Ninety percent of understanding what is wrong is the patient's history." Another physician noted the importance of communicating with family members by stating, "If there are family members present, I talk to them." Several physicians noted the importance of communicating with nurses. As one physician said, "It is helpful to have the nurses on board. They can tell the patient information about treatment. This keeps everyone on the same page." Another physician commented, "I'll talk to the nurse, to see if they have a different story or any different information [about the patient]."

When it came to communication between ED physicians and PAs, and ED physicians and specialists, one theme that arose was the importance of tailoring communication style. When asked about what constituted an effective interaction between PAs and ED physicians, one physician emphasized, "You need to have some kind of rapport. When the doctor or the PA is newer, you often need to have longer discussions, so you can get used to how each other works." In regards to communicating with specialists, one physician noted:

Communication can be difficult with specialists because you have to say it just right, and know the personality of who you are talking with. Some specialists want you to be very efficient. Others want you to be very formal with them.

When physicians were asked what would make their job easier, nearly all of them emphasized the importance of communication and teamwork in delivering patient care. One physician noted the importance of communication in the ED, both oral and written:

Having a great staff makes my job easier. When the nurses have everything ready, and the PAs have it all organized. A good EMR to quickly chart what you need to chart makes my job easier. Having people ready to answer the phone makes my job easier. Having a system there to support you makes my job easier.

Another physician noted the importance of teamwork:

I would say now what makes the job easier is your team. I think everyone would say that. The team you are working with makes a massive difference . . . If you are working with a great team, a team that carries their own weight, *knows how each other thinks*, your job is going to be easier. It doesn't even matter the patient load or the type of patients you have, so long as you have a good team. You could walk out of a shift having seen the most patients in history of the ED, and won't even be able feel like it if you have a good team working with you. (Emphasis added)

Thus while this physician emphasized team interaction, he also alluded to a shared cognitive process. When asked who is on this team, the physician responded, "The docs, the PAs, and the nurses. It's all of them."

The familiarity shared among the entire work group seemed to be important to the ED physicians as they considered how best to apply their (cognitive) expertise. Several of the physicians told us that ED physicians were a different kind of medical doctor, preferring urgency and variety in their work. There was tedium and cynicism associated with seeing patients who were perceived as only looking for drugs or attention, but also compassion for those whose suffering seemed more genuine. The ED physicians displayed a kind of pragmatism associated with *clearing the board*, or moving through the list of patients who needed attention. One physician told us, "We have one decision with two choices: admit them, or treat them and send them home. That's all there is to it." But with the pace of a board that was never empty, what we saw might be best described as a combination of cognitive and communicative expertise, where the frequently interrupted thought processes of the physicians (and NPs and PAs) were somehow ameliorated with smooth communicative teamwork.

Summary

Our observations of interaction among physicians and others in the doctors' room was meant (1) to address a gap in the literature on the nature of consultations in the EDs of community hospitals and (2) to develop a broader understanding of how expertise works in the built-up environment of the ED. We used a mixed method design to capture interactions over a composite weekend. We discovered that expert consultative interactions included many more roles than only physician-to-physician interactions would represent. Using semantic network analysis we found expertise about pain to be the most central term in the 421 interactions we coded both among physicians as well as among physicians and others. In addition, our second cluster of terms suggested that coordinative communication captured a substantial portion of interaction in the doctors' room. Thus, we learned that ED expertise primarily involves extensive coordination in the treatment of a variety of kinds of pain. Using interviews, we probed more closely the physicians' views of those interactions and found substantial evidence to support a cognitive view of expertise, with a communicative view also strongly supported. We found that the sociological or professional view was supported but in a largely unspoken and taken for granted fashion.

Our study, while an initial foray into cognitive, sociological, and communicative aspects of expertise as it is constituted in an ED, does have several shortcomings. Our observations were confined to the doctors' room, so we might have had a different set of data if we had been able to include consultative behavior beyond its walls. In addition, as we were unable to record the comments of specialists or hospitalists with whom physicians consulted by phone, in some instances we were only able to code half-conversations. And while we were pleased to have collected data over ninety hours and many interactions, we still have only a case study in a single hospital of one variety. Nevertheless, our study has developed and explored a new way of thinking about expertise, using a combination of semantic network and qualitative analysis.

The purely cognitive expertise perspective on ED work was supported both in our semantic analysis that included esoteric and anatomical references related to pain, the most common topic we observed, as well as our interviewees' comments. The second strongest cluster of terms however was clearly communicative. This suggests that specific cognitive habits do indeed compose expertise, but that communicative behaviors are also necessary for that expertise to be applied in the ED setting. Somewhat ironically, the interviews and our observations suggested that the intersection of the cognitive and communicative views of expertise in the ED setting occurred in terms of interruptions. Berg et al.'s (2013) study of interruptions in a British ED counted an average of 5.1 per hour, most of which occurred in face-to-face settings. Chisholm et al. (2000) observed an average of closer to ten interruptions per hour in three US ED settings. We surely observed many more, and our interviewees supported this observation. In fact, our interviewees told us that in the early stages of a career, learning the details of the wide variety of cases and their appropriate management was a challenge that each eventually surmounted, but the constant interruptions require a different, more social set of skills and habits. This raises the possibility of thinking about expertise not only in terms of the stock of knowledge necessary to begin the hypothetical diagnosis process in medicine (Patel and Ramoni, 1997) but also in the cognitive and social management strategies necessary to manage those interruptions and to coordinate care.

Advancing the Study of Expertise

CONTRIBUTION

Our study offers a glimpse of expertise enacted in an archetypal setting. Few scientific, philosophical, or technical endeavors require the stores of urgently applied knowledge possessed by physicians and their close co-workers whom we studied here. We were able to show that in enacting expertise these medical workers engaged in copious communicative coordination behaviors with others. While consultation with other physicians, notably hospitalists, accounted of a minority of their interactions, their expertise in those interactions was part of a negotiation on behalf of patients. In particular, as we noted, individual physicians were found to possess stocks of expert knowledge, but in order to apply that knowledge they were required to work with others. And the work with others was part and parcel of interruptions to their work flow. It was virtually never the case that their work was undertaken and completed without interruption. We also were able using semantic network analysis to identify the most common topic of the expertise, pain. While this is of course particular to this work setting, and is not necessarily the only focus of medical work more generally, the approach reminds us that expertise is ultimately about something that concerns experts and their clients. Finally, by using the cognitive, sociological, and professional framework, we were able to parse out the relationship between knowledge application, status, and interaction.

In this connection, our work relates to and may be compared with that in the chapter in this volume by Buzzanell and Long. While their case of engineers focuses on creative expertise in design and problem-solving, it nonetheless concerns expertise enacted in a community of professionals similar to the ED. For example, they too found negotiation as a central part of expertise enactment. Regarding the status of physicians in the ED, our subject stands in rather sharp contrast to the ideas developed in Kuhn and Rennstam (this volume). Nowhere in our observations did we ever find the authority of the physician questioned. In other words, while expertise and authority are usefully distinguished, as Kuhn and Rennstam argued, in the ED setting they are institutionally combined in the role of the physician. However, as we note next, developments in technological and administrative aspects of physicians' work may lead to struggles over epistemic claims of authority and expertise in medical work-experts.

FUTURE RESEARCH

Our study does raise several possibilities for future research on expertise in the medical setting. One aspect of interaction that might be construed as consultative behavior which was beyond the scope of the present project due to legal constraints regarding protected health information, but which should be included in future research on expertise and communication, is the interaction between physicians, NPs, and PAs and the electronic medical record system. Extant literature, our observations, and our interviewees told us that ED personnel spend copious amounts of time entering and retrieving data from the EHRs, more time than they spend in patient care. Tipping et al. (2010) documented that hospitalists spend 34 percent of their time using electronic medical records, but Hayrinen et al. (2008) reported that EHRs consumed no more time than other methods of documentation. However, the role of the

EHR in knowledge depositing and retrieval vis-à-vis expertise has not been explored.

A related aspect of ED expertise that warrants further investigation is its management by hospital administrations and other macro-level constraints. Everything that happens in the ED is constrained by private health plan and governmental reimbursement rules. Ultimately these funding and regulatory sources stipulate what counts as applicable expertise. These are related to the EHRs because the EHRs are simultaneously the sites of clinical documentation and the mechanisms of reimbursement. As we continue to understand medical expertise and its manifestations, the role of external funders and rule makers like insurance companies, Medicare, and public health standards should be taken into account.

In conclusion, this study provided a look at consultations in the ED of a community hospital, a valuable and largely unresearched setting for studying expertise. Despite the fact that individually housed cognitive skills and resources are central to the manifestation of medical expertise in EDs, coordinative communication shapes its actual application.

REFERENCES

Agnew, N. M., Ford, K. N., and Hayes, P. J. (1997). Expertise in Context: Personally Constructed, Socially Selected and Reality-Relevant? In P. J. Feltovich, K. M. Ford, and R. R. Hoffman (eds), *Expertise in Context: Human and Machine* (pp. 219–44). Menlo Park, CA: AAAI Press.

Apker, J. (2011). *Communication in Health Organizations*. London: Polity.

Apker, J., Mallak, L. A., and Gibson, S. C. (2007). Communicating in the "Gray Zone": Perceptions about Emergency Physician Hospitalist Handoffs and Patient Safety. *Academic Emergency Medicine*, 14, 884–94.

Apker, J., Mallak, L. A., Applegate, B. A., Gibson, S. C., Ham, J. J., Johnson, N., and Street, R. L., Jr. (2010). Exploring Emergency Physician-Hospitalist Handoff Interactions: Development and Use of the Handoff Communication Assessment. *Annals of Emergency Medicine*, 55, 161–70.

Berg, L. M., Källberg, A. S., Göransson, K. E., Östergren, J., Florin, J., and Ehrenberg, A. (2013). Interruptions in Emergency Department Work: An Observational and Interview Study. *BMJ Quality and Safety*, 22, 656–63.

Chisholm, C. D., Collison, E. K., Nelson, D. R., and Cordell, W. H. (2000). Emergency Department Workplace Interruptions: Are Emergency Physicians "Interrupt-Driven" and "Multitasking"? *Academic Emergency Medicine*, 7, 1239–43.

Clauset, A., Newman, M. E. J., and Moore, C. (2004). Finding Community Structure in Very Large Networks. *Physical Review E*, 70, 066111.

Côté, M. J., Smith, M. A., Eitel, D. R., and Akçali, E. (2013). Forecasting Emergency Department Arrivals: A Tutorial for Emergency Department Directors. *Hospital Topics*, 91, 9–19.

Creswell, J. W., and Clark, V. P. (2007). *Designing and Conducting Mixed Methods Research*. Thousand Oaks, CA: Sage.

Eisenberg, E., Baglia, J., and Pynes, J. (2006). Transforming Emergency Medicine through Narrative: Qualitative Action Research at a Community Hospital. *Health Communication*, 19, 197–208.

Eisenberg, E., Murphy, A., Sutcliffe, K., Wears, R., Schenkel, S., Perry, S., and Vanderhoef, M. (2005). Communication in Emergency Medicine: Implications for Patient Safety. *Communication Monographs*, 72, 390–413.

Goffman, E. (1959). *The Presentation of Self in Everyday Life*. New York: Doubleday.

Hayrinen, K., Saranto, K., and Nykanen, P. (2008). Definition, Structure, Content, Use and Impacts of Electronic Health Records: A Review of the Research Literature. *International Journal of Medical Informatics*, 77, 291–304.

Kessler, C., Kutka, B. M., and Badillo, C. (2012). Consultation in the Emergency Department: A Qualitative Analysis and Review. *Journal of Emergency Medicine*, 42, 704–11.

Kessler, C. S., Afshar, Y., Sardar, G., Yudkowsky, R., Ankel, F., and Schwartz, A. (2011). Prospective, Randomized, Controlled Study Demonstrating a Novel, Effective Model of Transfer of Care between Physicians: The 5 Cs of Consultation. *Academic Emergency Medicine*, 19, 968–74.

Kessler, C. S., Asrow, A., Beach, C., Cheung, D., Fairbanks, R. J., Lammers, J. C., Tibbles, C., Wears, R., Woods, R., and Schuur, J. D. (2013). The Taxonomy of Emergency Department Consultations: Results of an Expert Consensus Panel. *Annals of Emergency Medicine*, 61(2), 161–6.

Lammers, J. C., and Proulx, J. D. (2016). The Role of Professional Logic in Communication in Healthcare Organizations. In T. Harrison and E. Williams (eds), *Organizations, Health, and Communication* (pp. 13–30). New York: Routledge.

Lammers, J. C., Barbour, J., and Duggan, A. (2003). Organizational Forms of the Provision of Health Care: An Institutional Perspective. In T. Thompson, A. Dorsey, K. Miller, and R. Parrot (eds), *Handbook of Health Communication* (pp. 319–45). Mahwah, NJ: Lawrence Erlbaum Associates.

Leicht, K., and Fennell, M. (2001). *Professional Work: A Sociological Approach*. Oxford: Blackwell.

Maughan, B. C., Lei, L., and Cydulka, R. K. (2011). ED Handoffs: Observed Practices and Communication Errors. *American Journal of Emergency Medicine*, 29, 502–11.

Nokes, M., Lavoie, N., Roney, K., and Davis, K. (2011). Professional Consultations in Emergency Medicine. Unpublished manuscript, University of Illinois at Urbana-Champaign.

Patel, V. L., and Ramoni, M. F. (1997). Cognitive Models of Directional Inference in Expert Medical Reasoning. In P. J. Feltovich, K. M. Ford, and R. R. Hoffman (eds), *Expertise in Context: Human and Machine*. (pp. 67–99). Menlo Park, CA: American Association for Artificial Intelligence; Cambridge, MA: MIT Press.

Shem, S. (1978). *The House of God*. New York: Richard Marek Publishers.

Starr. P. (1982). *The Social Transformation of American Medicine*. New York: Basic.

Stein, E. W. (1997). A Look at Expertise from a Social Perspective. In P. J. Feltovich, K. M. Ford, and R.R. Hoffman (eds). *Expertise in Context: Human and Machine* (pp. 181–94). Menlo Park, CA: AAAI/MIT Press.

Sternberg, R. J. (1997). Cognitive Conceptions of Expertise. In P. J. Feltovich, K. M. Ford, and R. R. Hoffman (eds), *Expertise in Context: Human and Machine* (pp. 149–62). Menlo Park, CA: AAAI/MIT Press.

Teddlie, C., and Tashakkori, A. (2009). *Foundations of Mixed Methods Research: Integrating Quantitative and Qualitative Approaches in the Social and Behavioral Sciences.* Thousand Oaks, CA: Sage.

Tipping, M. D., Forth, V. E., O'Leary, K. J., Malkenson, D. M., Magill, D. B., Englert, K., and Williams, M. V. (2010). Where Did the Day Go? A Time-Motion Study of Hospitalists. *Journal of Hospital Medicine*, 5, 323–8.

Treem, J. W. (2012). Communicating Expertise: Knowledge Performances in Professional Service Firms. *Communication Monographs*, 79, 23–4.

9 Learning Expertise in Engineering Design Work

Creating Space for Experts to Make Mistakes

PATRICE M. BUZZANELL AND ZIYU LONG

In engineering space, the fundamental means by which work is accomplished is design, often in team contexts. As Radcliffe (2014, 8; see also Atman et al., 2014; Cross, 1982) asserts:

Design is a defining characteristic of engineering. Engineering design is a recursive activity that results in artifacts—physical or virtual.... Design involves both the use of existing information and knowledge and the generation of new information and knowledge. For engineers, designing is both a creative and a disciplined process. Design requires leaps of the imagination, intuitive insight, the synthesis of different ideas and empathy with people who come in contact with any new product, system or process that is designed. Yet it also demands careful attention to detail, knowledge of scientific principles, the ability to model complex systems, judgment, a good understanding of how things can be made, the ability to work under severe time constraints and with incomplete information and limited resources.

As Radcliffe notes, design processes involve the utilization of existing knowledge and the generation of new knowledge. Yet, how designers make sense of what knowledge is needed in different design phases and in moment-to-moment design team interactions is not well understood. In particular, designers may appreciate, in general, the specialized knowledge that team members with different disciplinary backgrounds such as mechanical engineering or software development should bring to the project without being able to anticipate the depth and breadth of members' learning and ability to utilize their knowledge.

In the constitution of expertise in design teamwork, members may struggle with multiple processes. These struggles include: how expertise grows and becomes valued in everyday design decisions involving interactions with diverse stakeholders; how expertise shifts as members negotiate the ways that they pursue viable, feasible, and safe designs; how expertise expands through the creation and handling of ambiguities inherent in design review and critique; and how expertise layers in team recognition of, responsiveness to, and reflection on ethical dilemmas (Buzzanell, 2014; Cardella et al., 2014; Zhu et al., 2014). Because expertise is constituted communicatively and shifts throughout design processes, these struggles to identify, value, and integrate expertise are inherent in design itself. These struggles are embedded in the ways designers learn how to work within existing and needed novel information and knowledge structures, or within "disciplined" and "creative" processes, as Radcliffe calls these fundamental tensions.

In this chapter, we describe and analyze how individuals and teams engage with various stakeholders to create capacities for constructing expertise throughout design phases. Constituting expertise is a challenge. This process requires that designers embrace ambiguities and politics involved in problem defining and solving iterations:

Perhaps the stakeholders' needs are not defined as problems per se or perhaps they are able to articulate only surface concerns and not the fundamental issues with which they struggle on a daily basis. Perhaps, too, the power dynamics involved in the ongoing construction of lived experiences as problematic are so deeply embedded in their workplaces, home lives, communities, and/or other contexts that sorting through, explicating, articulating, and focusing attention on the problem may in itself be the primary effort in design.

Just as "problem" can be problematized, so too can the concept of "users" [in design] be scrutinized so that assumptions can surface and be discussed. In many situations, the users might be simply those for whom designs are created and delivered. However, there are many others who are implicated in design solutions and who might appropriate the solutions for practices and reasons never even considered by the originators of the solutions. In these cases, solutions might be ironically, inadvertently, ingeniously, and resistively appropriated. They might be modified without credit to the originators and to intellectual property rights. They might not actually solve the problem or might do so in such a short-term sense that new design processes are activated immediately to handle the "real" problems. Furthermore, the proposed and actual solutions might not be sustainable or might prompt unethical consequences that are difficult to foresee, such as in the case of intercultural ethics. (Buzzanell, 2014, 319)

Given the fluid nature of design, how expertise is constructed, reconfigured, and "fixed"/unfixed along the way means that individuals and teams use and/ or develop different technical and social knowledge. This ongoing process of "learning as we go along" upends conventional technical design considerations where one can be expert by operating within disciplinary knowledge and project "templates." Instead, expertise is constituted through interaction. In interaction, participants develop deep understandings of self and potential users' lives in specific socio-political-economic and cultural contexts. In interaction, different capacities for individual and team contributions to design processes and outcomes emerge in technical and social arenas.

The questions, then, are why and how expertise becomes constituted in particular ways at specific times and in certain contexts, such as multidisciplinary engineering design teams. We examine these issues by proposing (a) frames/resources for expertise processes and then delving into (b) the struggles in team-based engineering expertise processes, and (c) discussion of theoretical contributions and implications that can drive the analysis of expertise in engineering and other design processes.

Frames/Resources for Expertise Processes

In this section, we discuss our model for the frames/resources for expertise processes and incorporate the case of a global engineering design team in the Engineering Projects in Community Service (EPICS) called Transforming Lives, Building Global Communities (TLBGC).

There are three aspects to, and sources in, understanding expertise development: (a) how expertise is constituted communicatively in project-based design work (drawing from organizational communication); (b) how texts enable individuals and teams to develop expertise and align themselves into professional norms (drawing from professional communication); and (c) how design schemata are enacted, enlarged, and enriched in particular situations, with objects, and by whom (drawing from engineering education). Although presented as distinct areas, these components of Figure 9.1—constitutive, textual, and design—come together in the engineering community construction of expertise.

The three frames share overlapping boundaries and are interconnected with one another. All three frames highlight the role of communication in facilitating/constraining the emergence, development, and learning of expertise.

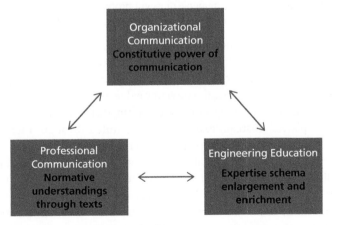

Figure 9.1 Frames/Resources for Expertise Processes

Rather than looking at expertise as resources, skills, and/or knowledge that resides in individuals, the three frames look at expertise as a collective communicative phenomenon that is fluid, enacted in local interactions, and situated in the broader contexts.

Each frame focuses on specific aspects of expertise. The organizational communication frame explores how expertise is constituted in talk-in-interactions. It frames expertise as collective actions/processes constituted in interactions. Guided by professional communication, the second frame illuminates how expertise is both bounded institutionally and unbounded. Expertise is codified through professional texts that regulate and discipline individuals and professional communities, but that also have fluid parameters that are negotiable (i.e. what it means to be an expert, what counts as expertise in specific contexts). The third frame draws from engineering education scholarship to explicate the continual co-learning and adaptation processes that occur in ambiguous real-world design processes. Taken together, these three frames provide more holistic understandings of expertise from its emergence and construction (i.e. constitutive power of communication), its professionalization/legitimation (i.e. normative understandings through texts), to its transfer and adaptation (i.e. expertise schema enlargement and enrichment).

COMMUNICATIVE CONSTITUTION OF EXPERTISE IN PROJECT-BASED WORK

Organizational communication scholars view organizing and expertise as processes through which organizations and expertise are constituted and performed in particular contexts (see Putnam and Boys, 2006; Putnam and Nicotera, 2009; Robichaud and Cooren, 2012). Kuhn (2012) argues that a constitutive approach takes communication seriously by "portraying communication as constitutive of social realities" with a focus on the production of meanings in social action; "seeing organizations not as containers for communication, not merely settings inside of which communication occurs, but intrinsically *as* communication;" "staying in the realm of communicational events both conceptually and methodologically" with mindfulness that communication is always contextually, politically, and materially situated; and "eradicating simplistic assumptions about meaning convergence as the *telos* of communication" (thus, embracing contradiction, ambiguity, and difference as order and disorder co-influence each other; Kuhn, 2012, 548–50). A constitutive approach to organizing and expertise means that expertise does not reside in the individual. Instead, expertise resides in complex collaborative and interactive practices to construct knowledgeability, meaning, and action in situ and in broader contexts that then also shape the communities that engage in such practices (Kuhn, 2014; Kuhn and Rennstam, this volume).

If generation of expertise is an interactive phenomenon, then it also is relational, with the qualities of and tensions defining the relationship (e.g. trust, care, ethics, paradoxes) essential to understanding expertise and knowledge processes. Because expertise is not individually but communally determined, regulated, and constructed, the discourses and materialities that constitute expertise through practice also are constructed in similar ways.[1]

As such, expertise is a political process[2] in which communities have vested interest and for which there often are unknown needs for generation of expertise within such collectivities. For instance, the TLBGC team is located at Purdue University[3] but focused on sustainable water-energy-education in collaboration with members of two rural villages in Ghana. To engage in this global engineering project, the team sought to interface productively with administrators and faculty of the Kwame Nkrumah University of Science and Technology (KNUST) as well as student members of the National Society of Black Engineers (NSBE). Team members sought to create linkages that were collaborative and dialogic. These linkages involved cultural information exchange and ongoing question asking to check assumptions and learn more about the contexts in which team members were engaging in design.

---

[1] Although not taking a constitutive and embodied approach, Loyd et al. (2010) noted that expertise recognition, sharing, and inclusion into decision-making was fostered by perceived congruence between experts' (powerful/powerless) speech style and status, with liking mediating the relationship. Such findings offer possibilities for noting the conditions in which expertise could be constituted interactively.

[2] The phrase political process can mean many different things without all referring to constitutive dynamics of power, privilege, difference, and control-resistance. Using different theoretical and methodological approaches, the following studies provide insight into the generation, recognition, and politicization of expertise. First, Aime et al. (2014) conceptualized power structures in groups as fluid power heterarchies whereby team members' competencies become aligned with situational demands and (il)legitimate interpersonal power. Second, Baumann and Bonner (2013) raised possibilities, based on findings of inconsistencies between results for rated expertise and for behavior, that members' behaviors toward experts may change more quickly than their perceptions do. However, when group members are aware of expertise, their discussions tend to incorporate the use of unique information and weigh this expert information more heavily in decisions. Finally, Tajeddin et al. (2012) found that decision-making shifts with individuals' recognition of a team member's expertise and then with the teams' recognition of expertise in group decision-making. In other words, awareness of colleagues' expertise emerges when group members know the person's performance feedback results and then recognize its utility at the group level for decision-making, especially when the expert is perceived to have greater knowledge than other group members.

[3] EPICS is a vertically integrated, project-based service-learning course that is multidisciplinary, multi-semester, and design focused. These different aspects as well as the mission of the individual teams have profound implications for how expertise is constituted. Stakeholders include project partners, i.e. people who represent or are actual users of designs. Because EPICS designs are start-to-finish processes, EPICS develops long-term partnerships and team transition procedures. EPICS team members learn technical and design processes in an environment that often is ambiguous and challenges their abilities to collaborate with and learn from others and from their mistakes (for advantages of this project-based learning, see Kolmos and deGraaff, 2014). We draw upon the TLBGC case *not* to represent it as an ideal experience but to describe some unique opportunities and challenges when projects are real-world, open-ended, and sometimes ill-structured.

These linkages were driven by sustained efforts not to privilege any one stakeholder over others in the design process, and worked toward creating sustainable solutions built upon local customs, relationships, materials, and knowledge.

Although the problem definition phase—identification of the problem, specifications, and other factors—seemed relatively straightforward at first, it became increasingly complicated and ambiguous. For instance, the local project approval processes displayed political dynamics between and among municipality and village chiefs, WASA (water and sanitation) committees, and other leaders and decision-making groups. Some of the most significant needs that emerged during these engineering design partnerships involved challenges to and development of EPICS and KNUST team members' intercultural communication, understandings of ethics, and expanded technical knowledge and skills. Through virtual interactions and document sharing via internet and social media affordances, team members collaborated to focus on their partnerships with each other and with the Ghanaian villagers.

In these partnerships, the issues became more than simply fixing water pumps, testing the quality of surface and well water, or figuring out more sanitary systems for human waste disposal. Indeed, team members struggled to understand how and why village practices became routinized. For instance, one villager kept the key to the water pump and only unlocked the pump at certain times of the day and for limited numbers of villagers. Because of inadequate amounts of pumped water, other villagers tended to cook with nearby surface water through which people and animals walked. Surface water dried up for months at a time. Villagers retained their open air trench for human waste disposal despite its propensity to overflow during rainy seasons and despite health hazards. To team members from the West, the use of the open air trench seemed nonsensical at first since villagers had a latrine built near the empty school buildings away from the center of the village. To pursue their engineering designs, team members needed to understand the everyday political dynamics, traditional status, and privilege in the village, and where social interactions among groups of villagers, such as women, occurred in village life. Developing these understandings meant that diverse ways of knowing (e.g. cultural, technical, social scientific) and capturing information came together as emergent expertise in sometimes surprising ways.

As the NSBE-KNUST team partners conducted research in the two rural Ghanaian villages, both the EPICS and NSBE-KNUST team members questioned the knowledge that they had been taught as they tried to make meaning out of human behaviors and a context that was far removed from their everyday student lives and upbringing. They also needed to make sense of and work with the existing resources at hand. "Quality," "safety," and optimal designs did not always equate with testable and sustainable prototypes. Team members' identities as engineers did not reside solely in disciplinary knowledge aligned with their specialties but became infused with localized, including indigenous, engineering and design characteristics. What was new information was compared with what was known from diverse knowledge bases. This fusion of emergent and received knowledge became constituted into expertise in the moment. Those who demonstrated the ability to visibly construct and use this expertise were acknowledged as experts, albeit temporarily given the changing nature of the design processes (for attributions of expertise, see Treem, 2012). Throughout, different forms, domains, levels, and sources of expertise were contested, constrained, and acknowledged or adapted. Expertise, then, became fluid and contextual; who and what was considered to be expert at any given time became ongoing challenges and opportunities. Moreover, expertise incorporated ethical considerations because of the need to ascertain short- and long-term consequences including fundamental changes in village community structure based on design implementations (e.g. see Ting-Toomey, 2010).

Thus, in the learning context as well as project-based teams more generally, there is a very real tension among people's knowledge, technical development, and ethical responses as well as the processes to negotiate these considerations. For instance, in project-based work, engineering educators want students who are engaged in engineering design to learn new things but also apply that which they know well. If they do not understand the depth and reach of their knowledge and overstretch themselves (even though the educational environment should be one in which one learns how to handle mistakes and lessen design fixation[4]), then their designs, especially prototypes and final solutions, might be unsafe. They also need to figure out degrees of safety and what safety means in particular contexts, since safety is not an all-or-nothing state. Safety is a huge occupational priority for engineers, as they negotiate tensions and/or contradictions among ethical decision-making and reasoning as well as professional ethical codes, professional norms, design principles (e.g. human-centered design or HCD), and learning. Through this first frame, we see how expertise relevant to particular contexts is constituted communicatively

---

[4] Design fixation is a "process by which engineering design team members become committed to a particular design solution to the extent that they may no longer listen to and process information that contradicts or expands their original design" (Buzzanell and Zoltowski, 2014, 165). Although temporary closure is essential to move design forward, fixation lessens the knowledge creation necessary to admit new data about particular design aspects and about how the design comes together as an evolving system. Teams that have experience in design processes often are able to sustain the ambiguities, contradictions, tensions, and ongoing information processing that is needed for quality designs (for novice and expert designers, see Crismond and Adams, 2012; Cross, 1982). Treem (2012) found that team members perceived as experts engaged in patterns of communication that visibly demonstrate their abilities to synthesize and use large amounts of information, go beyond and create new work procedures, and legitimize particular work practices. Attributions of expertise are particularly important in ambiguous situations.

in an ongoing, interactive process of becoming, stabilizing, and changing as teams do design.

PROFESSIONAL DEVELOPMENT OF NORMATIVE UNDERSTANDINGS AND EXPERTISE THROUGH TEXTS

Bhatia (2010) notes that professional communication seems to focus on the output or text but actually involves sophisticated interactions among the text, professional community, and particular context in which professional communication occurs:

> The interesting thing about professional communication is that what you see as the ultimate product is the text, which is made possible by a combination of very complex and dynamic range of resources, including those that in linguistic and earlier discourse analytical literature are viewed as lexico-grammatical, rhetorical, and organizational. Other contributors to the construction of professional artefacts are conventions of the genre in question, the understanding of the professional practice in which the genre is embedded, and the culture of the profession, discipline, or institution, which constrains the use of textual resources for a particular discursive practice. In other words, any instance of professional communication simultaneously operates and can be analysed at these four levels, as text, as representation of genre, as realization of professional practice, and as expectation of professional culture. (p. 33)

Drawn from the field of professional communication, particularly genre studies, expertise is evident and constructed in texts through an actor-institution or profession interplay (for professional communication, see Bhatia and Bremner, 2014; Kong, 2014). Through texts, individuals develop expertise in what to say and how to say things, which continues to develop over time into interpretive frames by which experiences and people are viewed and valued (Carr, 2010). These texts can be singular, such as legal briefs, or multimodal, such as a combination of documents, websites, Tweets, blogs, and other texts. For instance, TLBGC students documented their steps, contacts and sources, analysis of raw materials, and other details in their design notebooks. These notebooks not only functioned as a repository of ideas but also as a record of and agent in student learning. Because team membership transitioned in part from semester to semester, these design notebooks enabled knowledge and process transfer over the years in which teams and projects were in operation (akin to transactive memory systems, see Ren and Argote, 2011; design notebooks also functioned as intellectual property documentation).

Documentation was kept in sites such as Dropbox, google.docs, and secure portions of websites, as well as in paper notebooks and 3-D prototypes. Team members used Skype, videorecordings of village life, audiorecordings translated with explanations of context and linguistic choices, diagrams of clay-baked village homes and public areas, and other materialities in design processes.[5] However, it is the practices and logics that create and sustain professions and professionals that are embedded within and manifest through the texts that align with expertise. Moreover, texts and templates within which professional discourse makes sense, becomes persuasive, and enables project documentation can transcend occupational boundaries, such as in the case of PowerPoint for project documentation in business consulting (Shoeneborn, 2013).

Texts are contested sites. A community's disregard for, or elevation of, certain texts as essential to the training and visible competence of professionals can have far-ranging consequences. Texts inform professionals about daily, weekly, monthly, and cyclical or seasonal practices. Texts embed logics, arguments, and linguistic choices that are understandable and establish rational boundaries for work. Moreover, professional identities are formed and legitimized through professionals' text development, including reports, websites, accreditation documents, templates, and other texts. As Buzzanell et al. (2014, 208) note about professional communication, "Power and agency are significant considerations insofar as accreditations, certifications, policies, reports, and other texts have profound consequences. Inattention to political dynamics, cultural underpinnings, and document specifications can affect professions' (de)legitimization and (de)institutionalization." Moreover, when a communication constitutive perspective is used to examine genres of organizational and professional communication, such as PowerPoint, there may be a "clash between the constitutive affordances of professional and of organizational communication" (Shoeneborn, 2013, 1777) that may be "resolved through an asymmetric emphasis on the presentation function, rather than on the documentation function" (p. 1795).

From a professional communication perspective, expertise in the design setting is both bounded and unbounded. Professional communication is *bounded*, insofar as boundary-making processes creates environments for inclusion–exclusion, ways of thinking and doing that provide the basis for negotiating expertise. These boundary-making processes can be observed in the design conversations in which designers frame the design problems and articulate solutions. Lawson (2004) found that these conversations are full of references to specialized areas of knowledge, a pool of past experiences related to the problem at hand, and a repertoire of possible ways of problem-solving. Professional and expertise boundaries also become salient in designers' use of tools. For instance, engineering designers can rely heavily on simulations of

---

[5] The process of contextualized transcription and translation was similar to that described by Kisselburgh et al. (2010) in which researchers literally sat with translators to capture the nuances and rationales for linguistic choices, the background on media reports and educational systems, and family and national cultural knowledge. These contextual details were embedded in interview documents.

their design solutions or certain design methods, notations in the design notebook, and specialized software. These materials can enhance the accuracy of their design, test and select the prototypes, predict results, and proactively address the potential failures before the design solution is finalized (Guindon, 1990). These texts and practices constitute the person's professional identity and set expertise boundaries.

Likewise, expertise also can be *unbounded* as professionals/designers engage in constant searching for information and disciplinary knowledge. This search enables ongoing development and attributions of expertise (see Treem, 2012). It also helps designers determine what is known and unknown, and what might be valuable and needed for the design. In addition to this ongoing searching and interpreting to form threads of expertise in professional design work, the development of expertise is embedded within and re-institutionalizing or legitimizing professional communities.

In HCD settings, it is not uncommon to see an integration/breach of domain boundaries of expertise and professional routines. As design problems are often "ill-structured" (i.e. the problems are highly ambiguous and complex), designers engage in iterative processes of ideation-prototyping-analysis-evolution (Dorst, 2011). For example, in the TLBGC project about clean water, different threads of expertise were constituted to build a satisfying design as students and faculty advisors changed their plans of actions and worked with local community members. These threads included civil and mechanical engineering, chemistry, survey design, and interview techniques, especially knowing to whom it is appropriate to address talk and in what conversational order, and other knowledge bases. At the same time, group members had knowledge beyond their professional domain that could become essential in the design process. For example, one of the civil engineering students was very knowledgeable about the local culture/language and his language expertise helped the design team to build trust and gain insights that were essential to design processes. Team members' backgrounds and access to experts became layered and evaluated according to relevance and implications throughout as they work as engineering/design professionals. These experts shared knowledge about seasonal, gendered, dietary, and other West African customs, as well as about tribal political dynamics and local community-building.

DESIGN EXPERTISE FORMATION AND ENRICHMENT

In this section, we examine how engineering education views expertise development in particular situations, with objects, and by whom, drawing from engineering education research and instructional practices. Although there are instances where who/what counts as an expert or expertise in engineering professions provides valuable insights, how engineering students learn to cultivate expertise collaboratively in design itself and project-based teams is important for the projects themselves and for engineers' career development. For instance, when one of the EPICS teams had project groups developing software for girls, they invited women and men familiar with 3-D modeling and game development to their weekly team meetings for breakfast and conversation with the whole team. Not only were students developing technical skills but they also developed their problem-solving, question asking, and related competencies (for description of this ABIWT team, see Buzzanell et al., 2008, esp. 125–6).

As mentioned earlier, design can be simplified into problem-setting and problem-solving processes in engineering and other disciplines and work practices. For design thinking, the following key components have been identified that attest to the complexity of design processes, practices, and knowledge:

Thinking at the scale of systems, making estimates, conducting experiments, managing ambiguity through convergent-divergent inquiry, decision making under uncertainty, communicating in diverse languages (text, graphics, shape grammars, and mathematical models), and functioning as a part of an interdisciplinary team with teammates from demographically diverse backgrounds. (Atman et al., 2014, 205)

Design thinking becomes accomplished in locale-specific environments. For Johri et al. (2014), situative perspectives on learning emphasize knowledge as not inherent in the individual or in cognitive storage but as accomplished in doing, by interactions within specific social contexts through participation in meaningful action. Thus engineering offers a space of action. Whereas application of knowledge learned in past encounters can inform novel situations, they note that how knowledge is used in novel situations "remains a critical challenge for the situative perspective" (p. 49). In this view, activity is "partially structured through the use of material and semiotic resources that have evolved within and are associated with particular practices" in context (p. 50). The constitutive role comes into play as problem-setting and problem-solving—the essence of design—arises in the course of situated activity and activity's meanings. This means that engineering is collaborative, dependent on materialities such as artifacts, and engages in practice as a community—practices that transcend engineering's situated social processes (see Bucciarelli, 1988, 1994) and material processes (see Henderson, 1991) and focus on meaning-making, cross-boundary contexts, and interdisciplinary work for knowledge creation (Barley et al., 2012). Moreover, this also means that expertise is community generated and, in the process, is challenged, with different forms and sources of expertise being contested, constrained, and acknowledged or adapted.

Specifically, in project-based design work in learning and in employment settings, expertise is formed through interaction but there are multiple explicit and implicit forms and levels of expertise. There is expertise of a knowledge domain, design expertise, moral expertise, cultural knowledge, and so on. Levels of expertise may vary on a continuum from novice to expert. Different expertise can be embodied in individuals, technologies, and standards of practice in complex ways. How different expertise is negotiated and determined to be of value in problem definition and setting requires a situative perspective but also the organizational and professional communication framings that can surface such tensions and opportunities.

For instance, novice designers may find it difficult to move from technical design considerations and schemata where educational and practical experiences in their disciplines enable them to feel as though they are experts to HCD. Ideally, in HCD, designers develop deep and rich understandings of potential users' mundane lives, including their routines, beliefs, values, interests, needs, senses of themselves in their material worlds, and other aspects. These aspects are situated in very specific socio-political-economic and cultural contexts. They affect every decision that team members make and how they make sense of and constitute expertise to design appropriately. In the empathic dimensions of HCD, cultural humility (also known as critical empathy) and awareness that ethics is implicated in every decision are interwoven with technical design (Kenny Feister et al., 2014). Cultural humility or critical empathy is an approach to design that admits that designers can never truly know or fully understand others' lives (see Buzzanell, 2011, 2014; Groll, 2013; Remke, 2006; Tervalon and Murray-Garcia, 1998). As a result, designers collaborate with potential users and defer judgment about usability to user expertise (see experience-based expertise, see Collins and Evans, 2002).

As one example, TLBGC had an advisory board that included Ghanaian women activists for girls' rights, anthropologists, civil engineers, past presidents and current members of NSBE, communication specialists, and others. Based on feedback from the TLBGC advisory board, the team expanded the needs assessment and community survey from working primarily toward community entry deadlines to building relationships with the villages and with KNUST student and faculty partners. This feedback was obtained during mid-semester and end-of-semester design reviews when EPICS team members and their instructors realized that no one knew answers to certain questions. These questions included: whether the land on which the village water pump or surface water area were was communal property, how a particular man became the keeper of the water pump key, who dug the original well and why in that particular spot and depth, and how the men and women in the village conducted their daily, weekly, and seasonal work. Based on feedback, students changed design procedures and returned to specifications and information-gathering phases. As a result, the NSBE-KNUST team partners increased observations and videotapes for sharing with the EPICS team partners. They increased skyped debriefing sessions when the internet broadband service was available and sustainable.

The HCD process ideally creates space for team members to make, deconstruct, and reframe mistakes into opportunities to rethink and reconstitute the information and expertise needed for design that meets contextual challenges. Moreover, in the TLBGC case, design was complicated by historical and national roots of particular engineering disciplines (see Lucena et al., 2008) and work practices compounded by racial, ethnic, gendered, and global relationships in which members routinely questioned themselves about communicating in ways that exposed postcolonial underpinnings. In these ways, the TLBGC team partnered with NSBE-KNUST and strove to collaboratively design rather than assuming that US engineers were more knowledgeable or would come in and "fix" a problem with materials that were not easily obtained in the area. The bumpy and messy ways in which so many different partnerships, interests, and systems were negotiated into design expertise became key learnings for the team members and for the global engineering partnerships at the different institutions.

In sum, designers constantly create and undo boundaries for action and incorporate expertise in a fluid and sometimes surprising fashion. Expertise in HCD processes is constantly being formed and enriched.

Struggles in Team-Based Engineering Expertise Processes

Expertise is important in design settings because it suggests that the individual has the skills, knowledge, experience, and approaches to ambiguities necessary to solve problems effectively and properly (e.g. following safety procedures, local and national regulations, and standards or professional codes of ethics). As noted earlier, expertise does not only reside in the individual who is perceived as expert, but also within nested communities that gain more or less importance as designs shift and progress. These communities include different professionals as well as potential users and other stakeholders in the design process and outcomes.

Because of the complex, political, and fluid nature of expertise constructions, we describe some struggles that are common in constituting expertise in team-based engineering design processes. These struggles begin with (a) simplistic criteria for attributing expertise in initial design phases (e.g. based on engineering disciplinary background and prior work or co-op experiences). Struggles also include (b) over-reliance on "experts" with particular information and knowledge that may or may not be transferrable to the context in which designers are working. Moreover, there may be: (c) ineffective sharing of information and knowledge with political dynamics exacerbating difficulties in information flow; (d) difficulties with suspending disbelief, sustaining dialectics of creativity and discipline; (e) demystification of human dynamics regarding collaboration, negotiation, ethical considerations, and engagement so that dialogue might not be derailed; (f) knowing when to focus more on technical and social/human and/or space between; (g) engaging in cultural humility and the everyday ethical negotiations when collaborating for HCD; and (h) shifting amidst learning and performing, and working with different ways of feeling, knowing, valuing, and being while trying to avoid design fixation throughout.

Some of these struggles are due to dichotomous understandings of expert-novice and to ideas that expertise comes from without rather than being constituted through interaction. For instance, perceived relative distributions in expertise among those who work closely together can disrupt or support collaborative environments, according to Black et al.'s (2004) study of physicians and CT technicians. In these cases, patterns of professional dominance can occur. In these patterns, professionals may avoid individuals with lesser professional status even when these individuals have greater technological expertise but do not convey their learning and results in face-saving ways for the physicians. In this case, designations of expert and expertise might engender destructive processes. Thus, a reframing of expertise dichotomies (e.g. expert vs. novice, of expertise vs. lack of expertise) into multiple, shifting, and intersecting dialectics might prompt different questions and insights into expertise processes and the power to identity design team struggles in particular contexts. In the interactive constitution of collaborative work environments, these contexts include new technologies, occupational status of members, and individuals' abilities to interact effectively with others. These struggles cut across the three frames or resources for expertise.

Advancing the Study of Expertise

This chapter argues for a three-pronged framing to understanding expertise in engineering design processes. In doing so, its contributions lie in the intersections of constitutive, professional text-centered, and contextual (engineering) design logics and accomplishment.

THEORETICAL CONTRIBUTIONS

We argue that expertise is continuously (re)constituted through everyday talk-in-interaction, engagements with texts, and designerly ways of knowing

(Cross, 1982) and being (Tenenberg et al., 2014) in which designers embrace the thinking, values, and embodiment of design. Within project-based design, students learn not only how to utilize and deepen their disciplinary knowledge, but they also learn what it means to become, and be perceived as, an expert and how being an expert changes over time and in different contexts. Through their project-based work, they respond to and create ambiguities, ethical challenges, stakeholder partnerships, and empathic understandings of users to do design. They and their team advisors model how expertise evolves through the three prongs in our design expertise model, not only in EPICS but also throughout their careers. Thus, it is through teaching and learning negotiations, involving human and nonhuman agents such as design prototypes, that the long-term processes of professionalization take place for designers (see Cardella et al., 2014).

As we have discussed earlier with regard to the three frames or resource, taking a constitutive lens means that studying naturally occurring talk using a talk-in-interaction approach is needed to understand expertise. In this way, the discursive and material contributions to the interactional setting of expertise development in an engineering project-based design context can be highlighted. Such analyses are needed to understand the dynamics of expertise. These dynamics include asymmetrical power processes and practices that align with competitive and collaborative tensions between the different individuals and the communities that they represent. These tensions are manifest in the structures of expertise sharing and in members' identity negotiations. Whereas a traditional notion of expertise development might involve deference to the "expert" by a neophyte, given the nature of project-based team work, who is expert at any given time is an ongoing struggle.

When taking a professional communication lens, of importance to further research is the documentation of interactive practices in which team members engage with each other to support project-based goals while also understanding the depths and limits of the different forms of expertise, including technical, cultural, relational, and so on, that they bring to bear on the problem. The professional communication lens then highlights the bounded and unbounded nature of the enactment of expertise in design processes. On one hand, the enactment of expertise can be bounded by the texts, practices, norms, and culture of the profession and the institution. On the other hand, the enactment of expertise is unbounded as the design situation is in constant change in engineering project-based design work, rendering new frames to understand the issue, sets of questions, specifications of the prototypes, and new courses of plans that require different domains, levels, and threads of expertise.

The third lens on expertise formation and development highlights the constant interactions and sense-making that are involved in the constitution of expertise in project-based teamwork settings. It provides useful insights to investigate how individuals or group develop expertise, and continue to learn to avoid design fixation, accomplish goals, and establish professional identity. We suggest that cultural humility and critical empathy are important processes as design teams search, build, and enrich their schemata to co-constitute expertise needed at specific design episodes or phases with the local community.

As a whole, the theoretical and pragmatic contributions of this work center on the constitution of expertise as interactive and generative processes embedded within, changing, and re-institutionalizing the professional and potential user communities with which project-based team members identify. The implications for future research and practice range from greater understandings of identity and identifications as well as knowledge, face, and cultural context. With regard to the latter, ethnic, cultural, gendered, classed, and linguistic diversities brought to bear on project-based and decision-making teamwork by members might display different interactive structures and linguistic features (e.g. Du-Babcock, 2006), as might the strategic goals of the organization for which project members work or participate. Furthermore, there are implications for career processes and outcomes since different forms and performances of expertise can impact competence assessments, assignments, and promotions.

ANALYSIS OF EXPERTISE IN ENGINEERING

In this section, we pose some implications of the framework we present for expertise and knowledge, coupled with suggestions for methods that could pull forward a research agenda to explore new possibilities.

First, we propose to incorporate ethics and cultural humility stances as a means of integrating fully the technical and social into the expertise repertoire of HCD (see Groll, 2013). Design is essential in life as "an activity of transforming something given into something preferred through intervention and invention" (Aakhus, 2007, 112). Thus, the implications of integrating humility, empathy, and ethical reasoning into design expertise go beyond simply informing project-based engineering work, but also enriching everyday design understandings of professional and personal interactions and community engagement. To pursue this line of research, we recommend that participant observation, interviews, focus groups be conducted.

Second, expertise is generative. It is constantly being formed, refined, assembled, negotiated, deconstructed, and valued. To fully understand the emergence and evolution of expertise as a community of practice, we recommend a longitudinal approach that incorporates observations with videotaping, and analyses of reflections. Depending on the data, research can utilize techniques such as constructivist constant comparative analyses

from grounded theory that incorporates flexibility and researchers' position-
alities for themes, critical moments or events (Charmaz, 2000), and textual
analysis for Gantt charts.

Third, communication research can investigate more fully the role of feedback,
ambiguity, contradiction, and discursive-material interplays in design work. We
focus particularly on the role of design feedback and critiques in developing
novice designers' professionalism and expertise because feedback and critique
operate at the center of learning and collaboration in teams, the context in which
much design and engineering work is accomplished (see Adams and Siddiqui,
2016). Videotaping with critical discourse analyses and think-aloud protocol
methods can be useful to capture such processes. Furthermore, phenomeno-
graphic interviews and analyses would be beneficial because phenomenography
examines how individuals as members of particular occupational communities
or other collectivities understand and experience phenomena for the purpose of
understanding the variations in experiences with a particular phenomenon.
According to Marton and Booth (1997), the unit of analysis for phenomeno-
graphic research is the participant's way of experiencing something and the goal
is to form a hierarchy of variations in experiences with the phenomenon
(Marton, 1988; Marton and Booth, 1997; Zoltowski et al., 2012).

Finally, we encourage researchers using quantitative and qualitative analytic
methods "to be self-reflexive about the ways in which their textual practices
construct knowledge, researchers' subjectivities, and the subjectivities of participants" (Putnam and Mumby, 2014, 6).

Conclusion

To sum up, this chapter has discussed expertise in engineering space both by
providing an extended example of a global multidisciplinary engineering design
team and by focusing on project-based design as practice in both learning and
employment contexts. Drawing from organizational communication, professional communication, and HCD, we provided a three-pronged framing of
expertise that links the communicative constitution of expertise in project-
based work, professional development of normative understandings and expertise through texts, and engineering design expertise formation and enrichment.
This framing enables scholars and practitioners to converse about the dialogic
tensions and possibilities that surface when attention is centered on particular
discourses and materialities within and between these frames. Taken together, we
propose that expertise "becomes" through and transcending these three processes
within design that is team-based, multidisciplinary, and community-embedded.
This chapter contributes to understandings of the tensions, ambiguities, and
ambivalences around experts, expertise, and accomplishment of new knowledge.

▦ REFERENCES

Aakhus, M. (2007). Communication as Design. *Communication Monographs*, 74, 112–17. doi: 10.1080/03637750701196383

Adams, R., and Siddiqui, J. (eds) (2016). *Analyzing Design Review Conversations.* West Lafayette, IN: Purdue University Press.

Aime, F., Humphrey, S., DeRue, D. S., and Paul, J. (2014). The Riddle of Heterarchy: Power Transitions in Cross-Functional Teams. *Academy of Management Journal*, 57, 327–52. doi: 10.5465/amj.2011.0756

Atman, C., Eris, O., McDonnell, J., Cardella, M., and Borgford-Parnell, J. (2014). Engineering Design Education: Research, Practice, and Examples that Link the Two. In A. Johri and B. Olds (eds), *Cambridge Handbook of Engineering Education Research* (pp. 201–25). New York: Cambridge University Press.

Barley, W. C., Leonardi, P. M., and Bailey, D. E. (2012). Engineering Objects for Collaboration: Strategies of Ambiguity and Clarity at Knowledge Boundaries. *Human Communication Research*, 38, 280–308. doi: 10.1111/j.1468-2958.2012. 01430.x

Baumann, M., and Bonner, B. (2013). Member Awareness of Expertise, Information Sharing, Information Weighting, and Group Decision Making. *Small Group Research*, 44, 532–62. doi: 10.1177/1046496413494415

Bhatia, V. (2010). Interdiscursivity in Professional Communication. *Discourse and Communication*, 21, 32–50. doi: 10.1177/1750481309351208

Bhatia, V., and Bremner, S. (eds) (2014). *The Routledge Handbook of Language and Professional Communication.* New York: Routledge.

Black, L., Carlile, P., and Repenning, N. (2004). A Dynamic Theory of Expertise and Occupational Boundaries in New Technology Implementation: Building on Barley's Study of CT Scanning. *Administrative Science Quarterly*, 49, 572–607. doi: 10.2307/4131491

Bucciarelli, L. (1988). An Ethnographic Perspective on Engineering Design. *Design Studies*, 9, 59–168. doi: 10.1016/0142-694X(88)90045-2

Bucciarelli, L. (1994). *Designing Engineers.* Cambridge, MA: MIT Press.

Buzzanell, P. M. (2011). Interrogating Culture. *Intercultural Communication Studies*, 20(1), 1–16.

Buzzanell, P. M. (2014). Reflections on Global Engineering Design and Intercultural Competence: The Case of Ghana. In X. Dai and G.M. Chen (eds), *Intercultural Communication Competence: Conceptualization and its Development in Contexts and Interactions* (pp. 315–34). Newcastle upon Tyne: Cambridge Scholars Publishing.

Buzzanell, P. M., and Zoltowski, C. (2014). Get your Message Across: The Art of Gathering and Sharing Information. In D. F. Radcliffe and M. Fosmire (eds), *Integrating Information into Engineering Design* (pp. 159–70). West Lafayette, IN: Purdue University Press.

Buzzanell, P. M., Fyke, J., and Remke, R. (2014). Professionalising Organisational Communication Discourses, Materialities and Trends. In V. Bhatia and S. Bremner (eds), *The Routledge Handbook of Language and Professional Communication* (pp. 207–19). New York: Routledge.

Buzzanell, P. M., Meisenbach, R., and Remke, R. (2008). Women, Leadership, and Dissent. In S. Banks (ed.), *Dissent and the Failure of Leadership* (pp. 119–34). Northampton, MA: Edward Elgar Publishing Inc.

Cardella, M., Buzzanell, P. M., Zoltowski, C., Cummings, A., and Tolbert, D. (2014). A Tale of Two Design Contexts: Quantitative and Qualitative Explorations of Student–Instructor Interactions amidst Ambiguity. Paper presented to the 10th Design Thinking Research Symposium (DTRS) conference, Analyzing Design Review Conversations, symposium held at Purdue University, West Lafayette, IN, Oct.

Carr, E. (2010). Enactments of Expertise. *Annual Review of Anthropology*, 39, 17–32. doi: 10.1146/annurev.anthro.012809.1049848

Charmaz, K. (2000). Grounded Theory: Objectivist and Constructivist Methods. In N. K. Denzin and Y. S. Lincoln (eds), *Handbook of Qualitative Research* (2nd edn, pp. 509–35). Thousand Oaks, CA: Sage.

Collins, H. M., and Evans, R. (2002). The Third Wave of Science Studies: Studies of Expertise and Experience. *Social Studies of Science*, 32, 235–96. doi: 10.1177/0306312702032002003

Crismond, D. P., and Adams, R. S. (2012). The Informed Design Teaching and Learning Matrix. *Journal of Engineering Education*, 101, 738–97. doi: 10.1002/j.2168-9830.2012.tb01127.x

Cross, N. (1982). Designerly Ways of Knowing. *Design Studies*, 3, 221–7. doi: 10.1016/0142-694X(82)90040-0

Dorst, K. (2011). The Core of "Design Thinking" and its Application. *Design Studies*, 32, 521–32. doi: 10.1016/j.destud.2011.07.006

DuBabcock, B. (2006). An Analysis of Topic Management Strategies and Turn-Taking Behavior in the Hong Kong Bilingual Environment: The Impact of Culture and Language Use. *International Journal of Business Communication*, 43, 21–42. doi: 10.1177/0021943605282373

Groll, L. (2013). Negotiating Cultural Humility: First-Year Engineering Students' Development in a Life-Long Journey. Unpublished dissertation, Purdue University, W. Lafayette, IN.

Guindon, R. (1990). Knowledge Exploited by Experts during Software System Design. *International Journal of Man-Machine Studies*, 33, 279–304. doi: 10.1016/S0020-7373(05)80120-8

Henderson, K. (1991). Flexible Sketches and Inflexible Data Bases: Visual Communication, Conscription Devices, and Boundary Objects in Design Engineering. *Science, Technology, and Human Values*, 16, 448–73. doi: 10.1177/016224399101600402

Johri, A., Olds, B., and O'Connor, K. (2014). Situative Frameworks for Engineering Learning Research. In A. Johri and B. Olds (eds), *Cambridge Handbook of Engineering Education Research* (pp. 47–66). New York: Cambridge University Press.

Kenny Feister, M., Buzzanell, P. M., Zoltowski, C., and Oakes, W. (2014). Making Sense of Ethics in Engineering Education: A Discursive Examination of Students' Perceptions of Work and Ethics on Multidisciplinary Project Teams. In *Proceedings of the 2014 IEEE International Symposium on Ethics in Science, Technology and Engineering* (pp. 1–5). Chicago: IEEE. doi: 10.1109/ETHICS.2014.6893409

Kisselburgh, L., Berkelaar, B., and Buzzanell, P. M. (2010). Collaborative Research in Global Contexts: Ethical, Institutional and Academic Synergies. In *Communication in e-Society: Innovation, Collaboration and Responsibility* (pp. 69–84). Shanghai: Shanghai People's Publishing House.

Kolmos, A., and deGraaff, E. (2014). Problem-Based and Project-Based Learning in Engineering Education. In A. Johri and B. Olds (eds), *Cambridge Handbook of Engineering Education Research* (pp. 141–60). New York: Cambridge University Press.

Kong, K. (2014). *Handbook of Professional Communication*. Cambridge: Cambridge University Press.

Kuhn, T. (2012). Negotiating the Micro-Macro Divide: Thought Leadership from Organizational Communication for Theorizing Organization. *Management Communication Quarterly*, 26, 543–84. doi: 10.1177/0893318912462004

Kuhn, T. (2014). Knowledge and Knowing in Organizational Communication. In L.L. Putnam and D. K. Mumby (eds), *The SAGE Handbook of Organizational Communication: Advances in Theory, Research, and Methods* (3rd edn, pp. 481–502). Thousand Oaks, CA: Sage.

Lawson, B. (2004). Schemata, Gambits and Precedent: Some Factors in Design Expertise. *Design Studies*, 25(5), 443–57. doi: 10.1016/j.destud.2004.05.001

Loyd, D., Phillips, K., and Whitson, J. (2010). Expertise in your Midst: How Congruence between Status and Speech Style Affects Reactions to Unique Knowledge. *Group Processes Intergroup Relations*, 13, 379–95. doi: 10.1177/1368430209350317

Lucena, J., Downey, G., Jesiek, B., and Elber, S. (2008). Competencies beyond Countries: The Re-organization of Engineering Education in the United States, Europe, and Latin America. *Journal of Engineering Education*, 97, 433–47. doi: 10.1002/j.2168-9830.2008.tb00991.x

Marton, F. (1988). Phenomenography: Exploring Different Conceptions of Reality. In D. M. Fetterman (ed.), *Qualitative Approaches to Evaluation in Education: The Silent Scientific Revolution* (pp. 176–205). New York: Praeger.

Marton, F., and Booth, S. (1997). *Learning and Awareness*. Mahwah, NJ: LEA.

Putnam, L. L., and Boys, S. (2006). Revisiting Metaphors of Organizational Communication. In S. R. Clegg, C. Hardy, W. Lawrence, and W. Nord (eds), *Handbook of Organization Studies* (pp. 541–76). Thousand Oaks, CA: Sage.

Putnam, L. L., and Mumby, D. K. (2014). Introduction: Advancing Theory and Research in Organizational Communication. In L. L. Putnam and D. K. Mumby (eds), *The SAGE Handbook of Organizational Communication: Advances in Theory, Research, and Methods* (3rd edn, pp. 1–18). Los Angeles: Sage.

Putnam, L. L., and Nicotera, A. M. (eds) (2009). *Building Theories of Organization: The Constitutive Role of Communication*. New York: Routledge.

Radcliffe, D. (2014). Multiple Perspectives on Engineering Design. In D. F. Radcliffe and M. Fosmire (eds), *Integrating Information into Engineering Design* (pp. 7–20). West Lafayette, IN: Purdue University Press.

Remke, R. (2006). (Ir)rationalities at Work: The Logics, Heart, and Soul of Head Start. Unpublished dissertation, Purdue University, W. Lafayette, IN.

Ren, Y., and Argote, L. (2011). Transactive Memory Systems 1985–2010: An Integrative Framework of Key Dimensions, Antecedents, and Consequences. *Academy of Management Annals*, 5, 189–229. doi: 10.1080/19416520.2011.590300

Robichaud, D., and Cooren, F. (eds) (2012). *Organization and Organizing: Materiality, Agency, Discourse*. New York: Routledge.

Shoeneborn, D. (2013). The Pervasive Power of PowerPoint: How a Genre of Professional Communication Permeates Organizational Communication. *Organization Studies*, 34, 1777–1801. doi: 10.1177/0170840613485843

Tajeddin, G., Safayeni, F., Connelly, C., and Tasa, K. (2012). The Influence of Emergent Expertise on Group Decision Processes. *Small Group Research*, 43, 50–74. doi: 10.1177/1046496411418251

Tenenberg, J., Socha, D., and Rot, W.-M. (2014). Designerly Ways of Being. Paper presented to the 10th Design Thinking Research Symposium (DTRS) conference, Analyzing Design Review Conversations, symposium held at Purdue University, West Lafayette, IN.

Tervalon, M., and Murray-García, J. (1998). Cultural Humility versus Cultural Competence: A Critical Distinction in Defining Physician Training Outcomes in Multicultural Education. *Journal of Health Care for the Poor and Underserved*, 9, 117–25. doi: 10.1044/policy

Ting-Toomey, S. (2010). Intercultural Ethics: Multiple Layered Issues. In G. Cheney, S. May, and D. Munshi (eds), *Handbook of Communication Ethics* (pp. 335–52). New York: Routledge.

Treem, J. (2012). Communicating Expertise: Knowledge Performances in Professional-Service Firms. *Communication Monographs*, 79, 23–47. doi: 10.1080/03637751 .2011.646487

Zhu, Q., Zoltowski, C., Oakes, W., Kenny Feister, M., and Buzzanell, P. M. (2014). Students' Perceptions of Ethics in Project-Based Team Context: Implications for Teaching and Assessing Ethical Reasoning in Engineering Education. 2014 Forum on Philosophy, Engineering and Technology (fPET), Blacksburg, Virginia Tech University, May.

Zoltowski, C., Oakes, W., and Cardella, M. (2012). Students' Ways of Experiencing Human-Centered Design. *Journal of Engineering Education*, 101, 28–59. doi: 10.1002/ j.2168-9830.2012.tb00040.x

10 Communication Expertise as Organizational Practice

Competing Ideas about Communication in the Market for Solutions

MARK AAKHUS, PUNIT DADLANI, RALPH A. GIGLIOTTI, CHRISTINE GOLDTHWAITE, ALLIE KOSTERICH, AND SURABHI SAHAY

This chapter examines how organizations operate as expert communication services competing with other organizations to solve communication problems experienced by stakeholders trying to address some social, political, environmental, or economic challenge or opportunity. Such organizations are interesting for the purposes of interrogating communication and expertise as they are essentially in the business of putting the two together. In so doing, these organizations pursue particular ideas about communication while crowding out other ideas about communication in the market for solutions. We aim to provide grounds for interrogating the nature of communication and expertise in an environment where organizations offer competing means, methods, and processes for stakeholders regarding expert ways of communicating. By focusing on ways organizations define and communicate expert services this perspective offers insight into the constitution of organizational expertise in the informational age.

The organizations of interest in this chapter were ostensibly built to provide expert communication services in the *market for solutions*, which Eggers and MacMillan (2013) describe as the opportunity space defined by the consequences of modern living on the environment, economy, society, and culture. The primary objective of these third-party organizations is to provide expert communication servicing for mediating and facilitating interaction among stakeholders from multiple disciplines and sectors. These expert services in communication are thus not the firms, corporations, government agencies, or foundations that offer particular environmental, economic, or social solutions in the market for solutions but instead offer ideas and methods for orchestrating how other organizations engage each other to achieve stakeholder collaboration.

A most recognizable communication expert servicing is seen in the various specializations that have emerged around the practice of messaging, such as public relations, public affairs, marketing, and advertising. An extensive market exists around the practice of messaging, with fierce competition in providing messaging solutions from innumerable sole proprietorships, partnerships, firms, and corporations. In terms of communication, these organizations are cultivating and developing knowledge about practices of communication and designing new communication practices. They take ordinary practices of communication—creating messages for informing and persuading—and seek to reinvent that practice for the purposes of resolving particular complexities and dilemmas of communication (e.g. informing, persuading).

In this chapter we attend, in particular, to the prospect of a related kind of communication expertise focused on orchestrating encounters between organizations and stakeholders. In terms of the market for solutions, these would be expert communication servicing organizations that generate value through their invention of, and competition over, solutions to the transaction costs of cooperation and collaboration among diverse stakeholders. These organizations provide communication designs or design advice to enable clients to construct communication that manages the exigencies of engagement and collaboration among diverse actors and macro-actors. Organizations that indicate specialization in the practice of orchestrating such interaction can be seen as being in the business of developing knowledge about interaction and its communicative possibilities for various arenas in the market for solutions. Our goal is to open inquiry into what these expert communication services know, or at least claim to know, about communication. Communication expertise, for the purposes at hand, can be characterized as knowledge about rules for interaction and expertise about designing interaction, through persuasion, procedures, and technologies. Such knowledge is used to achieve particular states or qualities of communication among multidisciplinary, multi-sector stakeholders seeking to collaborate to address some consequence of modern living.

The inquiry initiated here offers a subtle but challenging shift of attention in the broad pursuit of understanding communication and expertise. The view of communication and expertise developed differs from transmissional views that treat communication as a vehicle of knowledge sharing within and among organizations or communication as an interactive context in which knowledge emerges in particular ways. Instead, a design stance is taken (e.g. Jackson and Aakhus, 2014) that gives attention to the knowledge about communication that is developed and deployed to shape how communication happens. We begin by providing a brief account about how the relation between communication and expertise can be conceptualized as *communication expertise*. We base our inquiry on a preliminary investigation of the self-descriptions of a variety of organizations offering expert communication servicing. What is of interest here is what these organizations assert to know about communication as seen in the professional language these organizations use to articulate their service for others. Other investigations into what these organizations actually know and do are left to future research. The inquiry illustrates a path forward in paying attention to communication in society in the reporting of its findings and for addressing key questions about organizations, knowledge, and expertise that motivate this volume.

Communication Expertise or Expert Communication Servicing

The communication expertise of organizations is engaged here by first following Craig and Tracy's ideas about grounded practical theory (GPT), which explains that theory can be reconstructed from practice by attending to the practical judgments about what an appropriate communicative action would be in a particular moment (Craig, 1999; Craig and Tracy, 1995, 2014). These judgments disclose theory in practice because they point to what an actor takes to be the relevant communicative problem and its solution as well as the normative rationale justifying the solution. An actor's communicative practice can be cultivated through reflection on the consequences a practical theory (i.e. problem and solution framing, rationales) has for communicative action. For present purposes, organizations providing expert communication servicing are seen as providing practical communication theories for their clients in order to cultivate better judgment about their communicative action.

Communication expertise is further engaged by following the related ideas about communication as design (CAD), which highlights the designability of communication practice through the invention of rules, procedures, and technologies for interaction to enable particular communicative possibilities (Aakhus, 2007; Jackson and Aakhus, 2014). These designs for communication, in the simplest sense, serve to enable joint activity by actors to resolve an exigency in their broader context. So, for example, activities are devised that generate reports to resolve informational shortcomings, that generate judgments to resolve grievances, that generate plans to resolve ambiguities about courses of action, and so on. Any design for communication makes assumptions about how communication works and ought to work in resolving some exigency, and thus is warranted (or not) by evidence of legitimacy and effectiveness in making the needed form of communication possible (Aakhus, 2002).

From these starting points, we present examples of organizations using the market for solutions concept as a guide combined with ideas from GPT and CAD. We chose organizations across five distinct arenas of specialization: consultancies, accelerators, hackerspaces, knowledge management, and electronic markets. Our aim was to highlight the diversity of communication work in offering innovations regarding the related exigencies. We chose organizations with both a local and global focus, along with organizations that deal with the production of physical and digital goods and services. As Barbour, Sommer, and Gill (this volume) state, "Expertise is not just an attribute, but it is a capacity for action." In that spirit the organizations were selected based on their capacity for inventing action and interaction for others. Even though the expert servicing among the organizations within each grouping differed, there was enough commonality to treat them as cohering around and developing a particular communication expertise. The differences within the groupings enabled us to say something more general about the expertise for each grouping.

Part of engaging in a practice involves representing how one engages in that practice to others, and it is the representation that is given attention here. To examine these representations we identified the self-descriptions of role and purpose for each organization by looking at the keywords, phrases, passages of text, images, logos, and the like that are indicative or representative of the service the third party offers. We then focused on the unique professionalized language that each organization presented and which served as a metadiscourse about the communication services provided by the organization. The representations were used to reconstruct how these organizations were engaging the practice of orchestrating communication activities for others. These representations do many things including the signaling of aspirations, differentiations, commonalities, and membership in a practice while also disclosing discrepancies, contradictions, and paradoxes in doing the practice. For the purposes here, we focused on the former as what is of interest is an initial articulation of the communication expertise promised by these organizations.

The categories for reconstructing practice from GPT and CAD were used to work through the bramble of jargon used by these organizations to establish their services. We looked for how the representations indicated: *Aspect*: the focal opportunity space within the market for solutions; *Problem*: how the organization framed the communication problem faced by clients; *Solution*: the principles and techniques for reflection or design offered by the organization to resolve communicative problems; and *Rationale*: the empirical and normative justifications for the effectiveness and legitimacy of the solutions (Aakhus, 2002). For each organization within each grouping of organizations, the similarities and differences for each of these categories were analyzed and a summative phrase for each category was developed that characterized that element of practice. An overarching vocabulary and logic of the expert servicing was developed to articulate what these organizations claim in regard to the practice of orchestrating engagement among many actors.

While the data that we worked from have obvious limitations and only scaffold particular empirical claims, they are sufficient for the present inquiry that seeks to further articulate communication expertise as an object of study.

Expert Communication Servicing

As noted, the specific expertise of concern here is the expert communication services provided by organizations that offer solutions to stakeholders regarding the facilitation and mediation of collaborations. Within this organizational space organizations differ in the forms and designs of solutions offered. Our goal is to reveal similarities and differences between types of expert communication servicing and the organizations providing this expertise.

Consultancies: Providing Process Expertise All Over the World

Consulting enterprises occupy an important role in this current solution economy by offering process expertise, whereby they promise to deliver other organizations into a new way of thinking to address complex social challenges through a variety of suggested solutions. These are admittedly abstract promises, but they point to the very process expertise these organizations claim about helping clients design how their organizations think through the restructuring of communication practices that enable sense-making and action. As this section illustrates, they each offer a particular invitation for interaction between consultant and client.

CONSULTANCIES AS EXPERT COMMUNICATION SERVICING

The consulting-oriented enterprises selected for analysis include McKinsey, Gap International, the Creative Class Group (CCG), and StartingBloc.[1] These consulting organizations serve a range of clients including prospective entrepreneurs, communities, economic and real estate developers, governmental agencies, corporations, and non-profit organizations. Notably, by loosely framing the core

---

[1] Organizations in this chapter were chosen to maximize the diversity of organizational attributes (i.e. location, size, history) within a common expert communication service space. We recognize that is a purposefully biased sample, however it is a useful means of reconstructing practice from GPT and CAD at the level of organizational specialization and facilitates comparisons across expert communication services, instead of limiting analysis to individual companies.

issue(s), a diverse pool of prospective clients may find legitimacy in the proposed core technologies. The underlying logic of practice is highlighted in the way all four actors intentionally frame the core social issue(s) at stake in this current moment—issues that are diverse across consultancy—and how their expert service enables organizations to address those issue.

Vocabulary of consultancy practice

The selected organizations encourage what they refer to as creativity, leadership development, and a new paradigm in approaching what McKinsey identifies as "chronic, complex societal challenges." Gap International's emphasis on "breakthrough thinking" presupposes an ineffective current frame of reference, whereas CCG defines the issue as a "great reservoir of overlooked and under-utilized human potential." As an interpretive device used to help make sense of one's world, the framing of core issue(s) by these enterprises sets the stage for their respective solutions. Table 10.1 highlights specific connections between the organizational vocabularies of these selected consulting enterprises and the logics of communicative practice.

The logic of consultancy practice

These four consultancies offer expertise in crafting spaces where organizational leaders can make sense of complex social issues through a new paradigm. Each consultancy presents distinct ideas about how to design communication and interaction in support of the client. Common to the core service is that the intervention provides a space for thinking through alternative ways of addressing social problems through techniques tailored to improve the client's thinking about how to effectively address the problem. Their process expertise is invited during important moments marked by change, disruption, and uncertainty.

Accelerators: Bringing the Outside in for Business Innovation

Corporate accelerators are services that *bring the outside in*—that is, they connect principal corporations with external entrepreneurs or startup organizations as a source for generating innovation. Organizations traditionally rely on closed systems of innovation, focusing on the internal development of knowledge and products (Lichtenthaler, 2011). Recently, however, there has been movement toward open innovation through interaction with other organizations and engagement with open source communities (Chesbrough,

Table 10.1 Vocabulary of Consultancy Expert Servicing

Summative phrase	Key Terms			
	McKinsey	Gap International	Creative Class Group	StartingBloc
Aspect Gap between traditional organizations and innovative entrepreneurs	"We help the world's leading organizations address chronic, complex societal challenges"	"transforming organizations and transforming the world"	"to change the world for the better"	"budding social innovators" who are committed to social change
Problem Limited frame of reference; organizations/members not reaching their full potential	"we believe that the health of our society depends on the health of its institutions"	Self-imposed and other-imposed limits	"overlooked and underutilized human potential"	The lack of social, economic, and environmental innovation
Solution Communication and interaction	"Our research helps to identify the most successful interventions for big, intractable problems"	"breakthrough" consulting strategies which "equip leaders with the organizational insight, the strategic framework, and effective leadership competencies to lead at exceptional levels"	"The Creative Communities Leadership Project gives emerging leaders the tools they need to generate greater economic prosperity in their region"	"We connect them to their tribe and give them access to the resources, co-conspirators, projects and support they need to create impact"
Rationale Expertise is communicated by the ability to put different uses into different contexts	"We are committed to making a positive difference to the world. We address societal issues because it's our responsibility, and because it improves the condition of the societies in which we, our families, friends and clients live and do business"	"Regardless of the scope of work, these consulting services, tools, and programs are for leaders who see changing the way people think as a necessary pathway for executing strategies and accomplishing their most ambitious objectives"	The cultivation of "next-generation thinkers and strategists" with the intention of "truly [achieving] economic progress and a more meaningful, more fulfilling way of life"	"StartingBloc is built on the belief that a small, committed group of people can change the world"

2003). This is epitomized through accelerators, which design new ways of interacting between legacy organizations and external innovators by offering communicative expertise in the form of mentoring, connections, and resources in exchange for access to and stake in ground floor innovation, and thus bridging the gaps that tend to limit innovation in the marketplace.

ACCELERATORS AS EXPERT COMMUNICATION SERVICING

Accelerators provide expert communication servicing grounded in the underlying logic of the practice of open innovation. This is achieved through the accelerator's approach to designing communication, in particular via ideas about the ways interaction should occur between external entrepreneurs and principal corporations.

Vocabulary of accelerator practice

Corporate accelerators tackle the communicative problem of interaction, specifically in bringing the outside (as in external entrepreneur or startup organization) into the principal corporation. Table 10.2 summarizes how four

Table 10.2 Vocabulary of Accelerator Expert Servicing

Summative phrase	Key Terms			
	timeSpace	NikeFuel Lab	Wayra	Citrix Startup Accelerator
Aspect Gap between traditional organizations and innovative entrepreneurs	"enhance society by creating, collecting and distributing high-quality news and information"	"mission is to bring inspiration and innovation"; "launch unique solutions"	Stimulate productivity	"foster the next generation of enterprise solutions"; "fresh approach to today's problems"
Problem How to bring the outside in	Lack of time, space to enhance the "collecting and distributing of high quality information"	Lack of accountable collaboration between traditional organization and entrepreneurs	Lack of access to resources, knowledge needed to bring good ideas to fruition	Lack of support for next generation of enterprise solutions
Solution Communication and interaction	"teach/learn alongside entrepreneurs and employees"	Measuring, collaborating	Interacting, connecting, networking, supporting	Investing, advising
Rationale Expertise is communicated by the ability to put different uses into different contexts	Communication and exchange between passionate entrepreneurs and award-winning legacy of *New York Times* staff	Access to proprietary data enables accountability in idea generation and product development	Financial backing and support of established global network enables growth	Investment and connections to valid clientele foster market validation and success

accelerators (NikeFuel Lab, timeSpace, Wayra, and Citrix Startup Accelerator) frame their service and their common view of their expert communication servicing.

The logic of accelerator practice

Although accelerators share a common logic of practice, they differ in their expert servicing in a variety of interesting ways. First, while all of the organizations focus on fostering innovation, NikeFuel Lab and Citrix are solution-focused, aimed at generating product opportunities; whereas timeSpace and Wayra are process-focused, aimed at enhancing collection, distribution, and productivity. In other words, NikeFuel Lab aims to expand the Nike+ product ecosystem and Citrix aims to expand the variety of enterprise product solutions. In contrast, timeSpace is interested in fostering mutual learning and development processes and Wayra is interested in expanding networking and support systems.

These differences in accelerator focus are further exemplified through a more detailed examination of the accelerators' various solutions and rationales. For example, NikeFuel Lab offers a solution grounded in measurement, based on the rationale that connections between Nike and external organizations who share commitment to data will create better solutions; whereas Citrix offers a resource solution based in funding and investment in order to develop successful business solutions. These ideas contrast with Wayra's solution, which is grounded in notions of networking and the process of connecting the right ideas with the right people, and timeSpace, which offers a solution of osmosis, a mutual teaching and learning that would occur between the host corporation and the external entrepreneurs alongside one another to enhance society by being a part of the process. Each organization offers different ideas about how to design communication and interaction. While the ideas vary in an explicit manner, the implicit, underlying idea is quite similar. In a sense, the expertise of accelerators is communicated by the ability to put different uses in different contexts.

Hackerspaces: Constructing Venues for Sharing Tools and Creativity

As the boundaries between work and community continue to blur, hackerspaces offer designs for interaction that empower independent creative and technical actors to individually and collectively engage in activities that have thus far been the domain of industry. Hackerspaces are self-governed organizations that provide expertise in facilitating grassroots experimentation and open innovation in areas related to computing, science, engineering, and digital fabrication. These organizations generate a communicative context supportive of participation and innovation by providing access to space, resources, and like-minded individuals. The hackerspace design offers communicative expertise for organizing and governance that addresses barriers that restrict access to innovation activities and grassroots participation in the form of membership and open-access events. These designs facilitate deliberate and serendipitous interaction, encourage socialization and identity formation, enable creativity and collaboration, and encourage learning and sharing.

HACKERSPACES AS EXPERT COMMUNICATION SERVICING

The hackerspace expertise is most evident in the explicit and implicit rules and principles for organizing interaction among participants. Entities like Noisebridge and others seek to create a supportive community based on the pursuit of art, science, and technology for "the betterment of society." Hackerspaces propose designs for interaction in support of the underlying logic of building community, encouraging collaboration and knowledge sharing. More than just enabling creative-technical activity through the availability of materials and resources, hackerspaces provide behavioral expectations, interaction protocols, and other norms for generating discourse and activity related to innovation.

Vocabulary of hackerspace practice

Organizations within the hackerspace category differ in the communicative expertise they offer in a number of distinct ways (see Table 10.3). Common across these examples of how the service is framed are terms related to creativity, activity, and community. Most notable however are ideas about access, belonging, and decision-making. Noisebridge's approach is the most inclusive of all, offering unrestricted access while presenting direct and explicit behavior guidelines. For example, "On average, we do not want people looking for a halfway house to sleep in, using the space to store their items, coming here to indefinitely 'borrow' or outright steal things, or being on the lookout for people to annoy; Talk to people and make friends; be sensitive to people's desire to stop talking and start hacking." Contrast this with NYC Resistor, a private space permitting public access only through events. The only expectations explicitly stated are, "Participate: We like friendly people who like to think about how things work."

These examples illustrate differences in how membership is conceived and enacted, and the rights and responsibilities afforded. Membership is a mechanism that controls the bringing of the outside in and the power to influence the operation of the hackerspace. These examples range from radically

Table 10.3 Vocabulary of Hackerspace Expert Servicing

Summative phrase	Key Terms			
	Artisan's Asylum	HacDC	Noisebridge	NYC Resistor
Aspect Building community and facilitating creative collaboration	"support and promote the teaching, learning and practicing of a wide variety of crafts; enable creativity"	"marshals the organization's technological knowledge to benefit the surrounding community; apply the results of its work to specific cultural, charitable and scientific causes"	"a hackerspace for technical-creative projects, doocratically run by our members; a non-profit educational institution intended for public benefit"	"Learn, Share, and Make things"
Problem How to build a network of technical-creative actors	Lack of opportunity for local and "global makerspace community, the arts, and the innovation economy"	Lack of opportunity for "talented people" to "serve the community"	Lack of "safe space to work, learn, and play"	Lack of shared space for hacker collective
Solution Craft and artisan interaction, community-based learning, and DIY activity	"not-for-profit organization furnishing education, tools, workspace, and community to empower dedicated fabricators, including hobbyists, artists, and early stage entrepreneurs, to create on large or small scale	"Free and open activities to share knowledge, skills, and ideas. A combined meeting space and workshop is stocked with specialized tools and supplies useful for the collaborative development of technological and artistic projects"	"Infrastructure and collaboration opportunities for people interested in programming, hardware hacking, physics, chemistry, mathematics, security, robotics, all kinds of art, and, of course, technology"	"Participate: We like friendly people who like to think about how things work; We are not equipped to accept visitors outside of our public nights"
Rationale Participation promotes hacker culture and community	"access to our facility and all shared equipment . . . opens you to an incredible community of artists, makers, and innovators"	"build an innovative community technology space and to contribute to the growing international movement of hackerspaces"	"promote collaboration across disciplines for the benefit of cultural, charitable, and scientific causes"	"Meet regularly to share knowledge, hack on projects together, and build community"

participatory (Noisebridge) to private enterprises (NYC Resistor), and differ in the degree to which decision-making power and process are enabled and made explicit. Noisebridge's wiki-based website provides detailed information. Decisions are made through consensus during weekly member meetings, in which non-members are invited to participate. Similarly, HacDC also outlines its governance structure in a public forum. In contrast, NYC Resistor provides little information on governance and decision-making and membership is by invitation only, "If you're interested in joining, come get to know us . . . After a while if we have a space open in the group and it's a good fit, you may be invited to be a member."

The logic of hackerspace practice

Across the exemplars (Artisan's Asylum, HacDC, Noisebridge, and NYC Resistor) considered here are ideas about how communication should work. While the prescriptions range from explicit to highly ambiguous, these organizations claim to follow a philosophy of inclusiveness and creativity to justify the expert communication service provided as a source of invention and innovation in developing the hackerspace as communication service.

Knowledge Democratizers: Legitimizing Grassroots Entrepreneurs and Innovation

Knowledge democratizers help reinvent and restructure interactions among stakeholders associated with the development of grassroots-level knowledge systems. They claim expertise in connecting the right stakeholders in authentic discourse to overcome knowledge erosion and the deeper institutional barriers to local democratic governance. Knowledge erosion, which is especially prominent in third world countries, occurs when grassroots local knowledge is not properly identified or documented, making it inaccessible to local people. Furthermore, this creates barriers that prevent innovators from claiming rights for their innovations and also stops innovators from getting proper rights for their innovation. Knowledge democratizers design new ways of collecting, documenting, and disseminating grassroots-level innovation for communities based on values that support the proper provision of rights to innovators. Their communication expertise is to help preserve and sustain knowledge through local relationships, grounding the transference of knowledge in community-based accountability.

KNOWLEDGE DEMOCRATIZERS AS
EXPERT COMMUNICATION SERVICING

Organizations that exemplify the expert service of knowledge democratizing include Honeybee, the Society for Research and Initiatives for Sustainable Technologies and Institutions (SRISTI), National Innovation Foundation of India (NIF), and grassroots-level incubators such as Grassroots Innovations Augmentation Network (GIAN). These knowledge democratizer organizations vary in the technologies and solutions that make up their expert servicing. For instance, while SRISTI situates itself as the body that communicates trust to the grassroots-level innovator by hosting events like Shodh Yatra, NIF aids the Honeybee Network in conserving knowledge by licensing innovations registered with SRISTI. GIAN is an incubator that was set up by the state government in collaboration with SRISTI to promote rural investments, which focuses on technology transfer as a solution for countering knowledge erosion. This suggests that each knowledge democratizer, even when supporting the Honeybee Network, brings with them their own technologies and solutions. In this particular case of knowledge democratizers, it is the sum of all these technologies/solutions offered by these four organizations grounded in the Honeybee ideology that underscores the market they see for their expertise. Despite these variations in services, knowledge democratizers share a similar vocabulary that highlights the alleviation of knowledge erosion issue and points to a logic of practice.

Vocabulary of knowledge democratizer practice

Knowledge democratizers frame the communicative expertise they offer in particular ways that point to the underlying practice of knowledge democratizing they are developing (see Table 10.4). Common across these examples of how the service is framed are terms related to local, grassroots, innovation, and knowledge. Table 10.4 highlights specific connections between the vocabularies of these selected organizations and the logics of communicative practice.

The logic of knowledge democratizer practice

The logic of knowledge democratizing is vested in devising techniques and strategies of communication that create a new institutional space for grassroots innovation that resolves the problems of knowledge erosion. The approach grounds this space by providing proper rights to the innovators by systematically documenting and disseminating the knowledge collected. The particular solutions they create to expand opportunities for partnerships and

Table 10.4 Vocabulary of Knowledge Democratizer Expert Servicing

Summative phrase	Key Terms			
	Honeybee Network	SRISTI	NIF	GIAN
Aspect Sustainability, grassroots innovation	"Value addition of local traditional knowledge and innovation"	Strengthen the creativity of grassroots inventors	"help India become an innovative and creative society and a global leader in sustainable technologies"	Focused on incubating and commercializing grassroots innovations
Problem Knowledge erosion, inauthentic communication, limited democratic governance	"Knowledge has been extracted, documented without any acknowledgement to the source of knowledge"	"seldom have we provided opportunity to creative innovators and traditional knowledge holders to do research themselves"	"preserve fast eroding knowledge"	Important to set up mechanisms that encourage local innovation
Solution Create a new institutional space for sustainable diffusion and innovation, use of local language accountable documentation	Attempt to build up people-to-people communication. Six local language versions of magazine	"Shodh Yatra is to undertake a journey for the search of knowledge" ICT initiatives to connect across region, language, and culture	"Rigorous procedures are formulated and followed during innovation analysis" Expand policy and institutional space	Commercialized many technologies through processes like outright technology
Rationale Authentic discourse and cross-pollination, optimization of design	"Cross-pollination of ideas without taking away the nectar from the flower forever" philosophy of discourse, which is authentic, accountable and fair"	"respect and reward creativity at the grassroots"	Get due reward for their innovations: "knowledge experts need optimization in design process or product formulation by merging with modern science and technology inputs"	"new avenues of targeting the untapped markets"

collaborations are based on principles of authentic discourse that respect and reward creativity at the grassroots level.

Marketmakers: Creating New Frameworks for Market Exchange

Marketmaker organizations provide expertise for orchestrating internet-based market transactions to facilitate the exchange of ideas, products, and services via information technology infrastructure. Marketmakers view traditional market-based exchanges as constraining individual freedom by requiring particular transactional structures and surveillance that benefit corporate rather than individual interests. Marketmakers provide alternatives to the traditional market infrastructure that aim to: (1) reduce transaction complexity and increase security by connecting individuals directly rather than through multiple mediating layers; (2) allow the renegotiation of the normative features of market organizing situationally; and (3) internalize individual trust and market mechanisms of regulation to be within or constituted by the particular market considered. These organizations thus provide communicative expertise through IT tools/services that empower individuals to build and interact in alternative markets that are in line with such individual interests.

MARKETMAKERS AS EXPERT COMMUNICATION SERVICING

Vocabulary of marketmaker practice

Marketmaker organizations implement their communicative expertise through information technologies that anonymize, autonomize, and internalize normativity in the digital market space. Table 10.5 summarizes, through the logic of practice, their communicative expertise.

The logic of marketmaker practice

The organizations within the marketmaker category offer important variations on the communicative expertise in market making. First, while all of the organizations advocate for an alternative to the traditional interaction space of "the market," Bitcoin and Tor (instrumentalists) offer core technologies that can be used as interactants see fit, whereas Silk Road and Atlantis (valuists) provide market infrastructure that cater to more value-laden counter-market demands, such as the sale of illicit drugs or weapons. The object of application, in other words, for the core technologies of the instrumentalists, who frame their communicative expertise as providing open-source resources for facilitating

Table 10.5 Vocabulary of Marketmaker Expert Servicing

Summative phrase	Key Terms			
	Tor	Bitcoin	Silk Road	Atlantis
Aspect Market transaction structures	Tor is used by "ordinary citizens who want protection from identity theft and prying corporations, corporations who want to look at a competitor's website in private, people around the world whose Internet connections are censored"	"The first decentralized peer-to-peer payment network that is powered by its users with no central authority or middlemen"	Silk Road claims that there is a need for ways for individuals in society to organize that get around the controls that the state puts on how and what individuals can transact upon	Atlantis sees anonymous markets as having "room for competitor markets" for transacting with the most reliable service
Problem How to remove regulatory and normative interference from market interactions	Ongoing trends in law, policy, and technology "threaten anonymity as never before, undermining our ability to speak and read freely online"	The need for alternatives for transacting that are free from social (institutional) as well as more tangible vulnerabilities (information security)	The need to balance anonymity and trust for enabling self-structured market transaction spaces; the need for a "center of trust" that has trustworthiness and defensibility from institutional authority	Reliability of alternative market transaction structures: "There is a lot of potential in this market, and if they (Silk Road) aren't willing to make the big moves we will do it for them"
Solution Decentralized control of market interactions through collective autonomy & emancipatory organizing	The solution appears to be collective as serving the collective good as Tor tools help in "maintaining civil liberties," by communicating with whistleblowers and finding support for issues with social stigmas	Framed as a collective, open, and democratic type of experience or design: "free to choose" "controlled by users around the world" where the "design is public"	anonymous marketplace based on "libertarian principles" that connects vendors to purchasers of virtually any product/service over secure, encrypted channels that avoid all official or regulated intermediaries	Claims "feedback is crucial" and that reliability and security are top concerns as they want "sellers to be able to make sales all hours of the day" and have the "free trade market evolve and prosper"
Rationale Communicative expertise involves redefining and self-structuring of market normativity	Ongoing trends in law, policy, and technology "threaten anonymity as never before, undermining our ability to speak and read freely online"	Provides what other intermediaries did but with much more *just and competitive* terms to offer such as "payment freedom," "very low fees," "security and control," and "transparent and neutral" transactions	Portrays societal institutions ("the State") as being in surveillance and control ("thieving murderous mitts") of society and the liberties of individuals	Aligns itself with the business to customer model where it can offer the best service for vendors and customers, a strategy that makes their product more legitimate to individuals because of the traditional idea of competition that it invokes

autonomous interaction, is less structured into the core technologies provided than the valuists, who see their expertise as providing a formalized interactive scaffolding for resisting and "revolting" against market regulation.

Second, Bitcoin and Atlantis play off of existing systems by providing more efficient services than existing options, such as the financial markets or, in Atlantis's case, being more reliable than competitors. In these two cases, the existing market is reified as both Bitcoin and Atlantis provide alternatives to it that adopt a significant portion of what it already is. By contrast, Tor and Silk Road predicate a large part of their expertise on providing a distinct innovation, whether that is internet protocols for remaining anonymous/untraceable or creating the first online, anonymous black market. These organizations, in other words, set the stage for the market, and the addition of Bitcoin and Atlantis then expand and create market persistence.

Advancing the Study of Expertise

How do we make sense of the organizations considered here and the expert servicing they offer? The focal organizations of interest specialize in mediating differences among actors with various stakes in some social, environmental, or economic matter while facilitating joint action to address the matter despite the differences. Indeed, these organizations attend to communicative matters that may not otherwise be recognized by others in the market for solutions and seek to open up opportunities to further their work in cultivating and inventing communication practice that in turn advances the viability of their expertise. In taking a ubiquitous aspect of an everyday practice of communication—orchestrating encounters—as a focus and claiming to develop expertise on this matter of communication, an expert communication servicing becomes apparent. Attention to it is one important way an understanding of the nature of communication and expertise, and the constitution of organizational expertise in the information age, can be advanced. The inquiry here highlights *communication expertise* over communication and expertise by suggesting that actors specialize in communicative knowledge about the rules of human interaction and skill in designing those rules through techniques, procedures, and technologies intended to enable alternative forms of human interaction that achieve particular forms and qualities of communication. The present inquiry thus highlights expertise in communication's design and the actors that cultivate knowledge about how communication works and ideas about how communication ought to work to offer expertise about designing what is communicatively possible.

Prima-facie evidence of the communication expertise of the organizations discussed in this chapter is found in their vocabularies about their service, which points to these organizations as being built around inquiry into communication problems and the development of practical theory in society about communication. Precisely what they have developed in terms of knowledge about communication, how this knowledge is taken up by others, or whether it consequential is not addressed here. Such matters might be fruitfully addressed in part by work on knowledge transmission and knowledge emergence. It is also important to understand that expertise is projected and constructed in identity and impression management (e.g. Alvesson, 2001; Leonardi and Treem, 2012), especially as that expertise is entwined with extra-organizational perceptions, certifications, and messages that cast roles (Lammers, 2011) and is negotiated in interaction with different audiences (Hollingshead and Brandon, 2003). However, such attention may beg the crucial question about the nature of communication expertise. The inquiry here is meant to keep communication expertise in focus and is thus suggestive for going further in doing so.

CONTEXT: WHERE IS EXPERTISE?

Following early insights by Engeström (1990) concerning tools and Star and Ruhleder (1996) concerning infrastructure, we suggest that communication expertise is relational—that is, borrowing from Star and Ruhleder, expertise emerges for people in practice connected to activities and structures and it happens when some tension between local and global activities and structures is realized and resolved. The complexities of orchestrating multi-sector, multi-disciplinary collaboration open up these local–global tensions, and the organizations here appear to have emerged relative to various complexities or dilemmas particular to devising joint action among principal organizations to address some aspect of the consequences of modern living. That is, in setting out to solve some social, economic, environmental, or cultural problem, another order of problems arose concerning communication, such as devising new vocabularies for talking across sectoral and disciplinary divides and methods for interpreting initiative success and failure when different cultural backgrounds shape the sense of what is good and right. When these matters arise there is relevance for new actors, or new versions of old actors, specializing in practice of communication to find ways to make sense of and devise solutions to the complexities and dilemmas for principal actors. The expert communication service might fail and the service disappear from the scene or it might work and become part of the scene as a background enabler of the principal actors. Thus, "where is expertise" may not be the obvious or even the critical question. Indeed, in the spirit of Star and Ruhleder, it is very pertinent to ask "when is expertise?" GPT and CAD endeavor to articulate the problems and puzzles practical communication theories address, and "when" helps locate the conditions that give rise to communication expertise, its emergence and transmission.

COMMUNICATION: HOW DO EXPERTISE AND COMMUNICATION RELATE?

By asking "when is expertise?," an alternative, complementary path to the analysis of location and transmission opens. Echoing Barbour, Sommer, and Gill (this volume), communicative expertise is unique in that it is constructed and enacted through relationships. We argue that expertise is grounded in a particular organization's ability to bridge an opportunity space and formalize a relationship between other distinct parties. Indeed, such relationships in their moment are an object of expertise. The problem in asking "where is expertise" is that it frames expertise as a thing to be found and then transmitted to other users or stored for future use, thus perpetuating the presumption that com-municative analysis of expertise and knowledge is primarily a matter of understanding information-seeking behaviors and systems. This is not an unreasonable strategy but it treats communication as vehicle of expertise and comes at the cost of seeing that there is expertise about communication as a pervasive, significant "meaning engagement practice" (Mokros and Aakhus, 2002), as highlighted in the preceding analysis.

LEVEL: ROLE OF ORGANIZATION IN UNDERSTANDING EXPERTISE?

The organizations examined here are presumably built up around some evolving conceptualizations of how communication works and how it ought to work that inspires what the organization becomes and its course of action. If so, then these organizations cultivate their expertise about communication through the devel-opment and refinement of concepts, intuitions, schemas, processes, procedures, technologies, and artifacts that distinguish the expert servicing of one organiza-tion from another. Understanding the way in which these become assembled is crucial to organizational expertise, as an organization is the instrumentation or method for inquiry into communication problems.

While communication expertise happens relative to the meaning of societal exigencies and the interpretation of and intervention upon communicative complexities and dilemmas in addressing the exigencies, there is no guarantee that expert servicing is relevant or useful. The development of communication expertise, and the competition in service provision, has the potential to define societal exigencies in unexpected ways.

UNIQUENESS: WHAT DOES THE PRESENT APPROACH OFFER?

Within organizational studies, the area of organizational communication research offers two key starting points for making sense of organizations that provide expert communication servicing. One emphasizes communication as a vehicle of knowledge transmission and the other emphasizes how organization is emergent in communication. While each of these has much to offer, the approach here departs from these two starting points. The former does not effectively engage practice while the latter does not effectively engage the normativity of practice. Where the former has developed methods for tracking transmission, and the impacts of knowledge that could in principle be incorporated into practice, the latter has developed methods for mapping organizational emergence to articulate processes that comment on some aspects of practice. What is missing is a means for engaging communication expertise as practical knowledge and practical reasoning about constructing communication in terms of the ideas expert practices advance about how communication works and how it ought to work. The integration of GPT and CAD offers a fruitful way forward.

TECHNOLOGY: WHAT'S THE ROLE OF THE INFORMATION AGE?

The approach taken here treats technologies as extensions of practice, of communication practice in particular. Whether a technology is a software application, a device, a transmission line, or a stick for pulling ants out of an ant pile for dinner, it is the realization of an idea about how people connect to each other and the natural and built world around them. A technology, intentionally or unintentionally, is a design for interaction that makes particular forms of communication more or less easy. From the vantage point here, technology is not privileged over the demands of human communication, but advanced information technologies in particular appear to scaffold robust means for realizing ideas about communication while opening up possibilities for entirely new conceptualizations of communication practice—for better or worse.

The inquiry pursued here highlights that ideas about communication still matter and understanding the consequences of ideas matters even more. Hence, the need to develop a pragmatic, practice-based approach to understanding communication problems and our solutions to them, such as found in GPT and CAD.

■ REFERENCES

Aakhus, M. (2002). Modeling Reconstruction in Groupware Technology. In F. H. van Eemeren (ed.), *Advances in Pragma-Dialectics* (pp. 121–36). Newport News, VA: Vale Press.

Aakhus, M. (2007). Communication as Design. *Communication Monographs*, 74, 112–17.

Alvesson, M. (2001). Knowledge Work: Ambiguity, Image and Identity. *Human Relations*, 54, 863–86.

Chesbrough, H. (2003). *Open Innovation: The New Imperative for Creating and Profiting from Technology*. Boston: Harvard Business School Press.

Craig, R. T. (1999). Communication Theory as a Field. *Communication Theory*, 9, 119–61.

Craig, R. T., and Tracy, K. (1995). Grounded Practical Theory and the Case of Intellectual Discussion. *Communication Theory*, 5, 248–72.

Craig, R. T., and Tracy, K. (2014). Building Grounded Practical Theory in Applied Communication Research: Introduction to the Special Issue. *Journal of Applied Communication Research*, 42, 229–43.

Eggers, W., and MacMillan, P. (2013). *The Solution Revolution: How Business, Government, and Social Enterprises are Teaming up to Solve Society's Toughest Problems*. Boston: Harvard Business School Publishing.

Engeström, Y. (1990). When is a Tool? Multiple Meanings of Artifacts in Human Activity. In Y. Engeström (ed.), *Learning, Working and Imagining: Twelve Studies in Activity Theory* (pp. 171–95). Helsinki: Orienta-Konsultit.

Hollingshead, A. B., and Brandon, D. P. (2003). Potential Benefits of Communication in Transactive Memory Systems. *Human Communication Research*, 29, 607–15.

Jackson, S., and Aakhus, M. (2014). Becoming More Reflective about the Role of Design in Communication. *Journal of Applied Communication Research*, 42, 125–34.

Lammers, J. C. (2011). How Institutions Communicate: Institutional Messages, Institutional Logics, and Organizational Communication. *Management Communication Quarterly*, 25, 154–82.

Leonardi, P. M., and Treem, J. W. (2012). Knowledge Management Technology as a Stage for Strategic Self-Presentation: Implications for Knowledge Sharing in Organizations. *Information and Organization*, 22, 37–59.

Lichtenthaler, U. (2011). Open Innovation: Past Research, Current Debates, and Future Directions. *Academy of Management Perspectives*, 25, 75–93.

Mokros, H. B., and Aakhus, M. (2002). From Information-Seeking Behavior to Meaning Engagement Practice. *Human Communication Research*, 28, 298–312.

Star, S. L., and Ruhleder, K. (1996). Steps toward an Ecology of Infrastructure: Design and Access for Large Information Spaces. *Information Systems Research*, 7, 111–34.

Part IV

New Directions for the Study of Expertise, Communication, and Organizing

11 Explaining the (De)valuation of Process Experts in Contemporary Organizations

JEFFREY W. TREEM AND WILLIAM C. BARLEY

Is it possible to be an expert at searching for information on the internet? Answering this question calls into focus all of the different skills and abilities at play when conducting a search for information online. There is the operational aspect, which ranges from knowing how to navigate a webpage to skillfully using specialized operator terms to refine the search. Once you have search results you have to determine which are the most useful, trustworthy, and relevant sources of information. A search may return tens of thousands of results and you will need to decide when to stop looking at content and what information you will leave unused or unviewed. Then you have to decide what to do with the information you find: where to enter, store, and label the content. Finally, you likely want to share your results with others, so you have to determine the most effective way to present the information you have found in a manner that will be meaningful to those not involved in the actual search process.

Each of these skills and abilities is an area where individuals can be judged to be more or less competent, and therefore logic would dictate that it is indeed possible to be more or less expert in the task of searching for information on the internet. However, it is not immediately clear how to conceptualize the value of expertise in a process like internet search absent a specific goal orientation. Search is not a restricted activity, and anyone with a basic connection to the internet can access a search engine; therefore the value of this form of expertise is not tied to the exclusivity of participation in the practice.

Further, searching for information on the internet is not widely recognized as a domain of specialist practice, and does not in itself constitute a profession, a discipline, or even an occupational role (i.e. one is not likely to have a job title of Head Internet Searcher).[1] We can understand how the ability to effectively

---

[1] Here we are not referring to the specialist technical expertise involved in building, operating, or maintaining search engines, which overlaps with domains of computer and information sciences. Acting within those domains requires knowledge of specific computer programming languages and protocols that most individuals do not possess. Rather, our example is in reference to the everyday use of publically accessible search engines to discover and curate desired information.

locate the latest studies in a discipline is critical to becoming an expert researcher, accessing published updates in drug interactions is part of being an expert physician, and reviewing case law helps one perform as an expert attorney. When we view these actions as constituting expertise, however, we tend to attribute that expertise to the visible goal-oriented outcomes (i.e. research, medicine, or law) rather than the process itself (i.e. search). This tendency in attributing produces a bias in our perceptions of expertise that favors involving social practices and observable interaction, and discounts the importance of expertise in the many communicative processes—which are often not easily visible—that help constitute those practices (Treem, 2012). Our primary claim and object of inquiry in this chapter is that we neglect forms of expertise that focus on the *processes* that help facilitate expert practice.

We introduce the concept of *process expertise* to refer to expertise that is applicable to managing information and communication both within and across domains but does not, in itself, represent those domains' practices. Practice in a domain consists of what Collins and Evans (2007) classify as *specialist tacit knowledge* and takes two forms: contributory expertise and interactional expertise. Contributory expertise is the practice of actively participating in a specialist domain and is what we most commonly associate with expert performance. Contributory expertise has an embodied, material, or actionable quality—it can be understood as *doing*. When a physician performs a surgery, an attorney cross-examines a witness, or a plumber installs a garbage disposal they each respectively exhibit contributory expertise in medicine, law, and plumbing. Alternatively, interactional expertise is mastery of the language of a domain in the absence of actual practice in that domain. Interactional expertise is fundamentally communicative, and can be viewed more as *talking* the language of a domain. An author writing a textbook on surgery, a lawyer describing courtroom procedures to an associate, and a homeowner questioning a plumber about appropriate pipe fittings are each displaying interactional expertise in the respective domain.

Process expertise is similar to contributory expertise in that it represents a *doing* of something. It differs from contributory expertise, in that the "it" doing it involves is not easily aligned with a widely recognized domain of specialist knowledge. Process expertise often facilitates other forms of contributory expertise, and therefore can be viewed as adjacent to or overlapping with contributory expertise. Further, process expertise incorporates the materiality of work in ways not represented through interactional expertise. The concept of interactional expertise privileges individuals' use of language to engage with other human actors. This focus on language overlooks the important role that the ongoing production, maintenance, and use of communication artifacts (e.g. files, emails, paper, presentations) plays in organizational practices (Ashcraft et al., 2009; Cooren et al., 2012).

Process expertise deals with information that may inform practice in a specific domain, but does not necessarily replicate the language of that practice. For instance conducting a meta-analysis on the effect of a low-fat diet on long-term health requires contributory domain expertise related to statistics and health science. Communicating that study's results in a manner that is meaningful to other scholars requires interactional expertise in the accepted language of experts in those domains. In addition, we claim that the ability to navigate various research databases and identify all the relevant articles required for the meta-analysis is also a distinct form of expertise. In this case both the contributory expertise (the "science") and the communication about the practice (the interactional expertise) are shaped by the performance of the initial expertise in finding relevant articles and extracting information within them (process expertise).

Our goal in this chapter is not merely to advocate for process expertise as a distinct construct[2] worthy of our attention, but to explain why this type of expertise is often undervalued in contemporary work environments. We are conditioned to value work practices that are visibly associated with exclusive forms of domain knowledge. Despite its pervasiveness in organizations, process expertise is often marginalized as a complement to this type of expert work. By showing how process expertise manifests itself in organizations we aim to provide a framework for understanding its distinct value for individuals and organizations. Finally, we present an agenda for incorporating the study of process expertise into research on expert work and identify issues that will be relevant to the ongoing study of process expertise.

The Invisible Rise of Process Expertise

One consequence of operating in the information age (Castells, 2000) or the era of big data (Boyd and Crawford, 2012) is that individual and organizational success increasingly depends on the skillful acquisition, transfer, and storage of large amounts of information. The growing volume of information which is easily accessible to individuals across expert domains has made process expertise both possible and valuable. Rather than revealing how the information age has ushered the importance of this form of expertise, however, recent research has focused more on the ways information access has eroded the

[2] We characterize process expertise as a distinct construct in the sense that it refers to a specific form of action related to processes of information use that facilitate action. However, an alternative way to conceptualize process expertise would be as a form of contributory expertise *in* a particular organizational process (see the example of expertise in internet searching). However, because these types of contributory expertise are often not recognized as specialist domains there is value, both analytically and practically, in considering process expertise as distinct from contributory expertise.

exclusivity of domain knowledge. For instance, medical patients access databases of symptoms, diagnoses, and treatment plans and increasingly challenge the knowledge offered by physicians (Lowrey and Anderson, 2006), car buyers now have access to automobile listings and historical pricing that allows them to bypass the services of expert salespeople (Barley, 2015), and consumers can inexpensively purchase software that calculates tax obligations and incorporates the latest policy changes without relying on the knowledge of certified public accountants. This research demonstrates that developments in information and communication technologies (ICT) have dramatically changed the nature of professional work. Instead of relying on exclusive jurisdiction over information for claims of expertise, modern professionals exhibit what Brint (1994) calls "professional expertise," which consists of distinct technical skills and abilities that are valued in the marketplace for services.

The shift toward knowledge-based and technologically mediated work environments has meant that work practices increasingly involve information processes: processes to use information technologies; processes to organize information that goes into or comes out of those technologies; processes for evaluating the usefulness, completeness, and accuracy of information; or processes for representing this information to others. Ironically, organizations often use ICT, such as knowledge management systems, to try to automate many of the processes that make information useful to individuals in a particular context. Technologies such as group decision support systems (Poole and Holmes, 1995), expertise recommender systems (McDonald, 2001), and work flow platforms (Dourish, 2001) were all developed to facilitate processes associated with information management and use. The logic driving the proliferation of knowledge management platforms is that the technologies could capture the knowledge of professionals in a manner freeing them from information processing, so they may spend their time working on the things they know.

This perspective of viewing technology as an aid to expert practice treats the processes of its use as detached from the practice of expertise. What is missing from this story is the recognition of the various ways that individuals interpret, enact, apply, and manipulate communication technologies to their own ends, a sentiment which is at the core of many early critiques of knowledge management systems (Ackerman, 2000; Ackerman and Halverson, 2000; McDermott, 1999). Overlooking the importance of these process skills is a mistake. This is what Zuboff (1988) meant when she noted the increased role and importance of *intellective skills* that workers employ to develop meaning from the data produced by workplace technologies. We see process expertise as a way to conceptualize the variance in intellective skills among workers and to develop a framework for how these skills add value in organizations.

A key aspect of understanding the value of process expertise is how it can influence the performance of domain expertise. Leonardi and Treem (2012) provide an example of the close coupling between process and domain expertise in their study of a team of IT service technicians. In their case study, the team members had recently instituted a process for assigning work tasks that used information within a knowledge management system to determine who was most qualified for each job (i.e. who had relevant domain expertise). Some workers quickly recognized that this assignment process depended heavily on the information they entered into the knowledge management system and began to curate their information entry to appear more or less qualified for specific jobs. In this case the strategic use of the knowledge management system (a process expertise) influenced other workers' assessments of domain expertise. Ironically, these assessments also led to the strategic workers securing opportunities to develop greater domain expertise. As was the case with the internet searchers referenced earlier, this example illustrates how process expertise is readily transitioned into contributory domain expertise. The workers on this team were contributory experts in IT in that they actively responded to software and hardware issues within the organizations and worked to solve situated problems. At the same time, attributions of the workers' level of expertise in IT were shaped by their process expertise in using knowledge management technology.

One thing that makes process expertise particularly interesting, then, is that its importance is often devalued, discounted, or ignored by individuals and organizations. This devaluing is visible in the fact that the experts who perform technical, information, and clerical process work in organizations are often situated in low-status positions. For example, Kellogg (2014) documented the importance of process experts in her comparative study of health care reform at two hospitals. The doctors and lawyers involved in the planned reform all recognized that the skilled ability to screen and coordinate potential patients, a process expertise, was necessary to their reform's success. These professionals, however, viewed the expertise needed for patient coordination as outside of and below their jurisdiction and believed that developing it themselves would compromise their position as domain experts. Given this reluctance, successful reform only emerged in the hospital where a group of lower status professionals, community health workers, took on the task of developing and performing this expertise. Leaders of the change effort primarily valued specialist domain expertise (i.e. knowledge of medicine and legal policy) when considering the potential for health care reform. However, they quickly discovered that the ability to implement their change depended on an expertise with process elements (i.e. knowledge of how to schedule appointments and how to process insurance claims).

One driving factor behind the devaluation of process expertise, we believe, is that process expertise is rarely associated with the type of specific knowledge we associate with domain experts. We commonly talk about someone who is an expert *in* political science, or *at* chess. This view of expertise as bound to a particular area, ability, or exercise underlies the perspective that expertise emerges through long-term immersion and deliberate practice in a domain (Ericsson et al., 1993). Over time as individuals learn how to operate in a particular domain and their abilities develop, they develop competence, proficiency, and potentially expertise in the respective area of interest (Dreyfus and Dreyfus, 2005). This view of expertise as developed through situated exposure over time is one reason why we often use experience in a domain as a signal of expertise.

The assumptions that expertise emerges through prolonged exposure in a domain and through interaction with domain experts are most pronounced in studies of professions and professional work. Research in sociology and organization studies has demonstrated the steps professions take to set limits on who has the rights and authority to operate in specialist domains (Abbott, 1988; Friedson, 2001; Larson, 1977). Over time expertise development becomes institutionalized within professional spheres such that individuals must attain levels of education, licensure, or certification in order to authoritatively claim expertise in a specialist practice. For example, a lawyer must attend an accredited university, pass an exam administered by a local judicial jurisdiction, and remain in good standing with a legal administration in order to practice as an attorney. Similar restrictions and limitations are found in other professional service domains guiding the work of physicians, engineers, or accountants. The alignment of specialist expertise with institutionalized domains provides individuals with shared expectations regarding not only the nature of the knowledge that experts possess, but how experts in a particular domain are expected to act or communicate (Lammers and Garcia, 2009). In turn, as professions and their association with certain forms of expertise are sustained over time they become institutionalized and in doing so communicate more broadly, at the individual, organizational, and societal level, expectations as to what experts look like and where we should look to find them (Lammers, 2011).

We currently lack an effective way to communicate about process expertise and the value it provides. Because process expertise is difficult to see as distinct, it lacks the authority associated with visible, material performances (see Kuhn and Rennstam, this volume, for a discussion of materiality and authority). We see the lawyer arguing an appeal in front of a judge, but we do not see the process of pulling case law from the library; we see the academic manuscript in a scholarly journal, but we do not see the process of constructing the annotated bibliography that helped prepare the article. Without a specific domain of application, and the associated institutional logics, rules, and messages that guide our understandings of expertise, process expertise is likely to be viewed as an idiosyncratic knack. As Zuboff (1988) noted in discussing the growing importance of how workers interpret abstract data, "Without a context in which meanings can be assumed, people have to articulate their own rendering of meaning and communicate it to others." Yet, as this quote notes, we currently interpret this expertise in terms of the language of the domain of practice (i.e. who it is communicated to), and do not consider the process of "articulating their own rendering of meaning" as an expert practice in itself.

The Organizational Value of Process Expertise

We argue that processes that support domain practices can often be conceptualized as their own domain of expertise. Recognizing that individuals can be process experts offers us a way to better analyze organizational work. Three elements lead us to assert that individuals can operate as process experts. First, the presence of expertise is predicated on the existence of a range of proficiencies and it is certain that individuals may be more or less effective at executing work processes. For instance, in Treem's (2013) study of public relations professionals he observed that individuals varied in their proficiency at using email or productivity tools such as Microsoft Excel or PowerPoint. Workers perceived differences in how peers used these commonplace technologies and these perceptions influenced their attributions of their peers' capabilities as public relations practitioners. These judgments about expertise could be objective, such as based on some standard that allows empirical comparison, either relativistic, based on the distribution of expertise within a specific context, or perceptual in that individuals believe that someone is an expert in a domain. Second, process expertise is skill-, ability-, and action-based. It is something that people *do* as a part of work and has a material component. Given the practical nature of process expertise, it follows the same standards used for contributory and interactional expertise that prolonged immersion in the domain will produce expertise (Collins et al., 2007). However, the domain of interest in the case of process expertise is the performance of a particular type of process and not traditional development of domain knowledge. Although it is not easy to identify a specific type of training, background, or shared knowledge that process experts possess, they do behave in a manner that can be visibly distinguished from non-experts. Third, process expertise has value in the sense that it is desired by organizations, and aids organizational practices. Although experts are often viewed as possessing or exhibiting rare or esoteric knowledge, an alternative characterization of an expert is someone who can competently and reliable provide something of value (see Yoon, Gupta, and Hollingshead, this volume, regarding judgments of competency). Process experts meet this standard in that engaging them involves a confidence and trust they will be able to provide a specific form of expertise, and in turn that expertise will not need to be obtained or developed elsewhere.

That process expertise is not associated with traditional knowledge domains does not necessarily imply that it plays a less important role in the production of value in organizations. Upon examining the type of work that process experts perform, we can identify at least four ways these individuals contribute to organizational action that traditional domain experts do not. In the following, we outline four common organizational processes where process expertise can facilitate the production of value. Many of these processes are not new to organizational studies, and many domain experts have some level of ability in performing them. As we will demonstrate, however, when an individual possesses expert ability at these processes, this can greatly facilitate organizational action.

OPERATIONAL PROCESSES

This refers to the instrumental understanding of how to operate the technologies, tools, and artifacts that provide individuals access to domain information. For example, Barley (1986) documented how technicians, not doctors, in a radiology department developed expertise in how to operate a new CT scanner and interpret the machine's outputs. These technicians were not expert radiologists (contributory) nor could they competently participate in conversations about the antecedents, progression, and proper treatment of the illnesses they viewed (interactional), but they still became critical to the expert process of providing CT scans at the hospital. The expertise of the radiology unit was largely influenced by the technicians' process expertise. Operational process expertise is often associated with the practices of technicians operating on the periphery of specialist domains, and because technicians can find it difficult to identify with professionals, they may have less power or authority relative to co-workers in traditional professional roles (Zabusky, 1997). A consequence of this is that operational process expertise and the individuals who exhibit this type of expertise are often commoditized and treated as "hired guns" instead of full contributors to an organization or profession (Barley and Kunda, 2006). Despite the material contributions operational processes make to practices, the individuals skilled at these processes are often treated as detached from the visible expert performance of the organization.

Operational process expertise is likely to be most valuable at the initial stages of a technology's diffusion or its immediate introduction into organizations. It is during these times that differentials in process expertise are likely to be highest, and therefore those with process expertise will have greater opportunities to contribute to practices (e.g. Black et al., 2004). Attewell (1992) describes the diffusion of business computing among organizations and notes that organizations initially outsourced the process, not because they did not view it as valuable, but to avoid the effort needed to develop the expertise of effectively using the technology. As business computing processes became ubiquitous, informal computer "gurus" emerged on teams to help trouble-shoot problems and teach peers how best to use the technology (for a similar example related to computer skills see Collins, this volume). Similarly, Treem (2013) found that public relations professionals with expertise in processes of using social media or design software were afforded opportunities to work on broader number of teams relative to their co-workers who had more common and shared forms of expertise. It is important to note that in both the business computing and public relations examples the process expertise was of distinct value to the teams and individuals, but in neither case was it formally recognized as an official aspect of the individuals' work roles.

CURATIONAL PROCESSES

These processes facilitate the appropriate retrieval, aggregation, and consolidation of information. Curational processes manage the challenge of making sense of information in environments where individuals cannot possibly comprehend the totality of information available to them (Eppler and Mengis, 2004). This overload, which is exacerbated by the proliferation of ICT, has a negative influence on work by increasing the stress felt by workers and increasing the likelihood employees will leave an organization (Ayyagari et al., 2011; Karr-Wisniewski and Lu, 2010). Files pile up over time, databases become bloated, and information about operations and performance continue to grow and grow. Contemporary organizations, then, face the challenge of knowing how to store information in a manner that will allow for easier retrieval and utilization.

Research suggests that curational process expertise is both present and valuable to organizations. At the individual level, for example, workers vary in the systems they use for filing and storing emails, and their ability to manage messages influences the amount of stress created by email communication (Dabbish and Kraut, 2006; Whittaker and Sidner, 1996). Similarly, at the group level Rader (2010) notes how individuals rarely consider others when storing and documenting information, and that purposeful labeling of information can increase the likelihood that information will be useful to others. Another example of the value of curational processes is seen in the development of articles in Wikipedia. Although we think of the substantive content of Wikipedia in terms of subject entries, the organization of the article in terms of labels, structure, and integration with the platform is conducted by editors. These editors may have no knowledge at all about the respective topic of the article they work on, but their expertise in the process of article construction facilitates higher quality entries. Sundin (2011) refers to editors in Wikipedia as "janitors of knowledge," a label reflecting how these process-oriented workers are viewed as having a lower status than others. However, Wikipedia's operation as a quality reference tool depends intimately on its editors' curational process expertise.

Curational process expertise is especially valuable to organizations in the development of knowledge directories. Scholars applying principles of transactive memory theory have argued that technology might be helpful in developing explicit, visible directories of who knows what in organizations (Jackson and Klobas, 2008; Nevo and Wand, 2005). However, it is often difficult to get individuals to contribute and update accurate information in these systems. Research shows that individuals with curational process expertise can facilitate systems such as file repositories, knowledge directories, internal social networking sites, or expertise finders. For instance, McDonald (2001) described the use of "expertise concierges" in a software company who intimately knew other employees' areas of expertise and assisted people in finding experts relevant to their needs. The concierges' expertise was knowing where knowledge was located in the organization in order to coordinate connections.

It is not inherently necessary, however, that curators be knowledgeable or even conversant in each of the areas of expertise they curate (which would constitute contributory or interactional expertise), but only that they can effectively facilitate the organization and movement of that knowledge. In an example Farzan et al. (2009) described how individuals acted as "promoters" on an internal social networking site and were able to increase participation on the site by recommending relevant or interesting content. The enactment of curational process expertise can help organizations connect workers with information useful to them in their respective domains.

EVALUATIVE PROCESSES

These processes concern the evaluation of potentially incomplete subsets of information within ambiguous environments to determine whether that subset is a more or less accurate portrayal of the broader information context. One of the recurring conundrums of abundant information access is knowing when to stop collecting information. For example, when performing "media monitoring" tasks, public relations professionals actively monitor numerous media outlets to collect stories relevant to their clients. A common dilemma that media monitors face, however, is that the vast number of media outlets in existence make it functionally impossible to monitor them all while providing clients with a timely account of coverage. A key aspect of a PR professional's process expertise, then, is knowing when their account of coverage is sufficient to function for their clients' purposes.

Evaluative process expertise is valuable because it helps organizations act effectively and efficiently in what March and Simon (1958) would call an ambiguous informational environment. Evaluative expertise is particularly visible in contexts where there is a pressing need to assemble an accurate understanding of a context in a timely manner. Studies of 911 call operators (Tracy, 1997; Tracy, 2002), for example, demonstrate the value of individuals who have this form of expertise. By engaging in strategic inquiry to gather and assess information emergency operators rapidly evaluate potentially danger- ous scenarios in a manner that allows for the efficient deployment of limited expert resources (e.g. police, paramedics, and firefighters).

We saw similar process expertise in our own research about the important role that nurses played in coordinating the transfer of ill children between hospitals (Barley et al., 2011). The nurses we studied were neither contributory experts in the treatment of children, nor familiar with every practitioner in their environ- ment. They were, however, routinely attributed as being experts at facilitating the transfer process. By intimately knowing the pediatric transport process, nurses were able to rapidly construct an accurate portrayal of a child who was located in a remote location. In doing so, they could determine whether the information they had gathered was sufficient to deploy hospital resources, or whether they needed to engage in further data collection to construct an accurate portrayal of their patients. By performing this process, nurses minimized the time taken to transport patients between hospitals and the danger those patients faced in that process. The presence of evaluative process expertise meant that those respon- sible for exhibiting the specialist practice (i.e. physicians) could be confident they were working with the most accurate information available.

REPRESENTATIONAL PROCESSES

These processes involve the production of representations that display infor- mation in a manner that facilitates organizational goals. An extensive litera- ture from Science Studies has shown us the value of representational processes in the ongoing production, transfer, and establishment of knowledge (Daston and Galison, 2007; Latour, 1986; Lynch and Woolgar, 1990). For example, Vertesi's (2015) study of the NASA Mars Rover team showed how important the visualization process was to researchers' ability to produce knowledge. She showed how the process of visualizing data from the Rover's sensors led researchers to discover evidence of water in the Martian environment. At least in its initial stages, this visualization process was clearly performed by a process expert who was not attempting to apply contributory domain expertise—the reason scientists constructed their early data representations of the Martian soil was to figure out how to get their robot's wheels unstuck from a sand trap (not to check for evidence of water).

In addition to facilitating expert interpretation, skilled representation can support political and persuasive processes. The skillful production of PowerPoint presentations, for example, plays an important role facilitating strategic change (Kaplan, 2010; Stark and Paravel, 2008). Although we may discount the value of skilled "PowerPoint-ing" to organizational activity, research suggests that this form of representation plays an increasingly prominent role in organizations (Schoeneborn, 2013; Tufte, 2003). Barley et al. (2012) demonstrated how the skillful production of information representations was central to negotiating knowledge at an automobile engineering organization. By crafting representations that displayed information in particular ways, engineers sought to either facilitate knowledge exchange or produce non-negotiable closure in the ongoing design of the car. Providing evidence that this representational ability was a process expertise, not a domain expertise, the authors found that the practices associated with this set of skills were consistent *across* a number of contributory expert domains. Representational process expertise was critical to the ability of domain specialist to manifest practices (i.e. proceeding with a particular unit's proposed design), but it represented a distinct form of expertise, and teams varied in how successful they were in deploying this expertise.

As the preceding sections illustrate, the value of process expertise is not based on exclusivity or the mastery of esoteric knowledge, but the mastery of a process that often has the potential to be deployed across multiple domains of practice. We refer to this quality of process expertise as "transferability." This is an important difference between process expertise and interactional expertise, which Collins and Evans (2007) refer to as "parasitic" because its value *relies* on its position relative to a specific contributory domain. If that domain were to stop existing, or the interactional expert were to lose access to people working in that domain, their ability to provide value would diminish. By definition, process expertise allows an expert to easily find new applications when access to a current domain is lost.

The transferability of process expertise also makes this expertise potentially more valuable for individuals than more disciplinary forms of expertise. Because process expertise is not dependent upon a particular domain it may offer individuals greater flexibility in terms of the professions, organizations, and occupational roles available to these types of experts. Conversely, individuals who immerse themselves in a particular domain are likely to develop greater expertise related to that domain, but developing such a familiarity may also come at the cost of reducing transferability. Similarly, the transferability of process expertise may increase the cognitive flexibility of process experts. When a specialist expert is faced with a problem in their respective domain they may call upon knowledge gained from previous experience to form a response: they are using knowledge they *have*, an object orientation. Over time they become reliant on entrenched or narrow domains of knowledge and less capable of considering alternative options (Dane, 2010). Because process expertise is often enacted in service of different practices over time, process experts are called on recurrently to utilize dynamic information to form a response: they are trying to facilitate new knowledge through an emergent, situated process. This suggests two different, but potentially interrelated paths to expert performance: domain-based and process-based.

Process expertise is also valuable to organizations because, when it is effectively aligned with specialist practices, it can amplify domain experts' work while minimizing their external obligations. This attribute of amplification can be contrasted with efforts to integrate knowledge by fostering deep collaboration of multiple domain experts. This type of collaboration requires developing forms of communication that can span specialist domains of expertise. Because process expertise is aimed directly at facilitating multiple existing practices, it can be coordinated in a manner that minimizes this type of work. For instance, in the example of pediatric patient transfer provided earlier, doctors at the pediatric specialty hospital often relied on patient records from outside hospitals to inform diagnoses and treatment plans. Without a process expert they would need to search for this relevant information, interpret the unique notation and terms used by the referring hospital, and consider whether they could trust the accuracy of the information. All of these processes would require time and effort. This requirement was minimized by their access to individuals who had operational process expertise to access relevant databases, curational process expertise to locate and integrate patient information, evaluative process expertise to assess the accuracy and comprehensiveness of information, and representational process expertise to present the case to local physicians.

Advancing the Study of Expertise

Broadly, this chapter serves as a call to treat process expertise as a distinct concept, explain why process expertise has been neglected in research on expertise and organizing, and provide a framework for the study of process expertise. We see three distinct areas of inquiry where an increased focus on process expertise can inform theoretical and applied developments.

TEAM ASSEMBLY

Recently scholars have become interested in the "science of team science" which explores how groups may combine specialized expertise to increase productivity, efficiency, and innovative outcomes (Contractor, 2013; Hall et al., 2008). However, this field largely looks at combinations of individuals in terms of disciplinary expertise (i.e. Borner et al., 2010) and therefore may be overlooking process experts. Integrating process experts into the study of teams is important because research shows that cumulative specialist expertise alone does not predict successful performance, rather it is processes of coordination, communication, and interdependencies that are correlated with the outcomes of organizational groups (Faraj and Sproull, 2000). Because process expertise has value in relation to its ability to facilitate contributory expertise, it may be incorporated into team assembly in a variety of ways. For instance, process expertise could exist as a broker for specialist domain experts, and therefore experts would sit outside of disciplines serving in a supplier or contractor role. Alternatively process experts could be incorporated into disciplinary teams and develop interactional expertise that aided coordination in a specialist or technician role. Finally, domain specialists could develop process expertise themselves which would broaden the scope of their contributory expertise. Each of these configurations presents different challenges related to how to best utilize the individual expertise of members in a manner that will benefit team performance.

ANALYZING ORGANIZATIONAL EXPERTISE

Embracing process expertise allows analysts to move beyond the practice–performance dichotomy that characterizes research on expertise, because it offers a framework to view expertise both as something workers do, and something that produces a distinct organizational outcome. Studying process expertise as something that is dynamic and manifest in different ways incorporates the duality that Feldman and Pentland (2003) describe as existing between the ostensive nature of what processes are meant to be, and the performative nature of how they are materialized in organizations. The majority of extant research on expertise looks at one side of this duality, either considering an ongoing accomplishment situated in action (Kuhn and Rennstam, this volume), or as an object that organizations seek to acquire, develop, and sell (see Aakhus et al., this volume). An analysis that considers process expertise can allow for examinations of expertise across organizational levels by including both specific micro-level behaviors in service of a disciplinary practice, as well as the performance of the practice and the resulting outcomes for the organization. This allows us to heed the call of Nicolini (2009) to both zoom in to see how organizational communication is constituted by individual workers, and zoom out to see the enactment of this communication and subsequent outcomes for organizations. This framework allows researchers to pose new questions related to the ways organizations and individuals demonstrate, reveal, or obfuscate actions that are viewed as expertise.

INSTITUTIONALIZING PROCESS EXPERTISE

When evaluating the expertise of individuals we commonly consider visible attributes, behaviors, and experiences (Bunderson and Barton, 2011). For instance, in attributing expertise to an engineer you might look at whether they graduated with a degree in engineering from a prestigious university, or are licensed by the National Society of Professional Engineers. Because process expertise does not easily align with a discipline or profession it may not be easily identified by organizations and therefore overlooked in employee selection. An implication of this is that process expertise may increase in perceived value if it becomes associated with institutional forms that can confer valued signals of status, such as academic disciplines or professions. A current example of this is the emergence of data analytics as an organizational function and program of study at universities. Data analytics, which can be applied across domains and comprises processes of operating with, curating, evaluating, and representing various forms of data, can be understood as a form of process expertise. Interestingly, certificates and programs of study focused on data analytics are found in diverse disciplinary areas including schools of management, engineering, and arts and sciences, which demonstrates the transferability of process expertise. This context presents the opportunity to study the differential value of data analytics in different disciplines and what institutional markers shift the value of process expertise.

■ REFERENCES

Abbott, A. (1988). *The System Of Professions: An Essay on the Division of Expert Labor.* Chicago: University of Chicago Press.

Ackerman, M. S. (2000). The Intellectual Challenge of CSCW: The Gap between Social Requirements and Technical Feasibility. *Human–Computer Interaction,* 15, 179–204. Retrieved from <http://www.eecs.umich.edu/~ackerm/pub/00a10/hci.final.pdf>.

Ackerman, M. S., and Halverson, C. A. (2000). Reexamining Organizational Memory. *Communications of the ACM,* 43, 58–64.

Ashcraft, K. L., Kuhn, T. R., and Cooren, F. (2009). Constitutional Amendments: "Materializing" Organizational Communication. *Academy of Management Annals,* 3, 1–64. doi: 10.1080/19416520903047186

Attewell, P. (1992). Technology Diffusion and Organizational Learning: The Case of Business Computing. *Organization Science,* 3, 1–19. doi: 10.1287/orsc.3.1.1

Ayyagari, R., Grover, V., and Purvis, R. (2011). Technostress: Technological Antecedents and Implications. *MIS Quarterly,* 35, 831–58.

Barley, S. R. (1986). Technology as an Occasion for Structuring: Evidence from Observations of CT Scanners and the Social Order of Radiology Departments. *Administrative Science Quarterly,* 31, 78–108.

Barley, S. R. (2015). Why the Internet Makes Buying a Car Less Loathsome: How Technologies Change Role Relations. *Academy of Management Discoveries*, 1, 5–35. doi: 10.5465/amd.2013.0016

Barley, S. R., and Kunda, G. (2006). *Gurus, Hired Guns, and Warm Bodies: Itinerant Experts in a Knowledge Economy*. Princeton: Princeton University Press.

Barley, W. C., Leonardi, P. M., and Bailey, D. E. (2012). Engineering Objects for Collaboration: Strategies of Ambiguity and Clarity at Knowledge Boundaries. *Human Communication Research*, 38, 280–308.

Barley, W. C., Leonardi, P. M., and Treem, J. W. (2011). Information Triage: Evaluating Expertise to Support Distributed Collaboration. Paper presented at the National Communication Association Annual Conference, New Orleans, LA, Nov.

Black, L. J., Carlile, P. R., and Repenning, N. P. (2004). A Dynamic Theory of Expertise and Occupational Boundaries in New Technology Implementation: Building on Barley's Study of CT Scanning. *Administrative Science Quarterly*, 49, 572–607.

Börner, K., Contractor, N., Falk-Krzensinski, H. J., Fiore, S. M., Keyton, J., Spring, B., Stokols, D., Trochim, W., and Uzzi, B. (2010). A Multi-Level Systems Perspective for the Science of Team Science. *Science Translational Medicine*, 2(49). doi: 10.1126/scitranslmed.3001399

Boyd, D., and Crawford, K. (2012). Critical Questions for Big Data: Provocations for a Cultural, Technological, and Scholarly Phenomenon. *Information, Communication and Society*, 15, 662–79.

Brint, S. (1994). *In an Age of Experts*. Princeton: Princeton University Press.

Bunderson, J. S., and Barton, M. A. (2011). Status Cues and Expertise Assessment in Groups: How Group Members Size One Another Up...and Why it Matters. In J. L. Pearce (ed.), *Status in Management and Organizations* (pp. 215–37). Cambridge: Cambridge University Press.

Castells, M. (2000). *The Information Age: Economy, Society and Culture*, vol. 1. *The Rise of the Network Society*. Oxford: Blackwell.

Collins, H., and Evans, R. (2007). *Rethinking Expertise*. Chicago: University of Chicago Press.

Collins, H., Evans, R., and Gorman, M. (2007). Trading Zones and Interactional Expertise. *Studies in History and Philosophy of Science* (Part A), 38, 657–66.

Contractor, N. (2013). Some Assembly Required: Leveraging Web Science to Understand and Enable Team Assembly. *Philosophical Transactions of the Royal Society of London A: Mathematical, Physical and Engineering Sciences*, 371(1983). doi: 10.1098/rsta.2012.0385

Cooren, F., Fairhurst, G. T., and Huet, R. (2012). Why Matter Always Matters in (Organizational) Communication. In P. M. Leonardi, B. A. Nardi, and J. Kallinikos (eds), *Materiality and Organizing* (pp. 296–314). Oxford: Oxford University Press.

Dabbish, L., and Kraut, R. E. (2006). Email Overload at Work: An Analysis of Factors Associated with Email Strain. Paper presented at the CSCW, Banff, Alberta, Canada.

Dane, E. (2010). Reconsidering the Trade-Off between Expertise and Flexibility: A Cognitive Entrenchment Perspective. *Academy of Management Review*, 35, 579–603.

Daston, L., and Galison, P. (2007). *Objectivity*. Cambridge, MA: Zone Books.

Dourish, P. (2001). Process Descriptions as Organisational Accounting Devices: The Dual Use of Workflow Technologies. In *Proceedings of the 2001 International ACM*

SIGGROUP Conference on Supporting Group Work (GROUP '01) (pp. 52–60). New York: ACM Press.

Dreyfus, H., and Dreyfus, S. (2005). Peripheral Vision: Expertise in Real World Contexts. *Organization Studies*, 26, 779–92. doi: 10.1177/0170840605053102

Eppler, M. J., and Mengis, J. (2004). The Concept of Information Overload: A Review of Literature from Organization Science, Accounting, Marketing, MIS, and Related Disciplines. *The Information Society*, 20, 325–44. doi: 10.1007/978-3-8349-9772-2_15

Ericsson, K. A., Krampe, R. T., and Tesch-Romer, C. (1993). The Role of Deliberate Practice in the Acquisition of Expert Performance. *Psychological Review*, 100, 363–406.

Faraj, S., and Sproull, L. (2000). Coordinating Expertise in Software Development Teams. *Management Science*, 46, 1554–68. doi: 10.1287/mnsc.46.12.1554.12072

Farzan, R., DiMicco, J. M., and Brownholtz, B. (2009). Spreading the Honey: A System for Maintaining an Online Community. In *Proceedings of the 2009 International Conference on Supporting Group Work* (pp. 31–40). New York: ACM. doi: 10.1145/1531674.1531680

Feldman, M. S., and Pentland, B. T. (2003). Reconceptualizing Organizational Routines as a Source of Flexibility and Change. *Administrative Science Quarterly*, 48, 94–118.

Friedson, E. (2001). *Professionalism: The Third Logic*. Cambridge: Polity Press.

Hall, K. L., Stokols, D., Moser, R. P., Taylor, B. K., Thornquist, M. D., Nebeling, L. C., Ehret, C. C., Barnett, M. J., McTiernan, A., Berger, N. A., Goran, M. I., and Jeffrey, R. W. (2008). The Collaboration Readiness of Transdisciplinary Research Teams and Centers: Findings from the National Cancer Institute's TREC Year-One Evaluation Study. *American Journal of Preventive Medicine*, 35(2 suppl), S181–72. doi: 10.1016/j.amepre.2008.03.035

Jackson, P., and Klobas, J. (2008). Transactive Memory Systems in Organizations: Implications for Knowledge Directories. *Decision Support Systems*, 44, 409–24. doi: http://dx.doi.org/10.1016/j.dss.2007.05.001

Kaplan, S. (2010). Strategy and PowerPoint: An Inquiry into the Epistemic Culture and Machinery of Strategy Making. *Organization Science*, 22(2), 320–46. doi: 10.1287/orsc.1100.0531

Karr-Wisniewski, P., and Lu, Y. (2010). When More is Too Much: Operationalizing Technology Overload and Exploring its Impact on Knowledge Worker Productivity. *Computers in Human Behavior*, 26, 1061–72. doi: http://dx.doi.org/10.1016/j.chb.2010.03.008

Kellogg, K. C. (2014). Brokerage Professions and Implementing Reform in an Age of Experts. *American Sociological Review*, 79, 912–41. doi: 10.1177/0003122414544734

Lammers, J. C. (2011). How Institutions Communicate: Institutional Messages, Institutional Logics, and Organizational Communication. *Management Communication Quarterly*, 25, 154–82. doi: 10.1177/0893318910389280

Lammers, J. C., and Garcia, M. A. (2009). Exploring the Concept of "Profession" for Organizational Communication Research: Institutional Influences in a Veterinary Organization. *Management Communication Quarterly*, 22, 357–84. doi: 10.1177/0893318908327007

Larson, M. S. (1977). *The Rise of Professionalism*. Berkeley, CA: University of California Press.

Latour, B. (1986). *Visualization and Cognition: Thinking with Eyes and Hands.* In H. Kuklick and E. Long (eds), *Knowledge and Society: Studies in the Sociology of Culture Past and Present* (vol. 6, pp. 1–40). Greenwich, CT: JAI Press.

Leonardi, P. M., and Treem, J. W. (2012). Knowledge Management Technology as a Stage for Strategic Self-Presentation: Implications for Knowledge Sharing in Organizations. *Information and Organization*, 22, 37–59. doi: 10.1016/j.infoandorg.2011.10.003

Lowrey, W., and Anderson, W. B. (2006). The Impact of Internet Use on the Public Perception of Physicians: A Perspective from the Sociology of Professions Literature. *Health Communication*, 19, 125–31.

Lynch, M., and Woolgar, S. (1990). *Representation in Scientific Practice.* Cambridge, MA: MIT Press.

McDermott, R. (1999). Why Information Technology Inspired But Cannot Deliver Knowledge Management. *California Management Review*, 41(4), 103–17.

McDonald, D. W. (2001). Evaluating Expertise Recommendations. In *Proceedings of the 2001 International ACM SIGGROUP Conference on Supporting Group Work* (pp. 214–23). New York: ACM.

March, J. G., and Simon, H. A. (1958). *Organizations.* New York: Wiley & Sons.

Nevo, D., and Wand, Y. (2005). Organizational Memory Information Systems: A Transactive Memory Approach. *Decision Support Systems*, 39, 549–62. doi: 10.1016/j.dss.2004.03.002

Nicolini, D. (2009). Zooming In and Out: Studying Practices by Switching Theoretical Lenses and Trailing Connections. *Organization Studies*, 30, 1391–418. doi: 10.1177/0170840609349875

Poole, M. S., and Holmes, M. E. (1995). Decision Development in Computer-Assisted Group Decision Making. *Human Communication Research*, 22, 90–127. doi: 10.1111/j.1468-2958.1995.tb00363.x

Rader, E. (2010). The Effect of Audience Design on Labeling, Organizing, and Finding Shared Files. In *Proceedings of the SIGCHI Conference on Human Factors in Computing Systems* (pp. 777–86). New York: ACM. doi: 10.1145/1753326.1753440

Schoeneborn, D. (2013). The Pervasive Power of PowerPoint: How a Genre of Professional Communication Permeates Organizational Communication. *Organization Studies*, 34, 1777–801. doi: 10.1177/0170840613485843

Stark, D., and Paravel, V. (2008). PowerPoint in Public: Digital Technologies and the New Morphology of Demonstration. *Theory, Culture and Society*, 25, 30–55. doi: 10.1177/0263276408095215

Sundin, O. (2011). Janitors of Knowledge: Constructing Knowledge in the Everyday Life of Wikipedia Editors. *Journal of Documentation*, 67, 840–62.

Tracy, K. (1997). Interactional Trouble in Emergency Service Requests: A Problem of Frames. *Research on Language and Social Interaction*, 30, 315–43.

Tracy, S. (2002). When Questioning Turns to Face Threat: An Interactional Sensitivity in 911 Call-Taking. *Western Journal of Communication*, 66, 129–57.

Treem, J. W. (2012). Communicating Expertise: Knowledge Performances in Professional-Service Firms. *Communication Monographs*, 79, 23–47. doi: 10.1080/03637751.2011.646487

Treem, J. W. (2013). Technology Use as a Status Cue: The Influences of Mundane and Novel Technologies on Knowledge Assessments in Organizations. *Journal of Communication*, 63, 1032–53. doi: 10.1111/jcom.120617

Tufte, E. (2003). PowerPoint is Evil. *Wired* (Sept.). Retrieved from <http://archive.wired.com/wired/archive/11.09/ppt2.html>.

Vertesi, J. (2015). *Seeing like a Rover: How Robots, Teams, and Images Craft Knowledge of Mars*. Chicago: University of Chicago Press.

Whittaker, S., and Sidner, C. (1996). Email Overload: Exploring Personal Information Management of Email. *Proceedings of the SIGCHI Conference on Human Factors in Computing Systems* (pp. 276–83). New York: ACM. doi: 10.1145/238386.238530

Zabusky, S. E. (1997). Computers, Clients, and Expertise: Negotiating Technical Identities in a Nontechnical World. In S. R. Barley and J. E. Orr (eds), *Between Craft and Science* (pp. 129–53). Ithaca, NY: Cornell University Press.

Zuboff, S. (1988). *In the Age of the Smart Machine*. New York: Basic Books.

12 Managing Dispersed and Dynamic Expertise in Fluid Organizational Forms

BART VAN DEN HOOFF AND JULIA KOTLARSKY

In our highly connected knowledge society, we are witnessing the emergence of more "fluid" forms of organizing (Schreyögg and Sydow, 2010). Fluidity here refers to the fact that "the organization" is no longer contained by clearly set boundaries, but is characterized by relationships, structures, processes, capabilities, and information that "flow" between different entities. As organizational boundaries (defined by Santos and Eisenhardt, 2005, 491, as "the demarcation between an organization and its environment") become less clearly definable, these flows are increasingly unhampered by such boundaries—and what constitutes an "organization" is less easy to define.

Fluid organizations can be characterized by a shrinking core and an expanding (flexible) periphery (Child and McGrath, 2001; Gulati and Kletter, 2005), and can take a variety of shapes—from "meta-organizations" or "networks of firms or individuals not bound by authority based on employment relationships but characterized by a system-level goal" (Gulati et al., 2012, 573), to organizations that outsource all non-core activities to third parties (Dess et al., 1995; Gulati and Kletter, 2005; Oshri et al., 2015). We also see the growing popularity of open innovation, that is, relying on active engagement with external parties (along with internal sources) in search of innovative opportunities (Chesbrough, 2003), and crowdsourcing platforms that provide organizations with access to a virtual, on-demand workforce (Kaganer et al., 2012). These forms of organizing have emerged in response to the increasingly complex, dynamic, and globalized environment in which organizations are active (Friedman, 2005; Kumar, 2004; Jarvenpaa and Majchrzak, 2008; Majchrzak et al., 2007), the increasingly knowledge- and information-intensive character of our economy (Child and McGrath, 2001; Gulati, 2010), and the rise of information and communication technologies (ICT) that have enabled the flexible integration of actors across temporal and spatial boundaries (Hinds and Kiesler, 2002; Kellogg et al., 2006).

This development creates an interesting tension between *flexibility* and *fragmentation*. Although the flexibility achieved through such new organizational forms is crucial in meeting the requirements of today's increasingly complex and volatile economy, the inherent fluidity of organizations is, if taken to the extreme, almost contradictory to the essence of organizing (Schreyögg and Sydow, 2010). Achieving flexibility on the one hand (in response to dynamically changing environmental demands) and avoiding the risk of fragmentation on the other (where the organization loses coherence and dissolves into separate units or actors) is the main dilemma for managers in fluid organizational settings. This dilemma is especially relevant when we consider the role of *expertise* in these settings. As we will argue in this chapter, fluid organizational forms are related to the increasingly dispersed and dynamic nature of expertise. Organizations become more flexible in response to changing environmental demands as they can more easily tap into various sources of expertise as needed—irrespective of where these sources are located. On the other hand, the fact that both the nature of expertise and the sources of this expertise are continually changing also creates a risk of fragmentation, as the organization loses its memory, its specific expertise, and dissolves into fragments of uncoordinated activities. Consequently, organizations increasingly rely on *flows* of knowledge instead of *stocks* of knowledge, creating a flexible and fluid network of actors contributing expertise when and where it is needed. Coordinating expertise across multiple boundaries in such a dynamic setting, however, is a daunting task. On the one hand, the expertise provided by various actors, some with only a fleeting connection with the organization, needs to be integrated with the knowledge already present in the organization in order to enhance the organization's innovative capacity. On the other hand, all actors in the organizational periphery also learn from their interaction with the core and obtain new expertise, raising questions on how the organization can retain crucial knowledge with such permeable boundaries. We will discuss how expertise can be coordinated in such settings through multiple expertise coordination mechanisms, and will stress the role of organizational routines, codification, and creating links to experts in supporting expertise coordination.

In this chapter, we focus on the implications of this trend toward more fluid organizational forms for the coordination of dispersed and dynamic expertise in such organizations. (i) We unpack the increasingly dispersed and dynamic nature of expertise in complex, knowledge-intensive and rapidly changing organizations. (ii) We highlight challenges of coordinating such expertise in fluid organizational settings. (iii) We discuss the consequences of these challenges for innovation and knowledge retention in such organizations.

Dispersed and Dynamic Expertise in Fluid Organizations

A useful definition of expertise is provided by Oshri et al. (2007b, 54) who, building on Polanyi (1962), describe *expertise* of individuals or groups as "the ability to act knowledgeably in a specific domain." They argue that expertise is dynamic: it consists of embodied knowledge and skills possessed by individuals, learnt through action and therefore constantly evolving. Treem (2012, 25) presents a *communicative view* of expertise, in which expertise is conceptualized as "an attribution that emerges through social interaction and is communicated to others through the process of organizing." In Treem's view, expertise is associated with observed *performance,* and needs to be *enacted* to be recognized by others.

Both these conceptualizations emphasize the dynamic, practice-related nature of expertise, which connects to the practice-based view of knowledge (Brown and Duguid, 1991, 2001; Cook and Brown, 1999; Orlikowski, 2002). This perspective suggests that knowledge is not external to, but embedded in the practices in which people are engaged. Yet, "expertise" and "knowledge" are not the same. As Kotlarsky et al. (2014, 609) highlight, "*expertise* is defined here as a 'knower's capacity to act,' and is differentiated from *knowledge* which is viewed as a tool used by 'knowers' to solve problems (Cook and Brown, 1999), or to transform their own expertise (Gherardi and Nicolini, 2000)."

Based on this, we conceptualize *expertise as an emergent and enacted ability to act knowledgeably in a specific domain, consisting of embodied knowledge and skills possessed by individuals, yet enacted and communicated through shared practices.* This means that by its nature, expertise is dynamic and complex, and difficult to capture and coordinate. As we will argue in the following paragraphs, the increasing demands for flexibility, speed, and uncertainty in the modern economy create new challenges for the coordination of expertise, as it becomes even more dynamic and dispersed. Being able to survive and thrive in this flexible, dynamic, and complex environment requires organizations to be adaptive rather than based on specialized routines, relying on horizontal collaboration between diverse groups rather than vertical chains of command (Barley, 1996; Volberda, 1996). A particularly relevant consequence of these new forms of organizing and the environment in which they take shape is the fact that the expertise on which these organizations rely increasingly becomes both *dispersed* and *dynamic.* Organizations rely on dynamic *flows* of knowledge between various partners instead of static *stocks* of knowledge within set boundaries, creating a flexible and fluid network of actors contributing expertise when and where it is needed. Thus, to reflect on our definition of expertise, for these new forms of organizing to be effective and efficient, expertise would require (i) enactment and communication of *dispersed* embodied knowledge and skills, and (ii) the ability to adapt and engage in dynamically changing practices.

DISPERSED EXPERTISE

First of all, organizations are becoming increasingly geographically dispersed in response to the globalization of the economy (Friedman, 2005). The growing globalization of markets for technology and knowledge workers means that organizations rely to a great extent on dispersed "centers of excellence" around a specific function, process, or technology, located where the required expertise can be most efficiently obtained, and where markets require that specific expertise (Demirbag and Glaister, 2010). Not only are organizations dispersed globally, though—as organizations increasingly consist of horizontal collaborations between diverse groups and/or individuals (Gulati et al., 2012; Kellogg et al., 2006), expertise is dispersed among the various members that are part of the organization. This especially concerns organizations' "flexible shell," consisting of often temporary engagements with various parties, or where tasks are outsourced (Gulati and Kletter, 2005; Kotlarsky et al., 2014).

Consequently, although new forms of organizing may be primarily aimed at lowering boundaries (or barriers) between individuals by making them accessible to each other (sometimes even referred to as "boundaryless" organizations—Ashkenas et al., 2002), they at the same time give rise to new, expertise-related boundaries, rooted in multiple contexts in which individuals are immersed. When experts who are dispersed across various organizations, units, and geographic locations engage in collaboration, their ability to relate to each other and integrate their knowledge may be challenged by issues associated with expertise-related boundaries such as differences in language proficiency and terminology use (e.g. Carlile, 2002; Carmel and Tjia, 2005), knowledge and experience asymmetries between globally dispersed team members (e.g. Oshri et al., 2008; Vlaar et al., 2008), differences in competences caused by different backgrounds and past experiences (e.g. Levina and Vaast, 2005), as well as different goals and conflicting motivations (e.g. Carlile, 2002; Jarvenpaa and Majchrzak, 2008). Coordinating expertise across such boundaries, as we will discuss, is a daunting task.

DYNAMIC EXPERTISE

Coordinating expertise is further complicated by the fact that new organizational forms require expertise to be increasingly *dynamic*, beyond the fact that it naturally evolves through application in practice. In fluid organizations, what kind of expertise is needed, where it is needed, and where it is found, is subject to rapid change. The requirements of flexibility, speed, and uncertainty mean that organizations are increasingly dependent on their adaptive capacity (Kellogg et al., 2006), as a consequence of which "organizational capabilities themselves have to become fluid to enable organizations to continuously create new (combinations of) resources" (Schreyögg and Sydow, 2010, 1252). This emphasis on adaptive capacity, and the capability to recombine resources, clearly relates to the extensive literature on *dynamic capabilities*. Teece (2007, 1319) defines dynamic capabilities as: "the capacity (1) to sense and shape opportunities and threats, (2) to seize opportunities, and (3) to maintain competitiveness through enhancing, combining, protecting, and, when necessary, reconfiguring the business enterprise's intangible and tangible assets." Expertise, of course, is a prime example of an intangible asset. The need to be able to dynamically reconfigure that intangible asset is clearly reflected by Eisenhardt and Martin (2000, 1106), who emphasize the increasingly dynamic character of organizational expertise and capabilities, which are in a continuously unstable state, and increasingly rely on "quickly created new knowledge." Kellogg et al. (2006) also discuss how rapidly changing demands caused their case organization to constantly recombine existing expertise and experience, "requiring ongoing information exchange among incoming and outgoing team members" (Kellogg et al., 2006, 28) to be able to address new problems and come up with innovative solutions.

In fact, this dynamic nature of expertise is also one of the foundations of new organizational forms. As Gulati and Kletter (2005) argue, the increasingly complex and dynamic nature of organizational environments, structures, and technologies lead to network-like forms of organization that increase access to the most recent expertise. The characteristics of these organizational forms, with a focus on networks, spontaneous interaction, improvised processes and teams, and lateral communication between a diversity of partners, all serve to maximize the organization's absorptive capacity in terms of new expertise. Routines and established organizational memory—or the "stored information from an organization's history that can be brought to bear on present decisions" (Walsh and Ungson, 1991, 61)—become less important than the dynamic capability to continually revise expertise in processes that are in constant flux (Schreyögg and Sydow, 2010).

To summarize, the increasingly complex and dynamic nature of organizational environments necessitates firms to adopt structures that enable them to access expertise that is as diverse and up to date as possible. Consequently, expertise is increasingly dispersed (across a variety of locations, organizations, individuals, and practices) and dynamic (subject to rapid change) in these new organizational forms. This raises a number of challenges for coordinating expertise in such organizations. These will be addressed in the next section.

Challenges of Coordinating Expertise in Fluid Organizations

In order to reap benefits from the expertise that is available within and around an organization, some form of *coordination* of this expertise is required. If expertise is not managed and coordinated, its potential as an organizational resource is not realized (Faraj and Sproull, 2000). In this chapter, we follow Faraj and Xiao (2006) in conceptualizing expertise coordination as "managing knowledge and skill interdependencies" (p. 1159). This takes place over time through various coordinated actions "enacted within a specific context, among a specific set of actors, and following a history of previous actions and interactions that necessarily constrain future action" (p. 1157). In more detail, expertise coordination entails knowing where expertise is located, knowing where expertise is needed, and bringing needed expertise to bear (Faraj and Sproull, 2000). Next to locating expertise and bringing it to bear where needed, the dynamic nature of expertise also emphasizes the importance of the *continuous* development and updating of expertise. Consequently, we identify three challenges in expertise coordination that result from the increasingly dispersed and dynamic nature of expertise: challenges related to (1) locating relevant expertise, (2) being able to apply relevant expertise, and (3) continuously developing and updating relevant expertise.

LOCATING RELEVANT EXPERTISE

Challenges in locating relevant expertise relate to (a) finding a relevant expert among geographically distributed colleagues, who often belong to different organizations, or (b) documents that contain relevant information. Usually it is a combination of a and b—finding an expert that can point to a relevant document, or studying documents and using pointers in the documents to find relevant experts (e.g. Kotlarsky et al., 2014; Oshri et al., 2008). As both experts and their codified knowledge are increasingly dispersed, and the expertise is increasingly diverse and dynamic, locating experts and their knowledge (let alone being able to relate one's own knowledge to their expertise) is increasingly complicated. Coordination mechanisms that serve to locate relevant expertise in an organization are the establishment and maintenance of social ties and development of a transactive memory system (TMS), which is a collective memory system for knowledge coordination in groups. The TMS relies on group members knowing who knows whom and who knows what, and can be enacted in both inter- or intra-organizational settings.

The importance of social ties in creating links between experts is often emphasized in research on coordinating expertise (Oshri et al., 2007a) and connected to the concept of TMS (Oshri et al., 2008). Efforts to develop and maintain social ties between dispersed individuals help to establish the structural and relational embeddedness of experts, which in turn motivates them to explore commonalities and to judge one another's expertise (Agterberg et al., 2010). Face-to-face meetings and exchanges are important here, but links between experts can also be integrated within flexible collaboration platforms that support various synchronous and asynchronous interactions (e.g. the way Microsoft uses Lync for collaboration with its Chinese vendors). Active links between experts enable the flow of knowledge, which is crucial in relation to the dispersed and dynamic character of expertise: where stocks of knowledge (in documents, information systems, and the like) are by definition limited in scope and easily outdated (Nissen, 2006), keeping knowledge actively flowing within a dynamically adapting network of experts enables an organization to build and maintain an adaptive capacity.

The adaptive capacity of such a network of experts depends to a great extent on experts' ability to utilize and build on each other's specialized knowledge. This is where the degree to which such experts can rely on a TMS that forms a collective memory system becomes important. This collective memory system enables the division of cognitive labor by creating specializations (different individuals specialize in different knowledge domains) and tapping into this specialized knowledge when working toward a common objective. As Kotlarsky et al. (2015, 4) explain, group members "use their individual metaknowledge about what other group members know to access knowledge of their expert colleagues from other specialist areas in order to complement their own knowledge when needed." Argote and Ren (2012) argue that a well-developed TMS is a micro-foundation for dynamic capabilities. A well-developed organizational-level TMS should achieve three goals to enhance dynamic or combinative capabilities: efficiency (the extent to which the capability accesses and utilizes the specialist knowledge held by individual organizational members), scope (the breadth of specialized knowledge the organizational capability draws upon), and flexibility of integration (the extent to which a capability can access additional knowledge and reconfigure existing knowledge). However, the boundaries related to the dispersed nature of expertise in fluid organizational settings are barriers to the development of such a TMS. In particular, geographical distance limits the necessary face-to-face interaction and makes it difficult to get to know relevant people (thus reducing chances of finding a relevant expert when some specialized expertise is required) (Sole and Edmondson, 2002), differences in culture and group identity negatively affect members' ability and willingness in terms of sharing expertise (Kane, 2010), and knowledge boundaries form barriers to TMS development in terms of syntax, semantics, as well as shared practices (Kotlarsky et al., 2015). Thus, creating a network of social ties, and a TMS, between the dispersed and often changing members of a flexible organization is a major challenge.

APPLYING EXPERTISE

Applying expertise in a fluid organizational setting is likely to involve decontextualizing expertise that was originally created (and thus embedded) in one context, and subsequently recontextualizing it within the new context. This means that expertise needs to be stripped down from "customer-specific" and confidential information, generalizing it in order to be able to reapply it in new contexts (Oshri et al., 2007b). In order to be able to decontextualize and recontextualize expertise, group members need to engage in a shared practice, which in turn means that they need to be able to overcome multiple boundaries—specifically the knowledge boundaries identified by Carlile (2002, 2004): (1) *Syntactic* knowledge boundaries concerning differences in terminologies, codes, protocols, routines, or other means of expression; (2) *Semantic* knowledge boundaries, related to the problem of different interpretations across different practices—differences in sense making, in meanings attached to certain phenomena; and (3) *Pragmatic* knowledge boundaries that emerge due to differences in interests, existing practices, goals, and other aspects that have become common sense, in particular knowledge domains. The pragmatic boundary is the most fundamental here, stemming from differences in practices which also lead to differences in terminologies as well as interpretations (Kotlarsky et al., 2015). Transcending these boundaries thus requires group members to establish a common goal (associated with the application of joint expertise) and to develop a common ground for sharing and adjusting the knowledge at a boundary (Bechky, 2003; Carlile, 2004), allowing for the recontextualization of local understandings in joint activity (Swan et al., 2007).

Establishing a shared practice in an organization that is dispersed and has a dynamically changing composition in terms of participants is of course a major challenge, complicating the extent to which joint expertise can be developed and applied in shared practices in fluid organizational forms. However, if such a shared practice is established, the organization is likely to reap various benefits. In particular, as Kotlarsky et al. (2014, table 2) demonstrate, the application of expertise in settings where expertise crosses knowledge boundaries signifies the transformation of expertise into something novel, which may take different shapes. For example, dealing with the pragmatic boundary transforms expertise through learning; while dealing with syntactic and semantic boundaries, as well as with knowledge asymmetry between globally dispersed members, transforms expertise through translating (Carlile, 2004), synchronizing, and co-creating novel understanding (Vlaar et al., 2008). This usually implies that the organizational expertise-base is growing, as reapplying something learnt from one project into a new one would benefit the organization if it becomes organizational knowledge.

The concept of "trading zones" (Kellogg et al., 2006) is also relevant for understanding how expertise could be applied. In a trading zone, members from different communities temporarily coordinate their actions through practices that enable them to interact across boundaries by agreeing on the general procedures of exchange in spite of their differing interpretations of what they exchange, and of the intent and meaning of the exchange itself. Thus, a trading zone is metaphor for a "place" where cross-boundary expertise coordination takes place. This is very much a performative view of coordination; that is, coordination takes place through recurrent actions of the participants. The practices through which they enact this trading zone are: (1) *Display* (making one's work visible to others through plans, schedules, etc.), (2) *Representation* (making work "legible" by expressing ideas and concepts in a form that is understandable to others), and (3) *Assembly* (reusing, revising, and aligning the work products of other communities in the construction of interdependent products). Again, engaging in such practices is severely hindered by the dispersed and dynamically changing nature of fluid organizations.

Although organizations operating under emergency or fast-response conditions are certainly not the only examples of organizations for which fluid forms of organizing can be essential, issues pertaining to locating and applying dispersed and dynamic expertise are very prominent in such organizations (Faraj and Xiao, 2006; Jarvenpaa and Majchrzak, 2008). This is a consequence of the fact that such organizations typically act under extreme time pressure and often need to find, on the spot, new and innovative solutions for emerging problems. When operating under conditions of urgency or emergency that are concerned with matters where lives are at stake (e.g. national disasters or terrorist attacks), the ability to integrate and apply knowledge of experts from different functional domains, different organizations, and often different countries may have significant impact on the success of disaster recovery efforts (Majchrzak et al., 2007). In a similar vein, fast-response organizations (e.g. Accidents and Emergency (A&E), fire brigade, police, and military) rely to a great extent on an interplay between structured and improvised coordination modes (Faraj and Xiao, 2006; Kotlarsky et al., 2014) that provide guidance and links between different areas for which different parties/individuals are responsible and also allow some flexibility (e.g. for dialogic practices) to accommodate specific circumstances that might be unique to a specific situation.

CONTINUOUSLY DEVELOPING AND UPDATING EXPERTISE

It is a major challenge in fluid organizations to keep up with what is going on: how the situation is changing, what different parties involved are doing, and how their expertise changes over time. Whereas the first two challenges discussed here are constantly faced by different individuals in teams in concrete situations, the third challenge is a continuous one at the organizational level: how can we coordinate the continuous development of expertise, and how can we keep different parties updated about any changes in expertise?

To face this challenge, it is imperative to identify and map interdependencies between the parties involved and establish liaison roles to address interdependencies between actions of different actors, teams, organizations, and other parties involved. Such liaisons should monitor changes in the environment, actions, or expertise that may affect the other parties at the interface, and alert or inform all parties that may be affected. For example, in dispersed organizations and interorganizational settings (e.g. outsourcing engagements) dedicated "account managers" from both client and supplier organizations coordinate knowledge flows between relevant actors in their organizations. Within large project or service-based organizations human "liaisons" or processes connect different parts of the organization aiming to provide an up-to-date picture about expertise, and also facilitate knowledge flows between different functions or groups. For example, dedicated liaisons associated with different Centers of Excellence for technologies and industries at Tata Consultancy Services coordinate and regularly organize events to inform other centers and business units about new technological developments (Oshri et al., 2007b).

We have mentioned earlier the importance of relying on *flows* of knowledge (rather than *stocks* of knowledge) and here we elaborate on the role that flows of knowledge play in developing and updating expertise in fluid organizational settings. To keep up with changes in business environment and in organizational membership, organizations are increasingly relying on coordination of *expertise*, rather than on coordination of *activities*, which was considered for years the major focus of coordinative action by scholars studying coordination from an information processing perspective (Kotlarsky et al., 2008, see their table 1). Kotlarsky et al. (2008) explain that, when adopting a knowledge-based perspective on coordination, coordination focuses on *experts' thoughts*, that is, how individuals interpret work and how they can understand what others think. Coordination mechanisms then enable coordination through their influence on knowledge processes by facilitating knowledge flows, making knowledge explicit, amplifying knowledge, and promoting the building of social capital. The increasingly dispersed and dynamic character of expertise in fluid organizational forms poses additional challenges for the coordination of knowledge flows.

Kotlarsky et al. (2008) suggest four categories of coordination mechanisms that can contribute to the coherence of knowledge flows in organizational settings that involve globally distributed members. First, *organization design mechanisms* facilitate knowledge flows by providing a structure through which knowledge workers can channel their expertise. To achieve coordination, the knowledge must flow, be connected, and various perspectives must be determined (Boland and Tenkasi, 1995). Organization design clarifies who is supposed to know what and who is supposed to communicate with whom. It therefore economizes knowledge flows. For this mechanism to suit the needs of fluid organizations there should be a stable core structure that connects key sources of core expertise (e.g. links between Centers of Excellence mentioned earlier) and serves as a backbone of the organization. In addition, fluid organizations should be able to deploy temporary organizational structures for specific contexts (projects, products, situations) that the organization is engaging in. Having templates for (temporary) organizational structures that suit specific circumstances and appointing "matching pairs" between geographically distributed counterparts in similar roles for distributed collaborations are examples of organizational designs that help to facilitate development and updating of expertise in fluid organizational settings.

Second, *work-based mechanisms* include plans, specifications, standards, workflow, categorization systems, and representations of work-in-progress, such as prototypes and design documents. They capture knowledge in a codified form, which is important to enable activity replication and commonality (Adler, 1995). Through the use of work-based mechanisms, knowledge and expectations are made explicit and thus are known and useful to other people working at different sites or times on interdependent tasks. As individuals accomplish their part of the collaborative work, work-based mechanisms capture their progress and make other parties aware of what has been accomplished by whom. This, in turn, triggers and facilitates interactions between parties involved in interdependent activities. In fluid organizations dispersed counterparts rely on tools and technologies to support multiple work-based mechanisms that define and guide their work.

This leads to the third category of mechanisms—*technology-based mechanisms*. These are important in dispersed organizations, as they enable rapid dissemination of expertise. Knowledge-intensive multinationals and service firms coordinate expertise using intranets, knowledge databases, and groupware. Both work-based and technology-based mechanisms thus rely quite heavily on codification. As already noted, however, increasing organizational fluidity creates an increasing reliance on flows of knowledge over stocks of knowledge. This means that it is questionable whether codification of expertise is sensible at all. That is not to say that codification is useless in facilitating the development and updating of expertise in fluid organizations—on the contrary. Kotlarsky et al. (2014) expand the widely accepted view of codification as making knowledge explicit, to include *codification of the "knower"* which identifies a person with expertise relevant to a problem. Codification of the knower provides links to knowledgeable individuals—experts—in situations when tacit and personalized expertise is required, thus enabling access to relevant expertise when needed. In their study within a globally distributed offshore-outsourcing setting that involved complex interorganizational arrangements, codification of the knower emerged as an important mechanism for the coordination of expertise. In this case (Kotlarsky et al., 2014) codification of the knower referred to representations of experts' identity, area of expertise, area of responsibility, role within the organizational structure of the project team, and a contact link to the expert for ready communication. Such codification can rely on both work-based and technology-based mechanisms.

Fourth, *social mechanisms* establish social capital and keep people updated about who knows and does what. Dispersed individuals rely on technology-enabled interactions but also occasional face-to-face encounters (e.g. team building) to get to know each other, negotiate points of view, and transform their understanding to generate innovative outputs; they have relational needs that are relevant for coordinating their work. This mechanism is mostly affected in fluid and dispersed organizational settings. A lack of occasions for face-to-face encounters between (globally) distributed members, and changes in membership in temporary or ad hoc teams lead to an erosion of these social mechanisms, which is likely to challenge an organization's ability to establish social capital.

To summarize, locating relevant expertise, applying it, and continuously developing and updating expertise in dispersed and dynamic organizational settings is challenging. It requires managers to pay specific attention to interdependencies between processes and individuals, and adopt organizational structures to establish and facilitate knowledge flows between them. The next section concludes this chapter by discussing tensions in managing dynamic and dispersed expertise and their implications for innovation and knowledge retention in fluid organizations.

Conclusions and Implications for Innovation and Knowledge Retention

So, what are the implications of the dispersed and dynamic nature of expertise in fluid organizational settings, beyond the challenges associated with the management of such expertise? Fluid organizational forms are often a result of a struggle toward improving competitiveness. Examples of fluid organizations that we mentioned in the introduction—networks of firms or individuals, organizations that are involved in outsourcing client–supplier relationships, open innovation initiatives, and crowdsourcing platforms—are all departures that once traditional firms took to gain a competitive advantage and/or remain competitive in the turbulent business environment. However, when resources, activities, and strategic objectives are no longer driven by interests of one firm but are aligned or shared by several parties, what implication does this have for innovation and knowledge retention? For example, how do organizations decide who has intellectual property over what part of a jointly developed innovation? Spin-off products with shared ownership and profit-sharing contracts are examples of possible avenues to benefit from joint innovations (Oshri et al., 2015).

As outlined, the emergence of fluid organizational forms fundamentally affects the coordination of expertise. Summarizing the argument from the previous section of this chapter, when we compare fluid organizations to more traditional organizations, we can draw the following conclusions:

- *Locating relevant expertise* is complicated by the development toward fluid organizations since expertise (both experts and what they know) becomes more dispersed and more dynamic. In a fluid organization, expertise is more dispersed, not only in a geographical sense (which is also the case for many more traditional organizations) but also across different organizations, groups, and individuals. It is also more dynamic, since the composition of fluid organizations is less stable (and thus who knows what is subject to change) and because requirements in terms of expertise (the expertise the "organization" needs to thrive) are rapidly evolving. Both these developments make it difficult to obtain a reliable insight into where relevant expertise is located, since both the *where* and the *what* (in terms of what is relevant) are changing.
- *Applying expertise* is complicated by the increasing fluidity of organizational forms because of the different, and changing, contexts across which expertise needs to be coordinated. The dispersed and dynamic character of expertise—in terms of who knows what and who does what—makes it difficult for people to engage in shared practices across the various boundaries that emerge (geographical, knowledge-related, cultural, identity-related, etc.). Such shared practices are crucial in the process of decontextualizing expertise from a specific context, and recontextualizing it in a different one. Compared to more traditional organizations, the dispersed and dynamically changing character of fluid organizational forms negatively influence the foundations for such shared practices in terms of face-to-face interaction, stable patterns of close collaborations, and learning on the job.
- *Continuously developing and updating expertise* is especially challenging in fluid organizational forms compared to more traditional organizations. Again, the fact that expertise is dispersed across different, and rapidly changing, contexts is the main complicating factor here. The distributed and dynamic character of expertise in fluid organizations means that the coordination of expertise needs to focus on keeping knowledge flowing, instead of efforts to store knowledge. Each of the expertise coordination mechanisms for enhancing the coherence of knowledge flows we discussed

before is more complicated in a fluid organization than in a more traditional one. In the more stable and coherent setting of a traditional organization, coordination mechanisms focusing on organization design, work, technology, and social capital are less complex than in the dispersed and dynamically changing fluid organizational forms. Organization design becomes more temporary and context-specific, the codification that is the basis for both work-based and technological mechanisms becomes less useful (except for codifying the knower), and network configurations are subject to constant change and lack the stability on which social capital can be built.

These observations are in line with one of our central conclusions: that fluid organizational forms, much more than traditional ones, rely on *flows* of knowledge instead of *stocks*. As expertise is increasingly dispersed and dynamic, efforts to codify and store what is known become less and less useful—the focus is on keeping knowledge flowing in a dynamic configuration of collaboration patterns. This has dual effects on the inflow and outflow of expertise. The retention of knowledge becomes problematic as a consequence of the changing configuration of the social network in which people work together. In the traditional organization, this is a relatively stable configuration in which social ties and a TMS are allowed to develop over time. In fluid organizational forms, however, this configuration has become less structured and more dynamic, creating considerable challenges for management in terms of preventing the outflow of critical expertise, since both the motivation and the ability to make individual knowledge collective may be negatively affected. However, the scope of the social network of both organization and employee will be widened through their increasingly flexible and varying (often temporary) contacts. This widening scope will facilitate the inflow of new potentially relevant expertise, benefiting the organization's innovative capacity. Keeping former employees in their network, organizations still profit from the expertise of those former employees. Likewise, building strong connections with flexible workers may not only help in retaining their relevant knowledge for the organization, but is likely to provide access to these workers' additional expertise (and contacts) as well. Consequently, balancing innovation and the retention of critical expertise requires organizations to be more open and flexible toward getting access to and utilizing expertise.

The changing configuration of organizations will inevitably lead to more knowledge flows between organizations as people enact their expertise in joint practices in varying constellations. It would seem hardly worth the effort to prevent critical expertise that these employees create or acquire during a particular collaboration from being used in a collaboration with another organization. Instead, organizations should focus on facilitating the flow of knowledge in a way that both provides continued access to current critical expertise, and the continuous inflow of new potentially relevant expertise. Managers should accept the fact that knowledge cannot be stored and kept away from other organizations, but that knowledge will always flow. Managing those knowledge flows as effectively as possible, in terms of both retention and innovation, is one of the central management challenges for managers of fluid organizations.

The previous observations relate to Schreyögg and Sydow's (2010) points about the role of organizational memory. These authors conclude that much of the literature on new forms of organizing suggests that an organizational memory would be of decreasing relevance for these organizations, as past learning would only tie them to old ways of doing and would inhibit their capacity to continuously revise cognitions and change expectations. As Schreyögg and Sydow (2010) argue, however, an organization does need a certain degree of "minimal structure" in which an organizational memory (previously defined by Walsh and Ungson (1991, 61) as the "stored information from an organization's history that can be brought to bear on present decisions") would actually be an important part. An organization's memory is part of its culture, of its identity, and thus is part of what defines it as "an organization." This goes back to our previous observation that any fluid organization would require a certain stable core structure which forms its backbone and maintains its core expertise. So, related to the tension between the inflow and outflow of expertise is the tension of maintaining a certain organizational memory that provides the core competencies of the organization, its culture and identity, while at the same time allowing for constant redesign and reinvention of the organization and its dynamic capabilities.

Ultimately, it all boils down to a trade-off between flexibility and fragmentation. The trend toward organizational fluidity emerged in response to the increasing flexibility required by the complex and dynamic environment in which organizations are active. With changing, dynamic constellations of organizations and people, the expertise that is needed at a certain point in time, and in response to a certain requirement, can be organized flexibly. Without some degree of stability, however, such flexibility will easily develop into a situation of fragmentation. When there is no stable core structure that holds the organization together, that secures the interrelatedness of practices shared in these dynamic constellations and the expertise developed and applied in these practices, there is nothing that holds these different constellations together. Consequently, expertise will be fragmented across various individuals and other units, but never integrated or coordinated. Thus, instead of becoming fluid and flexible, the organization will dissolve into tiny fragments of uncoordinated practices and expertise, and essentially cease to exist.

Advancing the Study of Expertise

While many studies of expertise have looked into complex organizational settings, such as emergency response (e.g. Faraj and Xiao, 2006), disaster recovery (e.g. Majchrzak et al., 2007), globally distributed organizational settings (e.g. Kellogg et al., 2006; Kotlarsky et al., 2014; Vlaar et al., 2008), the focus of these studies was on understanding what happens to expertise (e.g. Vlaar et al., 2008) or how it can be coordinated despite specific challenges posed by the unique organizational setting (e.g. Faraj and Xiao, 2006; Jarvenpaa and Majchrzak, 2008; Kotlarsky et al., 2014; Majchrzak et al., 2007). Building on these studies, we argue that, while each organizational context studied has its own characteristics, they all represent a bigger trend toward new organizational forms that we capture under the term "fluid organization." Our central argument is that this bigger trend is characterized by dispersed and distributed expertise. In this chapter we conceptualized the nature of expertise in such organizational settings, analyzed challenges, and offered coordination practices to deal with the challenges. Our analysis and conceptualization builds on and extends the Transactive Memory Systems theory and emerging expertise coordination theory. Furthermore, we rely upon and relate to the existing literature on dynamic capabilities and organizational memory.

The dispersed and dynamic character of expertise complicates the communication and recognition of expertise, which connects our chapter with Liao, MacDonald, and Yuan's chapter in this volume. Where their chapter specifically focuses on the cultural boundaries that emerge in globalizing organizations, our focus is broader, including a diversity of boundaries that complicate not only the recognition of expertise, but also the application and continuous development thereof. Our chapter also raises questions about what constitutes collective expertise when the collective becomes increasingly fluid and difficult to define, which connects with Fulk's chapter. Fulk raises some interesting questions about how individual expertise is combined at the collective level, with implications for what constitutes "the collective" when groups, organizations, and networks become more and more dispersed and dynamic.

Future research could focus on understanding the link between individual and organizational or collective expertise in fluid organizational settings. In such settings, the interaction between dispersed experts may be studied from a network perspective, focusing on dynamic aspects of the network and how it changes over time or in response to specific events that trigger the formation of a new network to respond to specific events. Future research could also further explore the tension between flexibility and fragmentation, addressing the question of what constitutes an organization when boundaries become less and less clear. It would be interesting, for instance, to explore the question of to what extent a shared body of expertise is crucial in defining an organization, and to what extent such organizations are by definition of a temporary nature. If a collective builds up a common body of expertise, does that constitute a new organization? And when that expertise becomes obsolete, does that mean that the organization dissolves again? All in all, the interplay between fluid organizational forms and expertise seems to be a fertile ground for interesting research questions in many different fields.

■ REFERENCES

Adler, P. S. (1995). Interdepartmental Interdependence and Coordination: The Case of the Design/Manufacturing Interface. *Organization Science*, 6, 147–67.

Agterberg, M., Van den Hooff, B., Huysman, M., and Soekijad, M. (2010). Keeping the Wheels Turning: The Dynamics of Managing Networks of Practice. *Journal of Management Studies*, 47, 85–108.

Argote, L., and Ren, Y. (2012). Transactive Memory Systems: A Microfoundation of Dynamic Capabilities. *Journal of Management Studies*, 49, 1375–82.

Ashkenas, R. N., Ulrich, D., Jick, T., and Kerr, S. (2002). *The Boundaryless Organization: Breaking the Chains of Organizational Structure*. San Francisco: Jossey-Bass.

Barley, S. R. (1996). Technicians in the Workplace: Ethnographic Evidence for Bringing Work into Organization Studies. *Administrative Science Quarterly*, 41, 404–41.

Bechky, B. (2003). Sharing Meaning across Occupational Communities: The Transformation of Understanding on a Production Floor. *Organization Science*, 14, 312–30.

Boland, R. J., and Tenkasi, R. V. (1995). Perspective Making and Perspective Taking in Communities of Knowing. *Organization Science*, 6, 350–72.

Brown, J. S., and Duguid, P. (1991). Organizational Learning and Communities-of-Practice: Toward a Unified View of Working, Learning, and Innovation. *Organization Science*, 2(1), 40–57.

Brown, J. S., and Duguid, P. (2001). Knowledge and Organization: A Social-Practice Perspective. *Organization Science*, 12, 198–213.

Carlile, P. R. (2002). A Pragmatic View of Knowledge and Boundaries: Boundary Objects in New Product Development. *Organization Science*, 13, 442–55.

Carlile, P. R. (2004). Transferring, Translating, and Transforming: An Integrative Framework for Managing Knowledge across Boundaries. *Organization Science*, 15, 555–68.

Carmel, E., and Tjia, P. (2005). *Offshoring Information Technology. Sourcing and Outsourcing to a Global Workforce*. Cambridge: Cambridge University Press.

Chesbrough, H. W. (2003). The Era of Open Innovation. *MIT Sloan Management Review*, 44, 35–41.

Child, J., and McGrath, R. G. (2001). Organizations Unfettered: Organizational Form in an Information-Intensive Economy. *Academy of Management Journal*, 44(6), 1135–48.

Cook, S. D., and Brown, J. S. (1999). Bridging Epistemologies: The Generative Dance between Organizational Knowledge and Organizational Knowing. *Organization Science*, 10(4), 381–400.

Demirbag, M., and Glaister, K. W. (2010). Factors Determining Offshore Location Choice for R&D Projects: A Comparative Study of Developed and Emerging Regions. *Journal of Management Studies*, 47, 1534–60.

Dess, G. G., Rasheed, A. M., McLaughlin, K. J., and Priem, R. L. (1995). The New Corporate Architecture. *Academy of Management Executive*, 9(3), 7–18.

Eisenhardt, K. M., and Martin, J. A. (2000). Dynamic Capabilities: What are They? *Strategic Management Journal*, 21(10–11), 1105–21.

Espinosa, J. A., Cummings, J. N., Wilson, J. M., and Pearce, B. M. (2003). Team Boundary Issues across Multiple Global Firms. *Journal of Management Information Systems*, 19(4), 157–90.

Faraj, S., and Sproull, L. (2000). Coordinating Expertise in Software Development Teams. *Management Science*, 46(12), 1554–68. doi: 10.1287/mnsc.46.12.1554.12072

Faraj, S., and Xiao, Y. (2006). Coordination in Fast-Response Organizations. *Management Science*, 52(8), 1155–69.

Friedman, T. L. (2005). *The World is Flat: A Brief History of the Twenty-First Century.* New York: Farrar, Straus & Giroux.

Gherardi, S., and Nicolini, D. (2000). To Transfer is to Transform: The Circulation of Safety Knowledge. *Organization*, 7(2), 329–48.

Gulati, R. (2010). *Reorganize for Resilience: Putting Customers at the Center of your Business.* Boston: Harvard Business School Press.

Gulati, R., and Kletter, D. (2005). Shrinking Core, Expanding Periphery: The Relational Architecture of High-Performing Organizations. *California Management Review*, 47(3), 77–104.

Gulati, R., Puranam, P., and Tushman, M. (2012). Meta-Organization Design: Rethinking Design in Interorganizational and Community Contexts. *Strategic Management Journal*, 33, 571–86.

Hinds, P., and Kiesler, S. (2002). *Distributed Work.* Cambridge, MA: MIT Press.

Jarvenpaa, S. L., and Majchrzak, A. (2008). Knowledge Collaboration among Professionals Protecting National Security: Role of Transactive Memories in Ego-Centered Knowledge Networks. *Organization Science*, 19(2), 260–76.

Kaganer, E., Carmel, E., Hirschheim, R., and Olsen, T. (2012). Managing the Human Cloud. *MIT Sloan Management Review*, 54, 23–32.

Kane, A. A. (2010). Unlocking Knowledge Transfer Potential: Knowledge Demonstrability and Superordinate Social Identity. *Organization Science*, 21(3), 643–60.

Kellogg, K. C., Orlikowski, W. J., and Yates, J. (2006). Life in the Trading Zone: Structuring Coordination across Boundaries in Postbureaucratic Organizations. *Organization Science*, 17(1), 22–44.

Kotlarsky, J., Scarbrough, H., and Oshri, I. (2014). Coordinating Expertise across Knowledge Boundaries in Offshore-Outsourcing Projects: The Role of Codification. *MIS Quarterly*, 38(2), 607–27.

Kotlarsky, J., van den Hooff, B., and Houtman, L. (2015). Are We on the Same Page? Knowledge Boundaries and Transactive Memory System Development in Cross-Functional Teams. *Communication Research*, 42(3), 319–44.

Kotlarsky, J., van Fenema, P. C., and Willcocks, L. P. (2008). Developing a Knowledge-Based Perspective on Coordination: The Case of Global Software Projects. *Information and Management*, 45(2), 96–108. doi: http://dx.doi.org/10.1016/j.im. 2008.01.001

Kumar, N. (2004). *Marketing as Strategy: Understanding the CEO's Agenda for Driving Growth and Innovation.* Boston: Harvard Business School Press.

Levina, N., and Vaast, E. (2005). The Emergence of Boundary Spanning Competence in Practice: Implications for Implementation and Use of Information Systems. *MIS Quarterly,* 29(2), 335–63.

Majchrzak, A., Jarvenpaa, S. L., and Hollingshead, A. B. (2007). Coordinating Expertise among Emergent Groups Responding to Disasters. *Organization Science,* 18(1), 147–61.

Nissen, M. E. (2006). Dynamic Knowledge Patterns to Inform Design: A Field Study of Knowledge Stocks and Flows in an Extreme Organization. *Journal of Management Information Systems,* 22(3), 225–63.

Orlikowski, W. J. (2002). Knowing in Practice: Enacting a Collective Capability in Distributed Organizing. *Organization Science,* 13(3), 249–73.

Oshri, I., Kotlarsky, J., and Willcocks, L. P. (2007a). Global Software Development: Exploring Socialization and Face-to-Face Meetings in Distributed Strategic Projects. *Journal of Strategic Information Systems,* 16(1), 25–49.

Oshri, I., Kotlarsky, J., and Willcocks, L. P. (2007b). Managing Dispersed Expertise in IT Offshore Outsourcing: Lessons from Tata Consultancy Services. *MIS Quarterly Executive,* 6(2), 53–65.

Oshri, I., Kotlarsky, J., and Willcocks, L. P. (2015). *The Handbook of Global Outsourcing and Offshoring* (3rd edn). London: Palgrave Macmillan.

Oshri, I., Van Fenema, P., and Kotlarsky, J. (2008). Knowledge Transfer in Globally Distributed Teams: The Role of Transactive Memory. *Information Systems Journal,* 18(6), 593–616.

Polanyi, M. (1962). *Personal Knowledge: Towards a Post-Critical Philosophy.* Chicago: University of Chicago Press.

Santos, F. M., and Eisenhardt, K. M. (2005). Organizational Boundaries and Theories of Organization. *Organization Science,* 16(5), 491–508.

Schreyögg, G., and Sydow, J. (2010). Organizing for Fluidity? Dilemmas of New Organizational Forms. *Organization Science,* 21(6), 1251–62.

Sole, D., and Edmondson, A. (2002). Situated Knowledge and Learning in Dispersed Teams. *British Journal of Management,* 13(S2): S17–34.

Swan, J., Bresnen, M., Newell, S., and Robertson, M. (2007). The Object of Knowledge: The Role of Objects in Biomedical Innovation. *Human Relations,* 60(12), 1809–37.

Teece, D. J. (2007). Explicating Dynamic Capabilities: The Nature and Microfoundations of (Sustainable) Enterprise Performance. *Strategic Management Journal,* 28(13), 1319–50.

Treem, J. W. (2012). Communicating Expertise: Knowledge Performances in Professional-Service Firms. *Communication Monographs,* 79(1), 23–47.

Vlaar, P. W. L., van Fenema, P. C., and Tiwari, V. (2008). Cocreating Understanding and Value in Distributed Work: How Members of Onsite and Offshore Vendor Teams Give, Make, Demand, and Break Sense. *MIS Quarterly,* 32(2), 227–55.

Volberda, H. W. (1996). Toward the Flexible Form: How to Remain Vital in Hypercompetitive Environments. *Organization Science,* 7(4), 359–74.

Walsh, J. P., and Ungson, G. R. (1991). Organizational Memory. *Academy of Management Review,* 16(1), 57–91.

13 Conceptualizing Multilevel Expertise

JANET FULK

Communication scholars are accustomed to conceptualizing expertise as a property of individuals rather than larger units.[1] Theories focus on how individuals develop, communicate, practice, and apply expertise (e.g. Ackerman et al., 2003). Scholars consider such questions as: what personal characteristics distinguish experts from non-experts (e.g. Wang et al., 2011)? Do experts "possess" expertise or is it created in practice (e.g. Collins and Evans, 2007)? How is a person's expertise strategically (e.g. Leonardi and Treem, 2012) or socially (Fulk and Yuan, 2013) constructed? What factors influence whether a person's expertise is accurately recognized by others (Yuan et al., 2013)? How do people communicate their expertise to others (Treem, 2012)? Considerable literature also focuses on how the expertise of different individuals is combined in groups, organizations, and networks. That is, when individuals are in collectives (dyads, groups, organizations, etc.), how can their individual expertise be leveraged for the good of the collective? In this vein scholars study, for example, how to compose teams to have the optimal mix of individual expertise (e.g. Contractor, 2013), how effective transactive memory systems divide up the expertise requirements across the individual members (Hollingshead, 2010), and how to promote collaboration and knowledge sharing among different domains experts (Jarvenpaa and Majchrzak, 2008). From this perspective, expertise is still imagined to reside in individuals whose knowledge and activities need to be assembled, coordinated, and managed for the benefit of the collective.

This chapter asks a somewhat different kind of question: can expertise itself also reside in part in relationships at the collective level, over and above individual expertise? Does a team, group, organization, or industry, for example, as a collective have and/or practice expertise beyond the expertise of its participants? If so, a variety of additional questions arise. What does collective expertise look like compared to individual expertise? How is collective-level expertise related to individual-level expertise? What theory

[1] The chapter was supported in part by a grant from the National Science Foundation, IOC 0822814.

can be applied to conceptualize the practice of multilevel expertise? How can multiple levels of expertise be measured? This chapter explores these issues in an attempt to assess the viability of the concept of expertise as residing in a collective as well as in its individual participants. In the process, a case is made not only for the concept of collective expertise, but also for the idea that, when collective expertise can be found, it is important for scholarship to consider expertise as a multilevel concept, and not just an individual or a collective concept.

The chapter begins with a very brief summary of fundamental conceptions of individual expertise, followed by an overview of foundational work on multilevel theorizing that focuses on the relationships between individual and collective levels of concepts. With this background, ideas from the theory of community ecology are applied to highlight different ways that expertise can be composed and compiled at the collective level, and how the collective level may in turn influence individual expertise. The goal of the discussion is to increase scholarly consciousness of the role of the collective itself in practicing expertise over and beyond that of its individual members. To this end, examples are provided from both the natural world and human collectives. The natural world examples serve several purposes. First, they highlight systems and processes that contribute to collective expertise that have already been well documented in the natural sciences. Second, they illustrate that the existence of collective expertise does not always depend on collective human cognition. Third, they are derived from a theoretical framework based in the theory of community ecology as it has been developed to apply to communication and organizational processes. The chapter concludes with some caveats and suggestions for future directions in exploring and measuring expertise as a multilevel concept.

Background

INDIVIDUAL EXPERTISE

Much has been written about experts. Expertise generally is based on mastery of knowledge in a particular domain or subject area. Expert knowledge goes beyond familiarity with primary source materials in a domain; it involves wisdom or competence in what a person can do given mastery of source materials. Thus, individual expertise is "located in specialists' practices rather than books" (Collins and Evans, 2007, 23). (For more detailed reviews, see chapters in this book by Collins and by Barbour, Sommer, and Gill).

Expertise is relational in that expertise is judged by comparison to non-experts, and expertise is a social attribution developed based on social rules, relations, and interactions. There also are multiple dimensions of expertise that individual experts practice over and beyond mastery of a technical domain, such as Collins's periodic table of expertises or Barbour, Sommer, and Gill's taxonomy of expertise. The focus on *practice* in definitions of expertise is particularly helpful for two reasons. First, practice can imply a relationship between the expert and the target of the practice (e.g. person, object, or both). The focus on relationships in addition to individuals is consistent with the concept of multilevel expertise explored in this chapter. Second, collective expertise in the natural world can involve "doing" in ways that are consistent with human knowledge but does not imply that animals can have cognitive command of esoteric knowledge in the way that humans can. This focus facilitates learning from findings in the biological sciences (e.g. Wilson's sociobiology (2005), or community ecology theory (e.g. Hawley, 1986)).

MULTILEVEL EXPERTISE: A SIMPLE EXAMPLE

Imagine a collection of pelicans flying in formation. Each bird is practicing some important individual expertise in flying. A more nuanced explanation appears when the pelicans are viewed as a collective. The birds as a unit apply organizing processes that maximize their collective flying capability well beyond that of even the most expert individual flier. First, they fly in either V formation or a straight line, so that only the very front of the flock has to experience the pressure of flying directly into the wind. The stroke of each bird's wing creates an updraft that a carefully positioned following bird can seize to reduce energy consumption by 20 percent of what would be required of a bird flying individually; even when the birds struggle to stay in formation, they achieve more benefits than flying alone or flying together without the formation (Derbyshire, 2001). Second, the birds take turns flying in the front versus back of the formation, alternating places so that no bird becomes overexerted and no bird gets a free ride (Naseer, 2010). The system is consistent with what humans know about aerodynamics and the physiology of exertion, but there is no need to assume that any individual bird possesses any of this human knowledge in order for it to be applied in practice at the flock level. This organization and system is an expertise in a domain that applies at the collective level and cannot be practiced by or attributed to any single bird. It is collective expertise. An analogous situation applies to airplanes manned by human pilots flying in formation. The V formation with turn-taking saves fuel so that a formation of pilots practicing the system can fly farther on a given tank of fuel; furthermore, the formation also confers strategic advantages in warfare.

This simple example highlights the need for a more complex conception of expertise that includes domains practiced by larger units than individuals. At the same time, however, just as no individual can practice this collective

expertise alone, so the collective also depends on the individuals to participate effectively in the system, so that collective expertise cannot be conceptualized as independent of individual expertise. In those situations in which
collective expertise is practiced, some method is needed for not only assessing collective expertise but also examining the interaction between individual and collective expertise. The next section reviews one well-accepted
approach to conceptualizing multilevel phenomena which facilitates conceptualizing expertise as at the individual level, at the collective level, and in
the interaction between those levels.

Multilevel Theorizing

Multilevel theorizing has been applied to understand the relationships between
any two levels of a variable (e.g. individual-to-group; team-to-organization;
organization-to-industry, etc.). Kozlowski and Klein (2000) argue that multilevel relationships can be described along a range anchored at either end by two
processes: composition and compilation. Compositional processes are those
in which "phenomena are essentially the same as they emerge upward across
levels" (p. 16). Antecedents and consequences are the same at the two different levels, so that higher level processes are simple aggregations. An example
from the biological world would be army ants, all of whom have the same
genetic capabilities and behave in the same fashion. The outcome of the swarm
is an aggregation of the actions of the individuals. The tiny army ants are able to
collectively take down large prey such as honey bees with "neither recruitment
among workers to food sources nor any other apparent form of cooperation
during foraging" (Wilson, 2005, 424). Kozlowski and Klein (2000) offer as a
human example the composition of organizational climate, which is a higher
level phenomenon derived from the average of individual perceptions of climate
within the organization. As this example illustrates, relations can be between
any two levels, and the levels need not be hierarchically adjacent to one another.

At the other end of the range from compositional are compilational processes, which Kozlowski and Klein (2000) describe as phenomena that "are
distinctively different as they emerge across levels," and also have "different
antecedents and processes at different levels" (p. 9). "There will be considerable dispersion and nonuniformity in the ways in which individual contributions are coordinated and combined to yield the compiled team performance
(Kozlowski et al., 1999)" (p. 64) and measurement can include "variance, pro-
portion, configural fit, and network characteristics, among others (Levine and
Fitzgerald, 1992; Meyer et al., 1993)" (p. 64). In compilation, "group members
have somewhat different mental representations of their collective task, based
on their specific roles within the team" (p. 36).

Compilational processes can be more or less complex based on whether individual experts have relatively similar or relatively different skill sets. When members of a collective have relatively similar levels of expertise at the different aspects of the collective's practice, the configuration of activities at the collective level may be important to collective expertise, but the assignment of experts to activities should not have a major impact on collective expertise. A simple example would be the expertise of gray wolves in hunting prey (Muro et al., 2011). The smallest and fastest (usually females) will take on the hunt while others tend to pack business at home. Typically there are not major differences among the hunters in task-relevant expertise. A few rules are followed. First, the pack approaches the prey and stops at a minimum safe distance. Second, a subset of the group will move in the opposite direction away from the pack and to the other side of the prey. They then charge the prey, driving it toward the rest of the pack hidden in the brush. Because each wolf has similar expertise and the roles are interchangeable, the pack is not dependent upon any single individual for any single role. However, once any role is assumed, the role player will have a slightly different representation of the task, but the representations fit together in compatible ways. If, instead, the wolves had specialized skills that differed by member of the hunting party (e.g. some were better than others at moving the prey toward the pack), the configuration of wolves for the task would require consideration of differences in individual expertise. Collective expertise would be higher when experts practiced parts of the task that were consistent with their level of specialized expertise

In the human world, consider a research group comprised of members with relatively similar levels of expertise in the practices of ideation, data analysis, and writing. Participants could take different roles for different projects of the group, and each member's mental representation of the project would differ depending on which role was assumed at any one time. As with the gray wolves, the particular configuration of which expert assumed which role for a project would not be a major factor in the level of expertise practiced at the collective level.

Kozlowski and Klein (2000) use the example of baseball team performance as a compilational process based on differentiated expertise in practicing different domains (left fielder, pitcher, etc.). Unlike with gray wolves, it makes a difference in the expertise of the collective who is assigned which function. One could not easily switch the pitcher and catcher roles and still maintain the same level of expertise at the collective level. Following up on the research team example, if the members of the team had different capabilities in ideation, data analysis, and writing, one could not easily switch the roles of the experts without influencing collective expertise. Indeed, compared to the situation where individuals practice similar levels of expertise, there are a much greater variety of possible levels of collective expertise depending on congruence of individual expertise and role assignment.

Having defined these two processes, Kozlowski and Klein go on to note that compositional and compilational processes are ideal types, and many cross-level influences involve varying degrees of both these two polar extremes. They argue further than once lower level attitudes and behaviors have been compiled and/or composed into the collective, the collective can then have influence downward on individuals. A simple example in keeping with Kozlowski and Klein's (2000) baseball example is the fate of the Chicago Cubs' outstanding first baseman Ernie Banks, who the 1960s was one of a minority of African-Americans to play major league baseball in the United States. Boyd and Harris (1973, 96) noted that "Ernie Banks ... was one of those players who was cursed to play out his career with an inferior team. It is no exaggeration to say that the difference between an Ernie Banks and a Mickey Mantle is the good fortune to play with a championship team. Ernie Banks never had that good fortune."[2] Again, from a multilevel perspective, lower collective expertise can be the result of insufficient individual specialist expertise, insufficient systems in place at the collective level, and/or insufficient expertise at participating in those systems.

Multilevel Expertise Reflected in Relationships

How does individual expertise get composed and compiled to the collective level which then has influences downward to the individual? Continuing with the analogy to biological systems, one overarching framework for examining these questions is community ecology theory (e.g. Hawley, 1986). This theory conceptualizes natural ecosystems as hierarchically organized, including levels of individuals, species, populations, and communities. Cooperation and competition for resources occurs both within and across levels. The key to understanding these processes is to focus on the relationships among the participants at all levels of the community. Although these theories primarily focus on populations and species, the patterns of relationships specified should be applicable to other types of collectives and their individual members, as has recently been proposed in ecological models of organizations (Baum and Singh, 1994; Margolin et al., 2015; Monge et al., 2008; Shumate and O'Connor, 2010; Shumate et al., 2005).

Community ecology theory identifies commensalist, symbiotic, and parasitic relationships (Hawley, 1986). Commensalism occurs among members of

[2] For those not familiar with the history of American baseball, Mickey Mantle is generally believed to be one of the greatest players in the history of the sport.

the same population that address the same set of environmental resources. Commensalist relations can be cooperative such that each party benefits, or competitive such that one party benefits at the expense of the other (Aldrich and Ruef, 2006). Symbiosis is a mutually beneficial pattern between members of different populations. Parasitism is also between populations but one population benefits at the expense of the other.

MULTILEVEL EXPERTISE GROUNDED IN COMMENSALIST COOPERATIVE RELATIONS

Cooperative relations can be distinguished in part based on whether they are practiced by individuals with relative similar versus differentiated expertise. As described earlier, nondifferentiated expertise can be found in hunting groups of wolves or in research teams where members are equally expert at ideation, analysis, and writing. Each individual participant has the expertise needed to fulfill any of the roles needed to achieve the collective expertise. Yet no one expert's practice can achieve the pattern alone, as was also discussed for pelicans or pilots in V formation.

By contrast, a classic example of a collective whose very existence depends on differentiated expertise is the honey bee (Mid-Atlantic Apiculture Research and Extension Consortium, 2015). There are three genetically different types of bee in the colony: queen, drone, and worker. The drone's sole function is to reproduce with the queen, after which it dies. The worker bees (sexually undeveloped females) maintain the colony by constructing nests, gathering food, and defending the colony. A complex division of labor exists among the worker bees based on the age of each bee. Coordination is accomplished through a communication system based on the distribution of chemical phero-mones among the workers as well as communicative "dances" in which worker bees engage. The hive as a collective has expertise embedded in the complex sets of relationships and patterns among the expert individuals. Collective expertise depends not just on structural features of the system (who does what when, for example) but also on communication and relationship patterns among spe-cialist bees.

Communication and relationship patterns also explain the relative col-lective expertise of Kozlowski and Klein's (2000) baseball teams. Consider the need to move the ball among the different individual positions. Baseball has systems that assist in making the individual experts work together. For example, what if the batter hits a ball toward the open area between second and third base? If there is a runner on first base, the shortstop will field the ball and deliver an expert throw to second base and then the second baseperson will throw the ball to first base, in the hope of a double play.

Alternatively, if there is no runner on first base the shortstop will throw directly to first base. The other players know this system and take appropriate actions and positions during play as well even if they are not directly involved in ball-handling. It is not simply the possession of the appropriate set of ball-handling skills that make a team successful; winning also depends on having and applying a set of rules, systems, and communicative protocols for how to handle emergent situations during game play. Indeed, collective level expertise becomes part of the requisite practical knowledge of each individual player, so that collective expertise helps to improve individual expertise. Just as the Yankees' collective expertise helped to propel Mickey Mantle to fame, the Cubs' relative lack of expertise hampered Ernie Banks.

An interesting example of how examining patterns of communication and relationships at the collective level uncovered collective expertise in organizations is presented in Contractor et al.'s (2011) study of the crashworthiness engineering unit of a major automobile company. The engineers on staff had varying degrees of individual expertise, experience, and seniority. Advice seeking was considered to be a standard part of crashworthiness work. Expertise was attributed differently to different individuals based on how frequently others sought their advice, highlighting not only the importance of individual expertise to the collective's success, but also how collective expertise was built on cooperative relationships. Contractor et al. also conducted a multidimensional network analysis of these networks to uncover additional patterns of expertise at the collective level. First, they included as nodes in the network the software and documents that also were consulted for advice (multimodal network). Second, they also considered multiple types of relationships among people and technologies (multiplex relationships). This approach led them to identify five different "structural signatures" reflected in the expertise network topography. For example, the topography produced by standard network analysis (unimodal uniplex) led to the conclusion that two years after implementing the new software it had replaced advice seeking among the human experts. The fully multidimensional network analysis, by contrast, led to the conclusion that after implementation of the software advice seeking was centralized on software for questions of what to include in the analysis; however, for questions of why a particular point should be included in the analysis the advice network was centralized on the junior analyst who had created the software. These alternative network topographies offer different interpretations of how collective expertise was compiled from the expertise of both individual experts and nonhuman sources. Cooperative relations among experts and expert technologies took different forms both over time and in relation to software available.

MULTILEVEL EXPERTISE GROUNDED IN COMMENSALIST COMPETITIVE RELATIONS

Competition across collectives

In the natural world, one type of competition occurs when resources are scarce and participants compete with other species for those scarce resources, leading some to survive and others to die. Competition can undermine ecological variety, with corresponding effects in the larger system. For example, in the Santa Barbara Islands off the coast of California in the United States, golden eagles moved in to compete with bald eagles whose population had been put at risk partly due to chemical contamination by DDT. When the golden eagles became the survivors and bald eagles were driven out, the population of island foxes went into serious decline. Golden eagles are predators to mammals but bald eagles are predators only to fish (National Park Service, n.d.).

A human example in which different collectives competed with each other at the expense of the overall system is presented in Monge et al.'s (1999) analysis of relationship patterns among different law enforcement organizations at the municipal, county, state, and national level. Experts in drug trafficking in the different organizations had a history of not sharing information or expertise across jurisdictional boundaries and sometimes even interfering with another jurisdiction's activities. Monge et al. describe roots of the competition in incompatible information systems, lack of trust in the context of risky undercover police work, power dynamics across jurisdictions, and a reward system embedded in asset forfeiture law that offered financial rewards for arrests by individual jurisdictions rather than multijurisdictional teams. There was little collective expertise across jurisdictions; rather, each jurisdictional applied its expertise not only individually but also without consideration of the expertise or task needs of the other jurisdictions. Since drug trafficking is not confined to single jurisdictions, the capabilities of the law enforcement system as a whole suffered.

Competition within collectives

When participants compete with other members of their own species in the natural world, the participants that tend to survive are those with capabilities favorable for the characteristics of a particular resource niche. The survivors reproduce and pass the valuable capability on to the next generation. A classic example is the giraffe. According to Darwinian evolution, over centuries the giraffe developed from a short-necked creature to one with a very long neck because it facilitated reaching food sources in the upper reaches of the trees. Given that there was some variation in neck length in the population of giraffes, the relatively shorter-necked giraffes had less access to food and lower survival rates and thus were not able to pass on the relatively short-necked trait to another generation. The longer necked creatures who survived, however, passed on their long-necked gene to their offspring (Monge and Oh, in press).

In the human world a classic example of within-species competition is Blau's (1964) study of two departments in an employment agency. One department changed its reward system to pay off individuals. People's rewards were determined by the number of people they placed in positions who stayed in those positions for at least thirty days. Not surprisingly, individual vocational specialists started competing for the applicants that were easy to place. The experts would hide information from others, provide incorrect information to others, and make placements they knew would last just over a month so that the person would come back and be able to be placed again for another thirty days. Needless to say, the performance of this unit fell far below the comparison unit that employed more group-oriented awards. Nothing had changed in the relative domain expertise of the vocational specialists in the two departments at the individual level, but collectively the practice of expertise was influenced by the system in which the experts participated.

Competitive relations fostering collective expertise

In some situations, however, competition might enhance collective expertise. Consider the process of natural selection and the survival of the fittest. If the resources available to the collective can be secured by individuals based on relevant expertise, then competition between experts to "become the best" can actually enhance the expertise available in the collective as a whole. A classic example in inter-collective competition is portrayed in *The Soul of a New Machine*, a story of the competition between two divisions of computer vendor (Kidder, 1981). Working independently and under somewhat different design constraints, both divisions had the same charge: design a new operating system in no more than one year. If they both met the deadline, only one of the division's systems could be implemented. The book chronicles the year of fits and start among the design experts who in the end delivered a higher quality system than they had imagined possible and did so in record time.

Competition has been found to be particularly beneficial in the context of crowdsourcing, "a decade-long trend toward solving science problems through large-scale mobilization of . . . external, unaffiliated actors to resolve a particular problem" (Lakhani et al., 2013, 108). Lakhani et al. (2013, 108) describe, for example, a two-week online contest to solve a "complex immunogenics problem" in which 600 experts from the biomedical discipline participated. The best solutions generated were more accurate and 1000 times faster than the benchmark. Other well-researched online crowdsourcing sites include, for example, Innocentive.com or TopCoder.com. The optimal design of such competitive contests has generated considerable research interest (e.g. Archak and Sundararajan, 2009).

MULTILEVEL EXPERTISE GROUNDED IN SYMBIOTIC RELATIONS

Symbiotic relations are based in mutually complementary relationships between different species. A classic example of symbiosis is the partnership between the orange striped clownfish species and the sea anemone, an invertebrate species that is found gripping onto underwater reef structures (Miller, n.d.). The sea anemone has long tentacles with stinging nematocysts at the end, designed to ward off prey. Nevertheless, the orange-and-white striped clownfish burrow right into the tentacles. They do not try to eat the tentacles, and in any case clownfish have a thick mucus layer that protects them if they accidentally get stung. The clownfish become guards for the anemones, charging forward aggressively toward any potential predators that approach. Clownfish also provide nutrients to the anemone through their own bodily wastes. The combination of different capabilities of the two sea creatures creates a collective quite different than what either species could have done on its own. Embedded in the relationships between the species is a system and pattern that leverages the unique capabilities of the two different species.

An example of multilevel expertise involving symbiosis in a human organization is online question and answer forums. Such forums typically include a variety of features: libraries of questions and their answers, profiles of individual contributors, the ability of all participants to "vote" on the quality of a question or answer, and reputation status of various members; interactions take place in the public space of the online forum. In a study of online expertise sharing in the field of software development via Stackoverflow. com, Bighash et al. (2015) point out that, although many researchers consider question askers as free riders because they typically do not contribute any answers, in actuality question askers are critical to the survival of the forum. Without questions there would be no answers. Bighash et al. note that there is expertise in question asking, and that poor questions get few or no responses and also harm the reputation of the questioner. The answerers benefit from the reputation points earned by the quality of the answer, and perhaps some unexpected learning along the way (Lakhani and von Hippel, 2003). The questioners that display the expertise needed to frame a well-constructed question benefit the community by eliciting a good answer that is available to all users. Interestingly, in the forum that Bighash et al. studied, the majority of participants only demonstrated one type of software-related expertise— asking or answering, but not both. The relations between the asking experts and the answering experts is symbiotic in that each needs the other's role, and the collective as a whole benefits from the relationship between the two in ways that neither role could accomplish on its own. The survival of the forum as a collective also depends in part on its system for recognizing and rewarding questioners and answerers.

MULTILEVEL EXPERTISE GROUNDED IN PARASITIC RELATIONS

Parasitic patterns are common in nature: Fleas taking advantage of dogs or aphids living on plants and eating the plant's sap. Some parasitic relations can be harmful to the collective, as when gall wasps infect black oaks and slowly kill whole forests of them (Abel, 2013). Other parasitic relations are more irritating than life threatening, such as the barnacles on the whale that are just itchy, but don't otherwise harm the whale.

In human multilevel expertise, one possible parasitic relationship is the counterintelligence spy who sells sensitive information to opponents. The spy parlays expertise in the intelligence field and access to sensitive data into a profit for himself, often with much damage to other members of the organization. A classic example is Aldrich Ames, an American Central Intelligence Agency (CIA) operative who passed sensitive information to the Soviet Union (and Russia after the fall of the Soviet Union in 1989) from 1985 to 1994, compromising a large number of fellow CIA double agents. His actions also damaged the CIA as a collective and set back US intelligence operations very substantially (Federal Bureau of Investigation, n.d.). Indeed, intentional or unintentional revelations of sensitive information by experts in ways that harm collective task forces, teams, and organizations are relatively common examples of parasitic relations.

Advancing the Study of Expertise

THE IMPORTANCE OF CONFIGURATION

As parasitic and some competitive relations exemplify, not just any system or pattern will produce a high level of collective expertise, and some will undermine collective expertise. Even in cooperative situations, the specific rules, patterns, systems, and structural signatures matter. For example, imagine that the birds flying in V formation do not have the second benefit of a system to share equally in the task of flying in front directly into the wind. What if, instead, smaller members of the flock were dominated by a set of bigger birds who could by threat require the smaller birds to fly the front of the V all of the time. The bigger birds could then rest comfortably in the trail blazed by the smaller birds. The flock as a collective would practice much less flying expertise, and likely some of the smaller birds would not survive the ordeal. Uninformed observers might even remark on the individual flying expertise of the dominant bigger birds which seemed to arrive at their destination much less winded than their smaller counterparts. In this case, we would see that a system at the collective level that favors a subset of individual experts rather than the collective as a whole is more likely to lead to inferences about individual versus collective expertise, even when system factors contribute to the diminution of collective expertise.

This example also illustrates the importance of understanding the interaction between individual and collective properties, in that the dominant individual experts took advantage of the aerodynamic system in place at the collective level to benefit themselves more than the collective. Scholars in evolutionary theory have described this situation as one of whole–part coevolutionary competition (Baum, 1999; Kauffman, 1993). In brief, the thesis is that the organization can be seen as a hierarchy of nested subgroups in which each level evolves simultaneously and is a node of selection. Agents at all levels attempt to optimize their fitness and thus be selected for survival. Evolution is faster and more effective at lower levels, leading to suboptimization rather than global optimization. Some solutions proposed by Baum (1999) include shared control systems, dynamic performance measures, restructuring to a more modular form into quasi-independent selfishly optimizing groups, and creating a division of labor such that each part needs the other parts to achieve the whole.

Symbiotic collective expertise also depends on configuration of capabilities. If a goby fish rather than a clownfish tried to work with the sea anemone, the goby would either be chased away by a clownfish or, in the unlikely event that it got past the clownfish guards, it would be stung by the anemone. Indeed, the goby has its own symbiotic relationship with the blind pistol shrimp: they live together in a hole dug in the sand by the shrimp (Small Science, n.d.). When a predator approaches the hole, the goby signals danger with tail flick that creates a vibration that can be felt by the blind shrimp who then retreats deep into the hole. The goby receives shelter and safety benefits from the hole that the shrimp has dug and maintains. Without the shrimp's digging, the hole would soon become filled with sand, exposing the goby to predators. The blind shrimp is protected by the goby's warning system. Again, the particular configuration of expertise and capabilities is critical.

Relationships also can be multiplex and involve multiple relations as Contractor et al. (2011) noted. For example, the goby fish sometimes will eat the pistol shrimp's eggs—a parasitic move in an otherwise symbiotic relationship. Collectives can simultaneously practice relations that are both cooperative and competitive. For example, the concept of co-opetition

(Brandenburger and Nalebuff, 1996) was put forward to conceptualize inter-organizational relationships in which organizations cooperated in one aspect of product cycle (e.g. research and development) while competing in another aspect (product markets). The need to maintain multiple types of expertise relations effectively in a collective adds additional complexity to multilevel expertise.

Contractor et al. (2011) also note that complexity arises when nonhuman elements are considered part of the human collective. They included software as a node in the expertise-seeking network at the crashworthiness lab. Given that domain expertise can include reliance on some codified knowledge, the software might be viewed as practicing expertise, and documents can be repositories of codified expertise like humans can be.

MULTILEVEL EXPERTISE AT OTHER LEVELS

Much of this chapter has focused on the relationship between the individual and the collective, largely because the individual is the most common site of attributions about expertise. However, the multilevel model applies across any set of levels. Going back to Kozlowski and Klein's (2000) baseball example, we could examine the collective expertise of the American League, to which one-half of the baseball teams belong, and compare it to its competitor, the National League. The analysis would look for systems and processes at the league level that influence the collective expertise of the baseball teams at a set. Configuration, in such a multilevel analysis, is important at both levels.

In addition to cross-level influences from multiple levels beyond the individual, each higher level can also experience cross-level influences from levels above and below it. Returning to the baseball example, the expertise of individual players is influenced by many factors at many levels. Players typically begin their training as youths in Little Leagues, schools, and on playgrounds as well as in high school and college baseball programs. Baseball programs in schools are part of a network that works with professional scouts looking for potential players to move to training camps and minor leagues. Activities are overseen by the Baseball Commission, which sets rules for recruitment and game play. Which player joins which team is in part a function of which players are mobile in any one year, and what total salary package is available to the team at the time. Salary budget is also a function of revenues, which depend on fan attendance and on sales of branded products to consumers. Thus, individual players' expertise and the expertise of the team as a collective depends in part on a system that they do not create and which privileges certain individual teams over others.

Measurement and Analysis

In the biological sciences, collective-level properties have been uncovered by a variety of methods. In the case of the pelicans and V formation, scientists from the French National Center for Scientific Research implanted heart rate monitors under the feathers of white pelicans in Senegal (National Public Radio, 2001). For the human piloted V formation, fuel consumption is easily measured. Unobtrusive measures in other human collectives might include examination of online or written records of interactions and relationships among individual experts. An emerging area is the use of digital signal processing to assess social signals. Sensors in mobile phones or wearable badges collect data on verbal and nonverbal relational communication behavior of individuals and collectives in relation to both humans and technology. The massive amount of signal data that has been generated is then analyzed by complex algorithms to detect patterns. The field is currently in its infancy, but is growing rapidly (e.g. Pentland, 2014). Among its many capabilities are recognition of collective action and automatic extraction of social networks. Also, studies have considered the reaction of humans to social signals sent by nonhuman actors such as avatars (see Vinciarelli et al., 2009, as well as Pentland, 2014, for reviews).

Computational models offer the option for uncovering complex, multilevel patterns that might otherwise be difficult to detect. Such models offer the opportunity to create more complex theories of collective expertise. Such models have been effective in studying collective systems in wolf packs (Muro et al., 2011) and penguins (Inside Science, 2012), for example. For penguins, an applied mathematician built a model of the shape and dynamics of the "huddle" penguins use to keep warm at night in the frigid Arctic climate. The huddle has a relatively round circumference and birds practice turn-taking for spots on the outer and colder edges ($-60°F$ and 100 mph wind gusts outside vs. $70°F$ in the very inner circle). Agent-based computational modeling also can help researchers to predict both the individual and collective outcomes of cooperative versus competitive configurations of expert practice in collectives of experts. In addition, models can also examine evolutionary dynamics as well as varying conditions of differentiated versus similar expertise (Elliott and Kiel, 2002).

In-depth observational study has been a mainstay of anthropological study of collectives. The research by Blau (1964) on the employment specialists' individual and collective behavior provides a good example for human collectives. Such depth of observation is likely to be particularly useful for examining the practice of tacit knowledge in multilevel expertise systems.

Multidimensional network analysis based on survey and observational data offers many advantages. Contractor et al.'s (2011) study on the crashworthiness lab offers an example for human collectives. This research is notable because it focused less on nodes than on relationships, as suggested by Monge et al. (2008) in their application of community ecology principles to human networks. The Contractor et al. study also demonstrated the need to focus on multiple relationships, since the structural signatures differed depending on which relationship became the focus. Similarly, we have suggested that there would be very different results at the collective level for the V formation in pelicans if both the V shape and turn-taking were not practiced. Finally, their work argues for inclusion of nonhuman expertise systems and repositories as well as human ones when studying multilevel expertise practices.

Conclusion

This chapter started with two key questions: can expertise itself also reside at the collective level, over and above individual expertise? How viable is a multilevel conceptualization of expertise? The conceptual analysis suggests a variety of questions that we as expertise researchers can keep in mind while theorizing and empirically examining expertise.

1. How much does an individual's expertise depend upon the nature and effectiveness of the systems that constitute expertise at the collective level?
2. How can a collective's expertise be enhanced or degraded by changes to the system that is employed at the collective level?
3. How can an individual's expertise be enhanced or degraded by changes to the system that is employed at the collective level?
4. How critical are collective properties to the ability of individual experts to function?
5. Where collective expertise is compilational, what specific algorithms and configurations most accurately describe how the individual contributions are combined in nonlinear ways within the collective?

Multilevel concepts and theorizing have come to a position of prominence in the study of communication and organization. As Klein and Kozlowski (2000, 211) note, "multilevel research is—at its best—complex, rigorous, and able to capture much of the nested complexity of real organizational life." As the other chapters in this book also have demonstrated, expertise is indeed complex practice in real organizational contexts.

■ REFERENCES

Abel, D. (2013). Wasps Infesting, Imperiling Area's Black Oaks. *Boston Globe*, Nov. 18. Retrieved from: <http://www.bostonglobe.com/metro/2013/11/18/mysterious-pest-threatens-trees-cape-and-martha-vineyard/JaQwwH66d1kIDrVUX11sqK/story.html>.

Ackerman, M., Pipek, V., and Wulf, V. (eds) (2003). *Sharing Expertise: Beyond Knowledge Management.* Cambridge, MA: MIT Press.

Aldrich, H. E., and Ruef, M. (2006). *Organizations Evolving* (2nd edn). Thousand Oaks, CA: Sage.

Archak, N., and Sundararajan, A. (2009). Optimal Design of Crowdsourcing Contests. *ICIS 2009 Proceedings.* Paper 200. <http://aisel.aisnet.org/icis2009/200>.

Baum, J. A. C. (1999). Whole-Part Coevolutionary Competition in Organizations. In J. Baum and B. McKelvey (eds), *Variations in Organization Science: In Honor of Donald T. Campbell* (pp. 113–37). Thousand Oaks, CA: SAGE Publications, Inc. doi: http://dx.doi.org/10.4135/9781452204703.n7

Baum, J. A. C., and Singh, J. V. (1994). Organizational Hierarchies and Evolutionary Processes: Some Reflections on a Theory of Organizational Evolution. In J. A. C. Baum and J. V. Singh (eds), *Evolutionary Dynamics of Organizations* (pp. 3–20). New York: Oxford University Press.

Bighash, L., Oh, P. Monge, P., and Fulk, J. (2015). The Creation of Information Goods in Online Knowledge-Sharing Communities. Paper presented at the 65th International Communication Association Conference, San Juan, PR, May.

Blau, P. (1964). *Exchange and Power in Social Life.* New York: John Wiley & Sons.

Boyd, B., and Harris, F. (1973). *The Great American Baseball Card Flipping, Trading and Bubble Gum Book.* Boston, MA: Little Brown & Co.

Brandenburger, A. M., and Nalebuff, B. J. (1996). *Co-opetition: A Revolutionary Mindset that Combines Competition and Cooperation: The Game Theory Strategy that's Changing the Game of Business.* New York: Doubleday.

Collins, H., and Evans, R. (2007). *Rethinking Expertise.* Chicago: University of Chicago Press.

Contractor, N. (2013). Some Assembly Required: Leveraging Web Science to Understand and Enable Team Assembly. *Philosophical Transactions of the Royal Society of London A: Mathematical, Physical and Engineering Sciences, 371*(1983). doi: 10.1098/rsta.2012.0385

Contractor, N., Monge, P., and Leonardi, P. (2011). Multidimensional Networks and the Dynamics of Sociomateriality: Bringing Technology inside the Network. *International Journal of Communication, 5,* 682–720.

Derbyshire. D. (2001). Why Birds Fly in Formation. *The Telegraph*, Oct. 18. Retrieved from: <http://www.telegraph.co.uk/news/worldnews/1359818/Why-birds-fly-in-formation.html>.

Elliott, E., and Kiel, D. (2002). Exploring Cooperation and Competition Using Agent-Based Modeling. *Proceedings of the National Academy of Sciences (PNAS), 99*(3), 7193–4.

Federal Bureau of Investigation (n.d.). Aldrich Hazen Ames. Retrieved from <http://www.fbi.gov/about-us/history/famous-cases/aldrich-hazen-ames>.

Fulk, J., and Yuan, Y. C. (2013). Location, Motivation, and Social Capitalization: The Use of Enterprise Social Networking Applications to Support Knowledge Sharing in Organizations. *Journal of Computer-Mediated Communication*, 19, 20–37.

Hawley, A. H. (1986). *Human Ecology: A Theoretical Essay.* Chicago: University of Chicago.

Hollingshead, A. (2010). Transactive Memory. In J. Levine and M. Hogg (eds), *Encyclopedia of Group Processes and Intergroup Relations* (pp. 931–4). Thousand Oaks, CA: Sage.

Inside Science (2012). Penguins: The Math behind the Huddle. Retrieved from <http://www.insidescience.org/content/penguins-math-behind-huddle/849>.

Jarvenpaa, S. L., and Majchrzak, A. (2008). Knowledge Collaboration among Professionals Protecting National Security: Role of Transactive Memories in Ego-Centered Knowledge Networks. *Organization Science*, 19, 260–79.

Kauffman, S. (1993). *The Origins of Life: Self-Organization and Selection in Evolution.* New York: Oxford University Press.

Kidder, T. (1981). *The Soul of a New Machine.* New York: Little Brown & Co.

Klein, K., and Kozlowski, S. (2000). From Micro to Meso: Critical Steps in Conceptualizing and Conducting Multilevel Research. In K. J. Klein and S. Kozlowski (eds), *Multilevel Theory, Research, and Methods in Organizations: Foundations, Extensions and New Directions* (pp. 211–36). San Francisco, CA: Jossey-Bass.

Kozlowski, S., and Klein, K. J. (2000). A Multilevel Approach to Theory and Research in Organizations: Contextual, Temporal and Emergent Processes. In K. J. Klein and S. Kozlowski (eds), *Multilevel Theory, Research, and Methods in Organizations: Foundations, Extensions and New Directions* (pp. 3–90). San Francisco: Jossey-Bass.

Kozlowski, S. W. J., Gully, S. M., Nason, E. R., and Smith, E. M. (1999). Developing Adaptive Teams: A Theory of Compilation and Performance across Levels and Time. In D. R. Ilgen and E. D. Pulakos (eds), *The Changing Nature of Work Performance: Implications for Staffing, Personnel Actions, and Development* (pp. 240–92). San Francisco: Jossey-Bass.

Lakhani, K., and von Hippel, E. (2003). How Open Source Software Works: "Free" User-to-User Assistance. *Research Policy*, 32, 923–43.

Lakhani, K. R, Boudreau, K. J., Loh, P. R., Backstrom, L., Baldwin, C., Lonstein, E., Lydon, M., MacCormack, A., Arnaout, R. A., and Guinan, E. C. (2013). Prize-Based Contests Can Provide Solutions to Computational Biology Problems. *Nature Biotechnology*, 31, 108–11. doi: 10.1038/nbt.2495

Leonardi, P. M., and Treem, J. W. (2012). Knowledge Management Technology as a Stage for Strategic Self-Presentation: Implications for Knowledge Sharing in Organizations. *Information and Organization*, 22, 37–59.

Levine, R. L., and Fitzgerald, H. E. (1992). *Analysis of Dynamic Psychological Systems* (vols 1, 2). New York: Plenum.

Margolin, D. B., Shen, C., Lee, S., Weber, M., Monge, P., and Fulk, J. (2015). Normative Influences on Network Structure in the Evolution of the Children's Rights NGO Network, 1977–2004. *Communication Research*, 42(1), 30–59. doi: 0.1177/0093650212463731

Meyer, A. D., Tsui, A. S., and Hinings, C. R. (1993). Guest Co-editors' Introduction: Configural Approaches to Organizational Analysis. *Academy of Management Journal*, 36, 1175–95.

Mid-Atlantic Apiculture Research and Extension Consortium (2015). The Colony and its Organizations. Retrieved from: <https://agdev.anr.udel.edu/maarec/honey-bee-biology/the-colony-and-its-organization>.

Miller, A. (n.d.). Intricate Relationship Allows the Other to Flourish: The Sea Anemone and the Clownfish. Retrieved from: <http://www.asknature.org/strategy/fb410d8500af30a5daf5b647954b7fa5>.

Monge, P., and Oh, P. (in press). Evolutionary Theory and Models. In K. Jensen (ed.), *International Encyclopedia of Communication Theory and Philosophy*. Hoboken, NJ: Wiley-Blackwell.

Monge, P., Fulk, J., Parnassa, C., Flanagin, A., Rumsey, S., and Kalman, M. (1999). Cooperative Interagency Approaches to the Illegal Drug Problem. *International Journal of Police Science and Management*, 2, 229–41.

Monge, P. R., Heiss, B., and Margolin, D. (2008). Communication Network Evolution in Organizational Communities. *Communication Theory*, 18(4), 449–77. doi: 10.1111/j.1468-2885.2008.00330.x

Muro, C., Escobedo, R., Spector, L., and Coppinger, R. (2011). Wolf-Pack (Canis Lupus) Hunting Strategies Emerge from Simple Rules in Computational Simulations. *Behavioural Processes*, 88, 192–7.

Naseer, T. (2010). Migrating Geese: A Lesson in Leadership and Collaboration. Retrieved from <http://www.tanveernaseer.com/migrating-geese-a-lesson-in-leadership-and-collaboration>.

National Park Service (n.d.). The Decline of the Island Fox. Retrieved from <http://www.nps.gov/chis/learn/nature/fox-decline.htm>.

National Public Radio (2001). The Pelican Experiment: Science Offers Proof that Flying in V-Formation Boosts Efficiency. Oct. 17. Retrieved from <http://www.npr.org/programs/atc/features/2001/oct/011017.pelican.html>.

Pentland, A. (2014). *Social Physics: How Good Ideas Spread: The Lessons from a New Science*. New York: Penguin Press.

Shumate, M., and O'Connor, A. (2010). The Symbiotic Sustainability Model: Conceptualizing NGO–Corporate Alliance Communication. *Journal of Communication*, 60, 577–609. doi: 10.1111/j.1460-2466.2010.01498.x

Shumate, M., Fulk, J., and Monge, P. (2005). Predictors of the HIV/AIDS INGO Network over Time. *Human Communication Research*, 31, 482–510.

Small Science (n.d.). Pistol Shrimp and the Goby Fish. Retrieved from <http://coglab.hbcse.tifr.res.in/teacher-resources/multimedia-resources/symbiosis/pistol-shrimp-and-the-goby-fish>.

Treem, J. W. (2012). Communicating Expertise: Knowledge Performances in Professional Service Firms. *Communication Monographs*, 79, 23–47.

Vinciarelli, A., Pantic, A., and Bourlard, H. (2009). Social Signal Processing: Survey of an Emerging Domain. *Image and Vision Computing*, 27, 1743–59.

Wang, J., Huffaker, D. A., Treem, J. W., Fullerton, L., Ahmad, M. A., Williams, D., Poole, M. S., and Contractor, N. (2011). Focused on the Prize: Characteristics of Experts in Massive Multiplayer Online Games. *First Monday*, 16(8). Retrieved from <http://firstmonday.org/htbin/cgiwrap/bin/ojs/index.php/fm/article/viewArticle/3672/3028>.

Wilson, E. (2005). *Sociobiology: The New Synthesis.* Cambridge, MA: Belknap Press of Harvard University Press.

Yuan, Y., Barzova, N., Fulk, J., and Zhang, Z. (2013). Recognition of Expertise and Perceived Influence in Intercultural Collaboration: A Study of Mixed American and Chinese Groups. *Journal of Communication,* 63, 476–97.

▉ AUTHOR INDEX

SUBJECT INDEX